Creating Miracles

Understanding the Experience of Divine Intervention

Creating Miracles

Understanding the Experience of Divine Intervention

Carolyn Godschild Miller, Ph.D.

H J Kramer Inc
Tiburon, California

Published by H J Kramer Inc
P.O. Box 1082
Tiburon, CA 94920

Editor: Nancy Grimley Carleton
Editorial Assistant: Claudette Charbonneau
Cover Art: Bernardino Luini, Angel
Cover Design: Jim Marin/Marin Graphic Services
Composition: Classic Typography
Book Production: Schuettge & Carleton
Luini painting: Courtesy of Pina Coteca di Brera, Milan, Italy
Photographer: M. Magliani/Superstock, Inc.
Permissions: Please see p. xvi.

Manufactured in the United States of America.
10 9 8 7 6 5 4 3 2 1

Library of Congress Cataloging-in-Publication Data:

Miller, Carolyn Godschild, 1946–
    Creating miracles : understanding the experience of divine
intervention / by Carolyn Godschild Miller.
    p.   cm.
    Includes bibliographical references.
    ISBN 0–915811–62–6 (pbk.) : $11.95 ($16.95 Can.)
    1. Course in miracles. 2. Miracles. I. Title.
BP605.C68M55 1995
299′.93 – dc20   94–48620
                                                            CIP

Until one is committed, there is hesitancy, the chance to draw back, always ineffectiveness. Concerning all acts of initiative (and creation), there is one elementary truth the ignorance of which kills countless ideas and splendid plans: that the moment one definitely commits oneself, then Providence moves too.

All sorts of things occur to help one that would never otherwise have occurred. A whole stream of events issues from the decision, raising in one's favor all manner of unforeseen incidents and meetings and material assistance, which no man could have dreamed would have come his way.

Whatever you can do, or dream you can, begin it. Boldness has genius, power, and magic in it.

Begin it now.

—Goethe

To Our Readers

*The books we publish
are our contribution to
an emerging world based on
cooperation rather than on competition,
on affirmation of the human spirit rather
than on self-doubt, and on the certainty
that all humanity is connected.
Our goal is to touch as many
lives as possible with a
message of hope for
a better world.*

Hal and Linda Kramer, Publishers

Contents

CONTENTS

Preface

Religions throughout the world claim that a "righteous" person will be miraculously sheltered from all harm. The Bible, for example, says, "No disaster can overtake you, no plague come near your tent; He has given His angels orders about you to guard you wherever you go" (Psalm 91:10–11). Many other spiritual traditions are equally explicit regarding the divine protection to which the faithful are entitled.

Yet everywhere we look, we find good people suffering, and no religion has succeeded in guaranteeing the health, safety, and prosperity of its members. Are the world's spiritual leaders simply mistaken in thinking that there really is a supernatural power watching over us? Is the problem that God holds us to some impossibly high standard of performance before judging us worthy of help? Or is it conceivable that there is some further step that even a person of great faith must take before God will intervene on his or her behalf—an invitation without which Divine Love itself cannot, or will not, interfere in human affairs?

Extraordinary as it may seem, I believe that I have discovered evidence of just such an "invitation" through studying the behavior of dozens of ordinary people who managed narrow escapes from seemingly hopeless situations. *In each case, the individual spontaneously did the very thing that many spiritual traditions say you must do if you want a miracle, only to find that a desperate situation took an unexpected turn for the better.* An impending automobile accident ended harmlessly, a serial killer decided to spare this particular victim, a "terminal" illness disappeared without a trace. I believe that the individuals who told me their stories stumbled upon an ancient formula for accessing miracles of deliverance, and that by studying their technique, you and I can learn to do the same thing.

Who Receives Miracles and Why?

People who believe in miracles often seem to think of them as special favors God performs on behalf of those who are especially deserving. However, my research suggests that this is not the case. Miracles are available to everyone. The problem is simply that we must make them possible by asking for them in the right way. Consider the case of Charles.

Charles

I recently appeared as the psychological "expert" on a daytime TV talk show dealing with miracles. Among the other guests was a man named Charles, who believes that he has been saved miraculously from several work-related accidents that had frequently been fatal to the people working around him. Charles is one of the "sandhogs" who dig the tunnels under New York City. This job has been rated as the second toughest in America (the first being salmon fishing in Alaska). The pay is good, but the work is extremely demanding and dangerous.

Charles recounted a breathtaking escape he had recently experienced when collapsed scaffolding sent sixteen tons of winch and steel crashing down three hundred feet through the underground platform where he had been working. Hearing a rending noise high above, Charles reported that he had had just enough time to curl himself into a little ball and pray aloud, "God protect me."

In this disaster, as in several previous ones, Charles escaped death by a hair's breadth. His best friend Anthony, who had been working beside him on the platform, was killed. My fellow guest told of immediately stripping off his boots and heavy clothing and then sliding thirty feet down a cable into the icy water below to search for his buddy. Charles had fully realized that if any electrical wires had been dangling in the water he would have been electrocuted, but his only thought had been to find Anthony and help him if he could. We will see the same fearless devotion to others displayed in many of the deliverance stories we will be considering.

Knowing of my interest in the reasons why miracles occur, Charles caught up to me backstage after the show to share his theory. "I'll tell you why some people get miracles and others don't. It's about being a good person. I always try to help others whenever I can, and I think that's why God protects me. I'm not particularly religious, but I try to be a loving, helpful person."

"The only problem with that," I replied, "is that it suggests that people who are *not* miraculously rescued must *not* have been good people. What about your friend Anthony, for instance. Wasn't Anthony a good, loving person? Didn't he help others?"

Charles looked stunned. "I never thought of it that way," he said. "Anthony was the best there is!"

"That's why I don't think that receiving miracles depends upon whether or not you are especially deserving. A great many wonderful human beings suffer dreadful injustice and hardship. I think that God loves everyone and would help all of us without exception. But we have to do our part to make these miracles possible."

What is the nature of the invitation that elicits divine intervention? My research suggests that it is a shift in consciousness into a peaceful, fearless, unconditionally loving state of mind in which one follows intuitive promptings without question. That Charles underwent such a mental shift is evident from his behavior. Any fears he might have had about his own safety were completely eclipsed by his loving concern for his friend.

As we shall see, miracles do not necessarily occur every time we beseech God for help, but they seem to flow naturally whenever we enter a peaceful, loving state of mind and follow inner guidance. Only then can we truly be said to have "turned the situation over to our higher power"—to use a phrase coined by the twelve-step programs such as Alcoholics Anonymous.

Even Atheists Experience Miracles

But perhaps you don't even believe in a higher power. No problem. My research indicates that divine intervention is experienced by people of all religions and no religion at all. The only difference is that believers are more likely to recognize surprising reversals of fortune as "miraculous," while nonbelievers mistakenly attribute them to "luck." Luck implies that these narrow escapes are random occurrences, but as we shall see, there is good reason to believe that they actually occur on cue whenever someone follows the appropriate procedure.

Religious people have traditionally thought of the supernatural power that makes miracles possible as "God." But some modern physicists are now finding evidence of an invisible, causal dimension out of which our minds create the things that occur within the physical world. This unmanifest realm of knowledge where possible futures are encoded as potential is highly reminiscent of what mystics call the "mind of God." And since this realm is not subject to the natural laws that govern events within our three-dimensional universe, it is quite literally "supernatural."

If you prefer scientific metaphors to spiritual ones, that's fine. As long as we can agree on the facts, there will be no need to argue over terminology. I believe that there is a guiding intelligence in the universe that is capable of changing physical "reality" under certain conditions. We may not be able to see "the hand of God," but if a supernatural power really exists, we ought to be able to observe its handiwork. And miracles are God's handiwork.

Road Testing Miracles

This book is broadly organized into two main sections. In Part One, we will explore the exciting, true-life accounts of people who escaped impending disaster after going into a meditative state of consciousness and following inner guidance. We will then consider the possibility that the positive outcomes that ensued were actually miraculous. This will involve a look at scientific objections to the possibility of miracles and consideration of alternative, nonmiraculous explanations for what I am calling "the deliverance phenomenon."

In Part Two, we get down to the nuts and bolts of receiving higher guidance and performing miracles, preparing you to "road test" the technique we have been talking about for yourself. Where the first part provides rational and empirical evidence for miracles, the second sets the stage for firsthand experience with divine help and guidance.

You need not wait for a serious physical threat in order to try out this miracle-working technique. All sorts of stubborn problems clear up quickly when we take the steps that permit divine intervention into our affairs. I think you will be delighted by the ease with which miracles occur when you sincerely invite this help. Since an invisible power within you is going to do all the "heavy lifting," accessing miracles is actually quite simple once you get the hang of it. A child could do it—indeed, a great many children *do* do it. And, after all, if miraculous solutions are really available for the asking, isn't it about time you asked?

Acknowledgments

This book is very much a group effort, drawing as it does upon deliverance stories told to me by dozens of friends, students, and colleagues. The extraordinary courage, creativity, and compassion of these people have been a great inspiration to me, and I believe that they will be equally impressive to those of you who read of their experiences. In order to safeguard the privacy of my storytellers, I have generally altered identifying details, and for the same reason, I will not acknowledge each contributor by name here. Nevertheless, I want to express my profound gratitude to everyone who shared a miraculous experience with me. Each one provided an indispensable piece of the puzzle.

I also owe an enormous debt to the following friends who struggled through early versions of the manuscript and guided its creation with their encouragement, suggestions, and criticisms: Dee Davis, Geri-Ann Galanti, Laurel Gord, Holly Harp, Eleanor Rolston, Hayden Schwartz, M. J. Shooner, Aviva Spann, and Caveh Zahedi. And Geri-Ann Galanti deserves my special thanks for her exacting work on several versions, and for having had the chutzpah to be brutally frank when necessary.

For helping and believing in me, I also want to thank my writing coach, Stuart Miller; my agent, Candice Fuhrman; my publishers, Hal and Linda Kramer; and my meticulous editor, Nancy Grimley Carleton. Without their encouragement and expert guidance, this book would not exist in its present form.

And most of all, I want to thank my husband, Arnie Weiss, who contributed to this work at every stage of the process and whose unfailing love is the greatest miracle I have ever known, or could ever hope to know.

Permissions

Grateful acknowledgment is made for permission to reprint:

Cartoons by Sidney Harris. Copyright © 1995 by Sidney Harris. Reprinted by permission.

Excerpt from *A Book of Angels* (New York: Ballantine Books, 1990) by Sophy Burnham. Copyright © 1990 by Sophy Burnham. Reprinted by permission of Ballantine Books, a division of Random House, Inc.

Excerpt by Terry Dobson as printed in *How Can I Help?* (New York: Alfred A. Knopf, 1985) by Ram Dass and Paul Gorman.

Excerpt from *Autobiography of a Yogi* by Paramahansa Yogananda. Published by Self-Realization Fellowship, Los Angeles, U.S.A. Reprinted by permission.

Quotations from *A Course in Miracles* (Tiburon, CA: Foundation for Inner Peace, 1975). Used by permission.

Introduction: Discovering Miracles of Deliverance

There is nothing [miracles] cannot do, but they cannot be performed in the spirit of doubt or fear. When you are afraid of anything, you are acknowledging its power to hurt you.

—A Course in Miracles

What if there was a way to protect yourself from physical danger and resolve painful interpersonal problems, just by changing your mind? What if your thoughts were invisibly programming the disturbing events that seem to "just happen" to you? What if you could summon a miracle to smooth your path through even the most difficult situation?

This is a book about people who may have spontaneously used an ancient spiritual technique to do just that. By altering their attitude in a particular way, they appear to have interrupted the flow of events around them, saving themselves—and sometimes others—from almost certain injury or death. It is my belief that these incidents were actual miracles, and that by distilling the common features of many such incidents, we can all learn to access "saving grace" in our own lives.

Perhaps I should begin by explaining how an experimental psychologist such as myself comes to be studying miracles. My interest in the subject began with my own narrow escape from what looked like certain death. Here is what happened.

Discovering Deliverance

I had driven up to the mountains near Los Angeles to enjoy the winter weather. The air in the city was balmy, but as I climbed the Angeles Crest Highway, it got colder. Patches of snow began to appear, and I got out to make snowballs and savor the season.

Back on the road, I was rounding a tight curve when I heard a bang and the car suddenly went out of control. As I pieced things together later, I realized that one of my rear tires had blown out on a turn, just as I was crossing a patch of black ice. I must have been going thirty-five or forty miles per hour.

The car went wild. I was briefly grateful for the fact that there was no one coming from the opposite direction as I skidded across the other lane. However, it was soon clear that my gratitude had been premature. Beyond the lane for oncoming traffic was a narrow scenic overlook area. And beyond that was the edge of a cliff. I was now hurtling sideways across the deserted parking area on a trajectory that would inevitably take my car over the brink.

It's hard to explain the next part, especially since it's difficult to see how there could have been time for so many thoughts and reactions. All I can say is that time seemed to expand.

First, although I don't think of myself as a brave person, I wasn't at all frightened. The magnitude of the danger seemed to place me beyond fear. What point was there in being afraid once the worst was inevitable? Concern about my safety gave way before a need to prepare for my death.

I remember being surprised by the fact that I was about to die. Hoping that I was mistaken, I looked the situation over again, but it was clear that I had more than enough momentum to skid over the edge. "Gee, wouldn't you think you'd know it if you were about to die?" I mused. "It's clear that no one survives a fall like this, but even now I don't feel as though I'm going to die. But maybe every-

2

one feels surprise and no one has any idea that they're going to die before they actually do. Still, you'd think you'd know at some level."

I wondered what dying was going to be like. Maybe I would suffer. Maybe the car would burst into flames the way cars do in movies when they go over cliffs. But then I thought, "It won't matter. I'll be out of my body by then." And another part piped up with, "Oh yeah! Like you know all about it!"

I vaguely regretted the fact that I had to die now. I wished that there were something I could do to get out of it. And then another part of my mind said, "Well, why don't you see if there is?"

So I searched my memory to see if there was anything I knew that might be useful. But all I could come up with was the idea that when you are skidding, you are supposed to steer into the skid. Had I read that in the manual for the driving test? I wasn't sure of the source, but I did recall that that was what experts say to do.

"Well, that's no use here," I told myself. "I'm already really close to the edge. If I turn the wheels in that direction, I'll just go over sooner."

But then I thought, "Well, what have you got to lose by trying? It's not as though you have a lot of options here." So I figured, "What the hell!" and turned the wheel into the skid.

By now I was practically at the edge. I figured that if there was any chance at all, I would have to steer into the skid until the last possible moment and then turn the wheel away from the precipice. And when I turned, it would have to be fast, but not too fast or I would skid again. How would I recognize the ultimate moment when turning would still be possible? It was probably already too late.

I became incredibly focused upon the feel of the car and the sight of the approaching cliff. It was as if the whole world had narrowed to this one problem. I was perfectly calm, as though it were some sort of totally absorbing intellectual exercise—figuring out just when and how to turn the wheel. And all the time I was watching myself with a sense of irony, since it clearly wasn't going to make any difference what I did. Even Mario Andretti couldn't have pulled this one off!

I sat there steering toward the cliff for what seemed like a very long time as the brink approached in slow motion. The ground had actually disappeared from view in front of me before a voice in my head said, "Now!"

At this signal, I turned the wheel smoothly to the right—fast, but not too fast. And to my astonishment, the car followed the wheel. I was out of the skid, and I swept gracefully away from the brink and back across the highway. With most of its momentum now exhausted, my car ran up on some boulders at the base of the cliff on the other side, and it was over.

I got out to survey the damage. The bumper was a little bent where I had run up on the rocks and, of course, my tire was flat, but otherwise the car was fine. Then I crossed the highway and looked at the skid marks in the dirt. The distance between the road and the edge of the cliff was about thirty feet. At the point where I had turned, the tire marks came to within three feet of the brink.

How long did it take my car to skid to the edge of the cliff? A car going thirty miles per hour covers forty-four feet per second. If I started the skid at about thirty-five miles per hour and the edge was some thirty feet away, it cannot realistically have taken much more than a second. Yet it was the longest second of my life. I felt as though I had had all the time in the world to think things out, make decisions, and execute them.

A few moments later, cars appeared from both directions and pulled over to help. Two men dragged my car off the rocks and whipped on my spare tire. Within minutes, I was starting for home as though nothing had even happened.

When I thought about the incident on the way back to Los Angeles, I was awed to realize that I had pulled off a driving maneuver no stunt driver would attempt. I also recognized that I could never have hoped to do it in ordinary consciousness. There

4

was something about my oddly peaceful altered state that allowed me to put total concentration into my driving. Combined with the slow-motion effect, it permitted me to calculate my reactions to a fraction of a second. The fearlessness I'd experienced in that state had also been critical. If I had been afraid as I approached the edge, I could not have thought clearly or held the car on course as long as was needed, and I would inevitably have skidded over the cliff.

Still puzzling over this incident, I mentioned it a few days later to my friend Carmela. "Now that's funny," she replied. "I had an experience just like that this week!" Here's what happened to Carmela two days after my accident.

Carmela

Carmela was strolling with her friend Fred on the bluffs near her home in Encinitas, California. It was a perfect day, and the path offered a spectacular view of the surf pounding on the rocks far below. When they came to a smaller path that snaked down the face of the bluff, Fred suggested they climb down it, and Carmela readily agreed.

"Now, I knew better than to do that. Every year there are news stories about people who are killed climbing on the bluffs. The ground is very unstable, and pieces are always falling away into the ocean. There are signs everywhere warning people to stay away from the edge, but I guess I've seen them so many times I don't even notice them anymore.

"Anyway, we started climbing down the path. It was so narrow that we had to walk in single file, and Fred led the way. We came to a place where it turned back up, and we were headed back to the top when the path suddenly fell away between the places Fred and I were standing. Then the path gave way behind me. I was perched on a little patch of ground that obviously wasn't going to be there for long either! I could hear the fallen earth crashing onto the rocks below, and I remember thinking, "Boy, was this ever a bad idea!""

5

"It should have been a frightening situation, but strangely enough, it wasn't. I found myself becoming completely calm. I realized that I had done a very foolish thing in coming down here, but it still seemed to me that everything would be all right. I went into meditation immediately and asked for help."

Carmela was a woman in her forties, and although she was in good physical shape, she'd never thought of herself as much of an athlete. Fred shouted encouragement and suggestions from above, but there was no way he could reach her or help directly. It seemed obvious that she could not go on standing where she was, so she instantly began climbing straight up.

"I reached up and found a toehold and a couple of handholds. As soon as I lifted my weight off of the patch of path, it dropped into the ocean, too. Now there was no alternative but to keep going.

"The whole climb was like that. Every time I moved my weight off a place, it crumbled and fell. Every toehold held just as long as I needed it and not a moment longer. I just kept moving."

Carmela reported that she actually felt quite cheerful as she worked her way up the nearly vertical face of the bluff. "It was an adventure—a challenge. I was totally absorbed in the task at hand, constantly scanning for places to get a hold on the cliff. Somehow, there always seemed to be another one just within reach. I never let it enter my mind that I might reach a place where I couldn't go any farther, or that I might fall onto the rocks. I wasn't afraid to die, but I didn't want to, so I just pushed that possibility right out of existence. I asked for divine help and trusted that I would be shown what to do. And I was.

"Fred raced up to the top of the bluff and was there to get ahold of me and pull me the rest of the way as I scrambled over the edge. We clung to each other and laughed with relief when it was over."

I was very struck by the fact that Carmela had had such a similar experience within a few days of mine. She, too, had been in danger of falling over a cliff to what seemed like certain death.

She, too, had entered a peaceful, fearless, intensely focused state of consciousness and then discovered skills and abilities she had not known she possessed. Some higher aspect of her own consciousness had seemed to watch over and guide her, too. The coincidence was so striking that I couldn't help thinking that it must mean something. But what?

Still working over these incidents in my mind, I mentioned them to one of my classes in the graduate program where I was teaching psychology. A student named Karen came up to me after the lecture and remarked in a confidential undertone, "Oh, by the way, Carolyn. It would still have been all right, even if you'd gone off the cliff. That's what happened to me." Intrigued, I asked for details. She related the following story.

Karen and Mike

Along with her boyfriend Mike, Karen had gone to make a family visit in the mountains of Colorado. Since the road was poorly marked, her brother met them at a nearby town so that he could lead the way to his new house. It was late at night before they started up the mountain.

Familiar with the road, Karen's brother drove quickly and confidently. Mike often saw his taillights disappear into the darkness ahead and had to hurry to keep from losing him altogether. As a result, he was going too fast to negotiate a tight turn that seemed to appear out of nowhere. A moment later, Mike had driven straight over the side of the mountain, and he and Karen were plunging into the darkness below.

Karen remembers feeling relaxed and amused as they sailed over the side. On the one hand, she knew that people who drive off cliffs in the Rocky Mountains don't live very long, but on the other, she was convinced that everything was going to be just fine. She reported that she seemed to go into an altered state of consciousness that was serene and even whimsical.

Time seemed to expand, and many thoughts drifted lazily

through her head. "Well," she thought ironically, "I guess this is why they tell you to wear seat belts!" Karen realized that neither she nor Mike was wearing one, but this thought was quickly followed by the reflection that it couldn't possibly matter with a fall of this magnitude. Despite the fact that logic told her she and Mike were about to die, she was absolutely confident that everything would turn out fine.

Strangely enough, it did. The car splashed down in the middle of a beaver pond just deep enough to break its fall. Once the waves subsided, Karen and Mike discovered that the water came to just below the windows. As cold trickles began to leak in through the doors, the two climbed onto the roof, where they huddled together, laughing and singing songs to pass the time.

Soon a motorist noticed their skid marks going over the edge and stopped to see what had happened. The two hailed him boisterously as he peered down into the darkness, and he went for help. Before long the car was towed out of the pond. It was undamaged and started up without difficulty.

The local people who gathered at the scene of the accident were doubly amazed. First, it was hard for them to believe that Karen and Mike had come through such a spectacular fall without so much as a scratch. But there was a further source of wonder. Although they passed the spot daily, no one had ever seen a beaver pond there before.

Could These Be Miracles?

The juxtaposition of these three highly unusual, yet strikingly similar, incidents made a strong impression on me. They seemed somehow to be cut from the same cloth. When I began mentioning them to other groups and classes, I found that often someone would chime in and say, "That's just like what happened to me!" And sure enough it was. I learned that a great many people had faced what appeared to be serious danger, only to go into an oddly peaceful altered state of consciousness and discover that things worked out fine.

Sometimes, as in my case or Carmela's, the positive outcome seemed to depend upon the skillful way in which the person handled the emergency. Other cases followed the pattern of Karen and Mike's accident, where the individuals involved could do nothing but rest in a peaceful state and await developments. Some of the people I spoke to attributed spiritual significance to their deliverance, while others never considered the possibility that it was anything more than good luck.

But every one of them instantly recognized the strangely peaceful and detached altered state. Some described it as having a playful quality, while for others it was characterized by self-confidence, compassion, or a sense of being guided by some benevolent higher power. Yet everyone agreed that they had experienced a peculiar sense of emotional distance, accompanied by the conviction that, somehow, everything was going to be all right. In a few cases, fear or anger was an alternative consciousness that seemed to compete for attention with the sense of peace, but for most, fear was conspicuous by its absence.

As intriguing as I found these stories, I don't believe I would have recognized their underlying significance if I had not been a student of metaphysics as well as a psychologist. On the one hand, I was learning about various spiritual thought systems that claim to teach one how to work miracles. On the other, I was being inundated with real-life stories of ordinary people who seemed to have spontaneously followed the procedures these spiritual systems recommended, only to find that a very dangerous situation worked out fine. Was it possible that these were actual miracles? Could it be that the "faith that can move mountains" is really only a vastly expanded understanding of the creative power of consciousness? Might miraculous solutions be within the reach of everyone?

Part One
Are Miracles Really Possible?

1

Believing the Unbelievable

Do you really believe you can plan for your safety and joy better than He can? You need be neither careful nor careless; you need merely cast your cares upon Him because He careth for you.

—A Course in Miracles

Brian

Brian had just received his doctorate in psychology and had been working at his first professional job in a maximum-security prison for only a few months when violence broke out. Prisoners seized weapons and hostages and began issuing nonnegotiable demands from the library building they were occupying. Tension mounted throughout the day as the National Guard arrived to surround the prison. Everyone waited breathlessly to hear the governor's response to the prisoners' demands.

Late in the afternoon, the warden stormed into Brian's office and shouted, "Goddamn it, you're the psychologist! You go in there and convince those prisoners to surrender!" Brian could only conclude in retrospect that he must have been more afraid of his boss than of the rioting inmates. Minutes later, he found himself headed for the library to tell a group of armed and desperate murderers that the governor had rejected all of their demands and that they had just better throw down their weapons and release their hostages, or else!

"Or else what?!" Brian wondered, uncomfortably aware of what traditionally happens to the bearer of bad tidings. "Or else shoot me, I guess."

Brian was conscious of guns trained on him from every direction as he took that long walk across the yard. The silence was so profound that he could hear the blood pounding in his ears, and it seemed as though everyone in the prison was breathlessly waiting to see what would happen to him. Obviously, whatever occurred, Brian was going to be right in the middle. It seemed largely a matter of whether he would be shot accidentally by the guards or intentionally by the prisoners once the fireworks began.

Unable to see how he could have gotten himself into such a situation, Brian experienced a growing sense of unreality. A few minutes ago he had been a nice middle-class kid trying to earn an honest living. Now all of a sudden he was Gary Cooper in *High Noon*. How, exactly, did something like this happen?

Despite his overwrought mental state, or possibly because of it, Brian found himself drifting into an amusing fantasy of himself playing this preposterous role in the best Hollywood tradition. He began to see himself as the Gary Cooper character in the Western — the lone figure of justice, warily moving down the empty main street of a frontier town. The prison guards became the townsfolk who watched from hiding as Brian went forth to fight their battle for them. That's right — Sheriff Brian, who would fearlessly confront odds that could only be beaten in a screenwriter's fantasy. Because a man's gotta do what a man's gotta do!

The next thing Brian knew, he had begun to parody himself and his grandiose fantasy. Pausing dramatically, he squared off against the library, hands flexing over imaginary six-shooters on his hips. He began to stalk toward the building in a ridiculous burlesque of the classic gunfighter swagger. Feeling the need for a little musical accompaniment, he shattered the tense silence by loudly whistling "Do Not Forsake Me, Oh My Darling," the theme from *High Noon*.

For a minute, guards and prisoners watched Brian's bizarre performance in stunned silence. Then they began getting it. Brian as Gary Cooper. Everyone acting as if this goofy kid was going to be able to face down a gang of armed killers. Suddenly everyone could see how absurd the situation had become.

Laughter rang out from all sides. Fed by the tension that had been building all day, it rose to hysterical heights. Guards and prisoners alike became helpless with hilarity as their anxiety poured out of them in foot-stomping, knee-pounding guffaws. People laughed until they cried—until they could barely stand up.

When it was over, Brian strolled into the library and explained the governor's response and the hopelessness of their position to the prisoners, who by now regarded him as a hell of a guy. Minutes later, he presided over their peaceful surrender.

The question we are going to be considering in this book is: Might this have been an example of an actual miracle? Is it possible that without realizing it, Brian did something that permitted divine intervention? Was the happy ending merely a piece of good luck, or could it have been something more?

Admittedly, when we see Brian's story standing alone like this, there is no particular reason to suspect supernatural involvement. The same thing can be said of the three anecdotes related in the Introduction, and, indeed, of all of the dozens of accounts we will be exploring in this book. Taken individually, all of them appear to represent nothing more than a lucky break. Danger threatens, but fortunately things turn out all right.

"Big deal!" I hear you cry. "Not all accidents, assaults, and illnesses end in disaster. What is so mysterious about the fact that the people you talked to escaped injury? Why should we drag in 'miracles' to account for something that can be understood perfectly well without them?"

My case for miracles revolves around the strange emotional reactions displayed by the people who told me of their narrow escapes. Like Brian, they all seemed to slip into an extraordinarily carefree state of mind and behave as though they were oblivious to danger. In retrospect, these people were themselves amazed at their own sense of well-being. Vague regret seemed to be about

15

the strongest emotion anyone reported when faced with the prospect of imminent death.

This surprising equanimity reminded me of the peaceful detachment one experiences in meditation. I couldn't help wondering if perhaps these survivors really had entered into a meditative state. This idea was all the more intriguing because I was aware that going into meditation is precisely what spiritual traditions throughout the world say you ought to do if you want a miracle. Again and again, people reported that they had done the very thing mystics claim will make miracles possible, only to find a highly dangerous situation taking an unexpected turn for the better. Could these really have been miracles?

What Are Miracles?

Author C. S. Lewis defined a "miracle" as an instance in which a supernatural power interferes in the natural world, and this is the definition I will be using here.[1] When most of us think of miraculous intervention, we envision a totally inexplicable event— one that *could not* have been caused by any natural means, and that *must* therefore have been caused by the power of God, possibly acting through an intermediary such as an angel, prophet, saint, or healer. For example, if the Red Sea parted for the ancient Hebrews as they fled the Pharaoh's army, or a body that was well-and-truly dead was resurrected from its tomb three days later, there can be no "perfectly ordinary" explanation for what occurred. Skeptics can argue that such things never really happened, but if they did happen, they were indisputably the work of a supernatural power.

The problem is that while wonders of this magnitude are undeniably fascinating, they do not really lend themselves to verification. If we call an event "miraculous" only in those rare instances where we can *conclusively* rule out every possible cause except a supernatural power, we will be confining our attention to a set of circumstances so singular that most of us will never have any firsthand experience with it. Futher, the evidence will only seem "conclusive" to the extent that we credit a stranger's story about what actually happened. Take, for example, this account by my friend Hayden and her mother Doris of an allegedly miraculous rescue during a family trip to the beach.

Hayden and Doris

When Hayden was twelve years old, her family went on a vacation to Daytona Beach, Florida. One day, Hayden's father had gone into town for an hour or so, leaving the little girl and her mother Doris to enjoy the off-season luxury of an enormous stretch of deserted sand and sea. Doris paddled around in an inner tube while Hayden held onto the outside. The two chatted contentedly, savoring the delightful contrast of cool water and hot sunshine.

Hayden thinks that they must somehow have lost all track of time, because the water suddenly got rough. Looking up, the pair was startled to realize that they had drifted far out to sea. The beach was just a line on the horizon, and the wind was carrying them out into the shipping lanes at a high rate of speed. The next thing they knew, several large swells washed over them from out of nowhere. Hayden was torn away from the inner tube and swamped by the waves.

A poor swimmer to begin with, the twelve-year-old struggled to the surface and fought to get back to her mother and the safety of the tube. Doris was frantically trying to reach her as well, but despite their best efforts, the distance between them just kept widening. Now thrashing around in panic, Hayden began to drown. Wave after wave rolled over her. She was dragged repeatedly beneath the choking surface, only to struggle weakly back into the air.

Finally, exhausted by her unequal contest with the sea, Hayden knew that she couldn't go on. As she was about to stop her useless struggles and let the waves take her under, a man appeared in the water a few feet away. Although there had been no one in sight the whole time they'd been at the beach, here suddenly was a strong swimmer right next to her!

Doris and Hayden agree that the man was dark haired and seemed to be in his thirties, although they didn't have time to notice much else or wonder where he'd come from. Hayden lunged for his outstretched hand, but she could not quite reach it. Since she had missed it by only an inch or so, she gathered her flagging strength and tried again. Again she missed, but only just.

"What I didn't realize," Hayden says today, "is that he was actually towing both of us to shore. Mother and I were trying as hard as we could to reach the guy, and he was somehow pulling us with him while staying just beyond reach. Although we'd been way out in the ocean, and although I never could quite reach his outstretched hand, we were moving toward the beach. And quickly, too! I suddenly looked up and found myself in shallow water quite close to the shore. At that point the man gently gathered me up in his arms and carried me the rest of the way up onto the beach.

"He lowered me to the sand, and I immediately began to vomit up the water I'd swallowed. Mother ran up onto the beach right behind us, and she fell to her knees beside me and held me as I retched."

Both women think that it took Hayden about a minute to finish retching up the water she had swallowed. Then the two of them settled back and looked around to thank their rescuer. But there was no one there.

"And I mean no one!" Hayden emphasizes. "Just as before, the beach and the water were empty as far as the eye could see. And the eye could see clearly for a good half mile in every direction!

"You've got to understand that this was a totally flat and featureless beach flanked on one side by a flat, calm ocean and on the other by a deserted parking lot. I wasn't vomiting more than a minute or two at the most, and an Olympic sprinter couldn't have gotten out of sight in that amount of time. There was simply nowhere he could have gone.

"Mother and I are both certain that there had been no one within a quarter of a mile of us before I started drowning, and it was clear that there was no one within a quarter mile now. The man had appeared out of thin air and then vanished back into it. He somehow towed both of us to shore against the wind and the current without touching either of us, carried me out of the water, and then simply dematerialized.

"I'm sure that some people would say we were just distracted and confused, but we both saw what happened and we both know beyond any possibility of mistake that this was not an ordinary human being. Mother and I both believe that we were rescued by an angel."

Believing the Impossible

In the last few years there have been a flurry of publications that recount astonishing incidents where angels appear to have rescued humans. I think that an unbiased person must at least consider the possibility that such things really happen. Nevertheless, it is clear that they don't happen every day. And unless they happen to you, how do you know what to believe?

If this rescue really occurred the way Hayden and Doris say it did, then some supernatural power must have intervened on their behalf. How can an ordinary human being materialize and dematerialize? If they were mistaken in thinking that he did this, we are still left to explain how an ordinary man could have towed them both to shore without physical contact. And if he were only a hallucination and they really swam in under their own power, who lifted Hayden out of the water and carried her up the beach?

It is difficult to see how the impression of these events could have resulted from either mental confusion or an honest mistake. If they were experienced by only one person, we might write them off as a momentary aberration, but both Hayden and Doris agree that they saw the same things. And while psychologists sometimes use terms such as *group hallucination* to account for inexplicable events witnessed by more than one person, the term has no real explanatory value. Science knows of no mechanism that can explain how two or more people could hallucinate the same thing at the same time.

The simplest explanation is, of course, that they are both lying. However, I know these women personally, and to me the idea that they would make up such a story and stick to it all these years seems no less incredible than the possibility that they really were rescued by an angel. Of course, you don't know them, so what convinces me may not convince you.

And that is precisely my point. If the argument for miracles rests upon tales of impossible occurrences told by strangers, it will never be truly convincing. Who knows whether the witness is at all credible? And even if he or she is credible, how far does that take us?

Most people today are aware of the inherent limitations of eyewitness testimony. Even jurors watching an alleged crime enacted before them on videotape often cannot agree about what they are seeing, despite an opportunity to review the material dozens of times. If that is so, then how much confidence can we place in the eyewitness testimony of strangers who claim to have experienced a miracle? However convincingly miraculous this aquatic rescue may have seemed to Hayden and Doris, those of us who hear of it at second hand are entitled to be skeptical.

Even the best scientific research on miracles involves this same limitation. For example, there is an international medical commission studying miraculous healings associated with the Shrine of the Virgin at Lourdes, France. This panel of distinguished Catholic physicians has found some sixty-four cases where no explanation other than a miracle is even remotely plausible. As a first attempt at rigorous scientific research on miracles, these findings are tremendously important.

However, they still leave you and me in the position of having to take someone else's word for what happened. Scientists have biases and make mistakes just like the rest of us. And there will always be equally qualified authorities arguing for the other side of any really interesting question. Even if we are prepared to accept what the "experts" have to say about miracles, how are we to decide which ones to believe?

Believing the Improbable

But the study of miracles need not revolve around impossible wonders that happen to others. If there really is a spiritual power that intervenes to heal and rescue humans, it seems unlikely that its activities would be confined to situations outside the realm of ordinary human experience. Once we know what to look for, I think we will find smaller, "garden-variety" miracles blooming in our own backyards, where we can look at them up close and form our own opinions about the way they work.

The approach to miracles we will be taking in this book largely ignores great wonders that strain one's credibility to the breaking point. Instead, we are going to focus upon true-life accounts of narrow escapes that fall somewhere between "the impossible" and "the everyday." These surprising reversals of fortune invariably occur after someone releases judgment about a dangerous situation and enters a peaceful altered state of consciousness.

By focusing upon these cases of deliverance, we can readily see the discrepancy between what seemed to be about to happen and what actually did occur after an individual slipped into a meditative state. As with Brian's account above, the positive outcomes to these stories are *surprising* given the way things were shaping up, but by no means *incredible.* You will have little trouble believing that such things could really occur.

The interpretation that these incidents may have been miraculous is usually mine, rather than the storyteller's. A person may have many complex psychological motives for asserting that he or she was the recipient of a miracle. But most of the people who told me their stories made no such claims, a fact that I think minimizes the likelihood that they were lying or exaggerating.

21

Although some saw the hand of God in what happened to them, most regarded their experiences as nothing more than fantastic luck.

And what makes me think they were anything more than that? When we look at many such incidents together, a pattern begins to emerge. What at first seemed to be only random lucky breaks suddenly come together to form a new category—one made up of instances where an endangered person releases fear and anger and slips into a meditative state, only to find the situation taking a surprising turn for the better.

We are going to see that the procedure these people spontaneously followed corresponds closely to the one associated with miracles by spiritual traditions throughout the world. After considering alternative explanations for what happened, we will look at some advanced thinking within modern physics in order to understand how a shift in consciousness might actually influence the course of events within the physical world. Best of all, after we have explored the procedure for accessing miracles, you will be in a position to try it out and see for yourself whether or not it works.

The existence of miracles is too important a matter to be left entirely to experts. If miracles are real, then learning to access them is crucial. And while scientific research on miracles is valuable, it is not going to resolve this issue to the personal satisfaction of anyone who is genuinely skeptical. Unless you can see miracles at work in your own life, they will not be real *for you*.

Is it possible that miracles are really nothing more than extreme examples of creative principles we are all using all the time? While there appear to be gifted miracle workers throughout the world who use these principles intentionally to manifest the physical "reality" of their choice, the mystics of many faiths suggest that every one of us is *unconsciously* employing them to create the world we see. By studying the "technique" of successful miracle workers, it is my belief that you can learn how to perform miracles consciously yourself. Perhaps you will even discover that you *already have* performed miracles, without realizing what you were doing.

Before we go on to consider how miracles might be possible, let us get a better feel for the basic deliverance phenomenon. In the next chapter, we will explore cases where the danger came through accidents. As you read each of these stories, pay particular attention to the unusual state of consciousness that invariably precedes the positive outcome, and consider how it may be influencing what happens.

2

Surviving Accidents

[Zen meditation] is a heightened state of concentrated awareness wherein one is neither tense nor hurried, and certainly never slack. It is the mind of somebody facing death.

—Yasutani Roshi

Let us begin by looking at some of the simpler stories involving accidents in order to get a feel for the basic deliverance phenomenon before discussing the more complex and psychologically interesting cases involving assaults. Like the three stories recounted in the Introduction, these incidents are relatively uncomplicated. They occurred quickly and involved no direct interaction with other people. Perhaps because of this simplicity, their underlying structure is readily apparent. As you read each story, notice the presence of the three critical elements—danger, a strangely peaceful and timeless mental state, and a surprisingly positive outcome.

Inner Peace Despite Impending Disaster

Carol

Carol was riding her motorcycle home from the grocery store when the car in front of her slammed on its brakes without warning. Unable to stop, Carol's bike smacked into the rear of the vehicle, and the next moment she found herself somersaulting through the air.

"I seemed to have a lot of time to think about things as I flew over the car. But I wasn't afraid. I knew that accidents like this often lead to death or brain damage or paralysis, yet I felt very sure that things were going to be perfectly all right. It was actually a kind of pleasant, carefree feeling. I don't know how I knew that everything would be okay, but I just felt that it would.

"And it was okay. Before leaving the supermarket I had shoved a big box of laundry soap into my backpack. When I landed on the pavement, I came down flat on my back and the soap box crushed beneath me, absorbing the impact. My helmet took care of my head. The spectators were flabbergasted when I bounced up a moment later laughing and brushed myself off. My bike was totaled, but I didn't get a scratch.

Carol's story reveals the dual consciousness of all of the people who told me their stories. On the one hand, they have a realistic idea of the probability of injury or death — a thought that would ordinarily inspire fear. On the other, they are at peace and somehow "know" that everything will turn out all right. Yet this acceptance is not based upon their conviction that they are going to be the ones to beat the odds. The sense of things being all right seems to exist *despite* the realization that they will probably be injured or killed. This is also seen in Mary's case.

Mary and Leonard

Mary was driving along the New York State Thruway with her husband Leonard beside her. It had been snowing, and the road was slippery. When another vehicle cut her off suddenly, she applied the brakes hard, and her car slid out of control.

"We were in the left lane, and we started to skid sideways across the thruway from left to right. That meant hurtling across several lanes of fast-moving traffic. There were cars all around us. I thought we were going to die.

"Strangely enough, I wasn't the least bit frightened. The whole thing seemed to happen in slow motion. The steering wheel was useless, and I just let go of it and waited calmly for the impact I knew would come.

"In the meantime, I seemed to do an awful lot of thinking. I felt regret about the fact that I was going to die now, although it didn't seem like a big deal. If my time was up, I could accept that. But then I thought about how unfair it was that I was going to kill Leonard, too. That really did seem like a shame.

"Our marriage had nearly been destroyed by his alcoholism, and now, after eighteen years of hell, he had finally gotten into Alcoholics Anonymous. He'd been sober for about two months at the time this happened, and all I could think was, 'Poor Leonard! After all these years the poor guy finally gets sober, and I go and kill him in a car accident! What a stupid waste!'

"The next thing I knew, I was pulling to a stop on the right-hand shoulder. Somehow we had skidded across the whole thruway without a collision. I can't tell you how relieved and grateful I felt. It was as if God had given us a second chance to get our lives straightened out."

Selfless Concern for Others

Again we see the slowing of perceptions that permits leisurely reflection upon a number of topics, despite the speed with which this skid across the thruway must have occurred. Time seems to expand within the altered state. And notice again the curiously fearless quality of Mary's thought process. She fully expects to die, yet her only real regret concerns her role in depriving her husband of *his* life.

This theme of concern for others was repeated again and again in the stories I was told. Instead of valuing their lives above all else, people who receive miracles of deliverance seem to accept their fate and then turn their concern toward others. This altruistic attitude is clearly seen in Julie's thought process.

Julie

It was late winter, and the single lanes for traffic in each direction were tightly hemmed in by five-foot walls of ice and snow thrown up there over many months by the snowplows. As Julie rounded a turn, she saw an oncoming car skid out of control and cross into her lane. It was moving fast on a collision course with her vehicle.

"I was electrified when I saw that car coming right at me. The awareness hit me like a shock. And then somehow I was perfectly calm, and everything was happening in slow motion. I could see that the other vehicle was out of control and that there was nothing the driver could do. We would inevitably collide unless I somehow got out of the way, but there was nowhere to go.

"I thought about pulling into the oncoming lane, but I immediately realized that there were other cars coming fast in that lane that would not be able to stop or get out of the way. The idea seemed to offer some hope that I could swerve around the skidding car and not be killed in a head-on collision, but it was clear that this would cause other collisions and many other people might be hurt or killed. That was no good.

"The only other option was to swerve into the wall of snow beside the road. It was covered with ice and looked solid. In my mind, it might as well have been concrete. I figured I would be killed instantly if I did that, but at least the other drivers and their passengers would be okay.

"It was as if I was mentally calculating the risks and the loss of life both ways. Either I died alone or I tried to live and put others at risk, too. Although I know it sounds impossibly idealistic, that's really the way it seemed in my mind. I felt very dispassionate about it—as if it was just arithmetic. It seemed clear that under the circumstances, it would be better for me to die alone. I felt a little sad when I realized that I would have to crash into that wall and die now, but that was all. I could see that it was for the best.

"So I jerked the wheel and hit the snowbank. I must have been going forty-five or fifty miles per hour. There was a jolt upon impact, and then everything became dark. Moments later, the car came to a gentle stop in complete darkness. I couldn't open the doors, so I just sat there, scarcely able to believe that I was alive and unhurt.

"It took a few minutes before I started hearing sounds around me. People who had seen the accident had pulled over and were digging me out. They were amazed and overjoyed when they got through the snow and found that I was perfectly all right. They said that they had never seen anything like the explosion of snow when I hit the bank, and they couldn't believe I had survived such an impact.

"I just sat tight, and in about twenty minutes they had dragged my car out of the deep tunnel it had made in the snowbank. It turned out that the people in the skidding car were fine. With me out of the way the driver had gotten his vehicle back under control and stopped safely. The people who had been approaching in the other lane all felt that I had saved their lives by pulling right instead of left.

"It was like a celebration. We all hugged one another, laughing with relief. We compared notes on what had happened and congratulated ourselves on being alive. It seemed amazing that a situation that had looked so grim could turn out to be absolutely harmless and even fun! My car was fine, and I was able to drive off with no problem at all."

"Team Spirit"

Notice the surprising degree of selfless concern for others reflected in this and other stories. Julie accepts the possibility of her own death as an unfortunate fact—almost the way one would accept the necessity of a trip to the dentist. In ordinary consciousness, the prospect of one's own death appears horrifying—unthinkable. Yet, in the peaceful altered state, these people simply accept the situation and quickly move on to display concern for the well-being of others. They seem to be operating from some larger perspective in which their own individual lives are not so terribly important.

It is almost as though people in this altered state regard themselves as team players. They want to continue their lives, but they recognize that what truly matters is the team's overall performance. This commitment to the larger effort will become even more striking when we explore some of the stories involving deliverance from assaults. There we will see people treat the men who are planning to murder them with genuine love and compassion. The "team" for which these individuals are ready to surrender their lives seems to include even their worst "enemies." The team appears to be humanity itself.

Alex's story may also be said to reflect this atmosphere of team spirit since he endangered himself by trying to help a companion.

Alex

As a young man completing his military service in Venezuela, Alex was riding on the back of an open jeep in a parade. There were three men sitting on the seat in front, and Alex was tightly wedged between two others, perched on the back of the vehicle.

The driver was rounding a corner at about thirty-five miles per hour when Alex realized that the man on his left had lost his balance and was falling over backward. By the time Alex saw what was happening, his companion was already practically out of the jeep.

Reaching out instinctively, Alex grabbed the man and tried to pull him back. But this only succeeded in unseating him as well, and he found himself toppling backward toward the pavement in slow motion.

Alex reports that as he fell, he went into a mental state of total acceptance. He knew that it was very likely that he would be seriously injured or even killed, but the knowledge did not disturb him. He remembers thinking that if it was God's will for him to die now, that would be all right. He experienced a state of complete surrender.

Both men fell out of the jeep, but while Alex's companion was badly injured, Alex himself experienced no ill effects from the fall. He believes that his spiritual state of surrender to God was what protected him.

Alex's sense of having been spared by God is also seen in many cases. To continue our "team" analogy, it is as though people who receive miracles are prepared to abide by the referee's decision, but are relieved when they are permitted to continue playing. Take, for example, Pat.

Pat

Pat was driving in heavy, fast-moving freeway traffic when there was a collision a few cars in front of her. Suddenly, cars were swerving madly back and forth, horns were blaring, brakes were screeching, and the air was filled with the sounds of crunching metal and shattering glass. Cars smashing into one another rebounded into adjacent lanes, where they crashed into other cars. There was a powerful chain reaction as the accident engulfed one vehicle after another.

To Pat, trapped in a middle lane with crashing vehicles before, behind and on either side of her, it seemed as though all hell had broken loose. Despite the speed with which things were occurring, Pat found herself flipping into a peaceful, dreamy state.

"I felt as if I was in a state of grace. Somehow, I was utterly serene and completely confident that I would be all right. Not that I thought my car would not crash—just that everything was somehow going to be all right whatever happened.

"When I finally got my car stopped and the dust cleared, I found that mine was the only vehicle anywhere near the accident that had not crashed. The scene was one of total devastation, and cars in front of mine, behind it, and on either side were all totaled.

And here I was in the middle of all this wreckage without so much as a dented bumper. I'd known that it would be all right, and it was. I know that God was with me that day."

Detachment

Pat described the altered state of consciousness as a "state of grace," giving it obvious spiritual connotations. Rita also believes that God preserved her.

Rita

A newly licensed teenage driver, Rita was on her way home from her job in downtown Chicago. Although it was rush hour and raining, traffic was still moving fast. This was before the change to the fifty-five mile per hour speed limit, and Rita estimates that traffic was moving at about seventy miles per hour despite the wet conditions.

She was in the far left lane when traffic unexpectedly slowed up ahead. Rita believes that it was her lack of driving experience that made her slam on her brakes. She was crossing a slippery, wet metal bridge at the time, and the car instantly spun out of control.

"You know, you'd expect to be really scared in a situation like that. But I wasn't scared at all. I felt completely calm. I thought, 'Well, I'm going to die now.' The car was swerving and spinning, and there were four lanes of speeding cars on one side and the concrete median strip on the other. I decided to let go of the wheel and close my eyes, because I figured that what was going to happen next wouldn't be pretty, and there wasn't a thing in the world I could do about it. I just thought, 'Oh well,' and waited to see what would happen.

"The next thing I knew, the car had come to a stop. I opened my eyes, and there I was looking into astonished faces as cars passed me. Somehow my car wound up facing the wrong way on the right-hand shoulder. I had spun across four lanes of speeding rush-hour traffic without hitting or being hit by anybody! Can you beat that?

"I just sat there for a few minutes, scarcely able to believe my luck. I know I said a prayer of thanks to God. And all the time people kept zipping past with their jaws sagging and their eyes big, wondering, 'How in the world did she get there?' It just blew their minds, and they looked so funny I had to laugh.

"Finally I started the car up and crawled very slowly the wrong way down the shoulder back to the on-ramp, where I got off. I drove the rest of the way home on surface streets. I still can hardly believe that I came out of something like that without so much as a scratch! And I've never gotten over the fact that I wasn't the least bit frightened while it was happening."

Rita was powerless once her car went out of control, and she recognized this fact. Instead of engaging in futile struggle, she quickly "turned the situation over" and retreated into a sense of inner peace to await the outcome. The positive result she received filled her with gratitude to the higher power she believed had spared her life.

Fearlessness

The next story provides another amusing illustration of the protective power of that strangely peaceful state.

M. J.

When the big Northridge earthquake jolted Los Angeles residents awake at 4:30 A.M., M. J. sprung out of bed with a smile on her face and an unshakable sense of peace in her heart.

"It was just like your miracle stories, Carolyn!" M. J. told me. "I realized I might be about to die, but whether I survived or not didn't seem to matter. In that moment, I was completely willing to accept God's will for me, whatever it was. Before I got sober two years ago, I used to be scared to death of earthquakes, and here I was in the middle of what seemed as if it might be 'The Big One,' feeling totally at peace.

"My roommate Antonia and I both stumbled out into the hall, where we braced ourselves in doorways until the first big tremors were over. Of course, the power was out, and it was pitch-black. She was really scared, but I just found it exhilarating—like an E-ticket ride at Disneyland."

The previous evening, M. J. had happened to notice a list of emergency precautions to take in case of earthquake, and once the first violent tremors subsided the women swung into action, finding flashlights, clothing, and shoes in the nearly total darkness that comes when the lights of a whole city are extinguished. Remembering warnings regarding drinking water, they quickly filled containers from the tap. M. J. kept up a flow of buoyant conversation throughout, trying to reassure Antonia that everything would be fine.

As the wrenching aftershocks continued, the two scurried downstairs to check on friends in another apartment. There, the four of them rode out the rest of the turbulent night, keeping one another company as they huddled in their respective doorways. Far from being frightening, the occasion assumed a partylike atmosphere for these folks.

"We really had a blast, Carolyn! These are all great people, and we just had the best time ever, cracking jokes and laughing ourselves sick as the aftershocks came rolling through. Finally it got light, and Antonia and I ventured back to our apartment. It was a total wreck! Well, not total.

"My room was the exception to the general devastation. I swear, it didn't look like it existed in the same time zone as the rest of the place, much less the same apartment. Everywhere else bookshelves had been torn off the walls, hanging pictures and mirrors were smashed, and furniture had been pitched all over the place. The floor was carpeted with broken glass and crockery.

"When I first looked into my own room, it seemed completely untouched. All of my angels were hanging on the walls just where they should be. The only thing that seemed to have moved at all was a low bookshelf by my bed. It had jumped two feet to the left. And when it landed, it had pitched my Alcoholics Anonymous Big Book onto my bed. When I saw it lying open there, I had to laugh. It was just as if God was offering me some really good reading material. That book was the only thing in the whole room that was out of place!"

Surrender

Like M. J., David also consciously turned to God in what he supposed might be his last moments of life.

David

David was on a white-water rafting trip with friends. He had been looking forward to this vacation from his video production business for a long time, and he was loving it. It was thrilling, laughing and hanging on for dear life as they plunged through one set of rapids after another.

Even when he was suddenly pitched out of the raft into the icy water, David was not overly concerned. After all, he was a healthy young man and a strong swimmer. He was wearing a life jacket. Spills were part of the fun. Of course, everything would be fine.

"But it wasn't. As I understood later, what happened was that the raft and I both got caught in strong circular currents that were holding us in one place. I got trapped under the raft. I kept bobbing up to the surface, but every time I did, my head hit the raft and I bounced back down. I kept struggling to swim out from under, but the raft was swirling around above me and I was being dragged by the current. Every time I came up, it was the same story.

"I was bobbing up and down this way for a long time. And

at some point it dawned on me that maybe this was it. Maybe I wasn't going to make it. It was like, 'Oh! Maybe this is where I die.' And I felt surprised, but not at all frightened. It was a very peaceful feeling. I just surrendered to the will of God and figured that if it was my time to die, it must be all right.

"So then I thought, 'Well, if I'm going to die, is there anything I ought to do?' And I immediately knew that there was. I've been a deeply committed Hare Krishna for many years, so of course I began to inwardly chant 'Hare Krishna.' Please understand that I really wanted to live. But if it was my time, I wanted to go with the name of God on my lips. So I tried again for the surface with the last of my energy, inwardly repeating, 'Hare Krishna, Hare Krishna.'

"And that time I made it! I popped up beside the raft, and everybody let out a shout and dragged me in. And I knew that it was Lord Krishna's will that I go on living."

It Doesn't Matter What You Call God

David's case underscores another point of critical importance. Although, as we shall see, most of the folks who told me their stories were spiritually oriented people, they did not share any particular religious path. David was a devotee of Krishna, but many others were Christians or Jews. A number followed no particular religion, although they dabbled in Eastern meditation, studied Native American rituals, or subscribed to the twelve-step program view of some undefined higher power that influenced their lives. If these were indeed miracles, it is clear that divine intervention was not reserved for members of any particular spiritual tradition.

Are These Mere Accidents?

Of course, it could be argued that these were all simply lucky breaks or that the altered state was responsible for the successful outcomes in some simpler and more obvious way. Perhaps being

35

at peace allowed the endangered individual to relax. People who are sleeping or intoxicated often fare better in accidents than those who react to danger by tensing up, and the same may be true of those who experience emotional detachment.

It is also possible that inner peace permitted the person to think clearly and react optimally. This was certainly true in my experience, where it was necessary to steer into the skid, and in Carmela's, where she had to climb the face of a nearly vertical bluff. It may have played a role in other cases as well.

Perhaps David swam more efficiently after becoming centered. Maybe Alex managed to hit the pavement in a better position because he was focused and relaxed. Possibly Pat may have done some fancy driving without realizing it, so that it was actually her own skill that saved her from the chain-reaction freeway accident.

Still, it is clear that people like Karen, Mike, Rita, and Mary, who simply awaited their fate, did not save themselves through their own skillful efforts. When we look at more of these deliverance stories, I think you will agree that more is going on in that altered state of consciousness than meets the eye. Many of my subjects had a sense of being guided out of danger by some higher power, and some said that a "loving presence" actually took over for them and spoke and acted in their place. There was often a sense of having been helped by a power greater than themselves. Perhaps this is pure imagination, but perhaps it is not.

Logically, there seem to be four possible explanations for these incidents.

(1) *Coincidence.* Perhaps in suggesting that the reversal of fortune is related to the peaceful mental state, I am seeing a pattern where none exists. Maybe people facing danger experience a variety of mental states, and I just happened to encounter those who (a) went into a peaceful, meditative state and (b) escaped relatively unscathed.

There may very well be other people out there who faced the prospect of death with a peaceful mental state and were killed or seriously injured. And perhaps others experienced rage or terror and nonetheless escaped without a scratch. Maybe this is all simply a random process. While the happy endings do seem unlikely until they occur, this does not necessarily mean that they are miraculous. After all, even highly improbable events do *sometimes* happen.

(2) *Luck.* Often when people talk about luck, they conceive of it as a random process, roughly synonymous with "coincidence." But sometimes it refers to a propensity of certain individuals to succeed where others would fail. Maybe my informants were actually "lucky" people.

(3) *Precognition.* Perhaps the individual somehow subconsciously foresees the future and recognizes that the danger is only apparent. The peaceful mental state might be a *response* to foreknowledge of the successful outcome, rather than the *cause* of it.

(4) *Miracles.* Maybe by going into a peaceful altered state the individual accesses inner guidance or some latent ability to influence events in the physical world. Perhaps the act of choosing peace over fear or anger in a dangerous situation somehow *makes* the situation turn out well.

If coincidence, luck, or precognition is the correct interpretation, then the peaceful altered state would not be causally related to the narrow escapes and there would be no "deliverance phenomenon." By suggesting that these were miracles, I am indicating a belief in the fourth possibility—that the endangered individual's altered state of consciousness influenced the outcome of events by inviting the intervention of a supernatural "higher power."

We might think of this higher power as a supernatural aspect of our own mind that possesses a latent capacity for altering events within the natural world. Alternatively, it might be some other supernatural entity with abilities a human being does not personally possess—that is, God, an angelic being, a spirit guide, or something similar. Such a being might act on the situation directly or by guiding the activity of the person going through it. For the time being, I will leave the question open and refer to the hypothetical agent of miracles simply as one's "higher power."

The Miracle Workers

Who were these people whom I suspect of having worked miracles? No one special. These are the stories of ordinary folks who reacted to threat with extraordinary courage, love, and faith.

As it happens, about 75 percent of the people who shared their stories with me were psychotherapists. These accounts were collected through a process of informal discussion, and since I was a psychologist working in an academic setting, the people with whom I was in contact tended to be psychologists, too, or people studying to become psychotherapists. Many were students in graduate-level psychology classes I have taught, while others were colleagues or fellow professionals who contacted me to contribute their own stories after hearing of my preliminary findings at professional conferences.

Because of the way in which these stories were gathered, it is impossible to know whether the experiences described are more common among psychotherapists than among members of the general public. However, it seems clear that education in psychology is not the determining factor. Even when the individuals later became psychotherapists, many of these experiences occurred before they began their graduate work. Nevertheless, some of the qualities that lead people to choose psychotherapy as a profession— e.g., relatively high intelligence, academic aptitude, the desire to help others—may ultimately turn out to be relevant.

I believe that it is also significant that so many of my informants tended to be spiritually oriented individuals. While most of these people were not conventionally religious, in every case in which the person's attitude toward spiritual matters is known to me, he or she has turned out to have participated in some spiritual or quasi-religious (for example, Alcoholics Anonymous) practice. Many had studied meditation, and several had considered a religious vocation at some point in their lives.

Although there were a few cases I encountered early on where I did not think to inquire about spiritual orientation, I suspect that almost all of the people I spoke with had an unusual degree of spiritual interest. As we shall see, centering the mind in peace appears to be essential for obtaining a miracle, and it is probable that this comes more easily to people who have practiced some form of prayer or meditation.

At the same time, if these were miracles, they were not reserved for the members of any particular religion. Divine help and guidance are reported all over the world and it is clear that no spiritual tradition has an exclusive contract with God. If my understanding of miracles is correct, *one need not even believe in God in order to receive the benefits of divine guidance.*

3
But Miracles Are Impossible!

Science is held in such awe in our culture that every scientist has a special responsibility to make clear to the lay audience where his expert knowledge actually yields scientifically verifiable results and where he is guessing, indulging in sheer speculation, or expressing his own personal hopes about the success of his research. This is an important task because the lay audience is in no position to make these distinctions.

—Noam Chomsky

The very idea of viewing miracles scientifically may strike some readers as absurd. Hasn't science proven that miracles *cannot* exist? This sort of confusion is so common that perhaps we had better deal with it before we go any further. After all, if reports of miracles are nothing more than pleasing fantasies, like stories about unicorns and perpetual motion machines, why should we waste our time on them?

Miracles are defined as instances where a supernatural power interferes with nature, and belief in their impossibility results from widespread acceptance of a philosophy of science called *naturalism*. As writer C. S. Lewis pointed out in his illuminating book *Miracles: How God Intervenes in Nature and Human Affairs*, naturalism is a theoretical position that defines "nature" as "the totality of that which exists."[1]

Now, of course, if we start from the assumption that everything that exists is part of nature, there can be nothing "supernatural."

Under this theory, everything real is rendered "natural" *by definition.* The alternative to naturalism is *supernaturalism,* a philosophy that holds that there are two kinds of things that exist in the universe. In addition to nature (creation), supernaturalists believe that there is also an original, self-existing entity that created nature and that continues to exist beyond time and space (God).

If naturalism is true, then miracles cannot exist. But is it true? To find out, we must decide whether naturalism or supernaturalism provides a more realistic account of the world we experience. Let us take a closer look at the worldview each theory supports.

Naturalism Versus Supernaturalism

First of all, naturalism holds that only physical things are real. This assumption denies existence to anything that cannot be perceived with the five senses. Supernaturalists, on the other hand, believe in the reality and importance of immaterial things, such as ideas, love, and God.

Naturalism is also a deterministic philosophy that assumes that everything that happens *must* happen, because it is part of a pattern set in motion at the dawn of time. According to this view, there is no such thing as free will. Although we humans have the impression that we are choosing what to do in each situation, naturalists believe that we are really just behaving as our brains have been programmed to do by our individual genetic makeup and our histories of reinforcement and punishment.

This means that we are not morally responsible for our actions. For example, the famous behavioral scientist B. F. Skinner argued that we shouldn't praise or blame people for the things they do, because they have no real choice in the matter.[2] If naturalism is correct, we are all simply automatons.

In contrast, many supernaturalists hold that human behavior is not predetermined—that we have free will and are responsible for our moral choices. They agree with naturalists that the physical universe operates according to natural laws, but they believe that those laws were established by divine intelligence rather than by blind chance.

There is a certain Eternal Law, to wit, Reason, existing in the mind of God and governing the whole universe.
—Thomas Aquinas

Is Naturalism More Scientific Than Supernaturalism?

Supernaturalism is actually every bit as scientific as naturalism. Since both theories agree that events in the physical universe ordinarily proceed according to natural laws, the scientific study of those laws is equally consistent with either point of view. There are, of course, versions of a supernatural perspective (for example, creationism) that are inconsistent with established scientific facts. But then, there are innumerable naturalistic theories that are equally unsupported by evidence.

Despite the occasional efforts of zealots to compel science to conform to religious dogma, most spiritually oriented individuals have no investment in believing that the natural world is one way rather than another. And how can we entertain the idea that supernaturalism is unscientific when many—and perhaps *most*—of the world's greatest scientists have themselves been religious people?

Science without religion is lame, religion without science is blind.
—Albert Einstein

Nevertheless, naturalism has undoubtedly been the more popular perspective among Western scientists in this century. If it is not really more consistent with established scientific fact, why should this be so?

Psychological Reasons for Scientists to Prefer Naturalism

I suspect that much of naturalism's considerable appeal may be due to the fact that if it were true, it would simplify the scientist's task. Scientists are concerned with investigating the natural world. When answers are slow in coming, they must continue searching, something they might not do if they were too quick to accept a supernatural explanation for the phenomenon under study. The problem is nicely illustrated in an amusing cartoon by Sidney Harris reprinted on page 44.

Clearly, if miracles are to be brought in to account for everything we do not presently understand, science would come to a standstill. There are certain assumptions we must make in doing research—not because we know them to be true, but simply because if we did not make them there would be no point in continuing. One of these is that miracles are not responsible for our results. Nevertheless, the fact that researchers must *assume* that miracles are not occurring does not mean that miracles never do occur. If I am to do research, I must also assume that no one is tampering with my instruments, but that assumption may occasionally turn out to be incorrect as well.

So we can readily see that naturalism embodies a good working strategy for scientists. Its underlying determinism is attractive for the same sorts of reasons. In a world where *anything* could happen at any time, no science would be possible. But to say that nature "ordinarily," or even "always in our experience," proceeds in a lawful manner is not the same as saying that it is *never* interfered with by a supernatural force.

The scientist's dilemma where miracles are concerned is neatly summarized in this excerpt from a paper by James Hansen.

A miracle is when something that cannot happen does anyway. It is not a question of the manifestation of hitherto unknown natural laws, if there are such that multiply loaves

43

and permit walking on water, but rather a temporary suspension of nature itself by some outside supernatural action. If this can happen, there is a problem. In science, exceptions do not prove the rule. Doing research at all means making at least a few basic assumptions: that nature is knowable, and that it is constant. Experiments can be done, and most important repeated. The genuine possibility of divine intervention as an unknown variable knocks the whole house of cards to pieces.[3]

A world that could be influenced by thought, free will, or a supernatural power would certainly be a more challenging object of study than one where everything was material and predetermined, but that is hardly the point. In fact, as we shall see, most contemporary scientists now accept the idea that thought and free will *do* exist. And some physicists are encountering an invisible, causal dimension of the universe that is arguably "supernatural," in that it stands outside of nature and is not constrained by natural laws. As attractive as naturalism has been to scientists, they are having to give it up in order to come to terms with the real complexity of things. And if miracles can be shown to exist, scientists will have to accommodate the reality of divine intervention as well.

Investigating God

But how do we go about obtaining scientific evidence of an invisible supernatural force? Despite the historical reluctance of Western researchers to investigate miracles, they are not really beyond the reach of science. Although God is not the sort of thing that can be measured with a yardstick or a scale, neither is gravity. As it turns out, theories about supernatural phenomena may be tested in much the same way as theories about anything else. Consider, for example, George's hypothetical experiment.

George

When I was working on my doctorate in experimental psychology, one of the class requirements was to design a study that would prove or disprove the existence of God. The professor's purpose in giving the assignment was, of course, to show us all that there was no conceivable way to do this. However, I still have fond memories of an ingenious research design proposed by one of my classmates.

George began his research proposal with a literature review, citing a passage from the Old Testament to the effect that if any man cursed God, God would instantly strike him down. Proceeding on the assumptions that God had inspired this biblical statement and that God would not lie, my friend went on to design the following experiment to test the hypothesis that God existed.

It involved hiring undergraduate volunteers (at the usual highly economical rate of five dollars per hour) to go out into a field and form three groups, one of which would curse God, while another praised God, and a third group of control subjects talked among themselves. The object, of course, was to compare the rate at which subjects in the three groups were struck down by lightning, plagues, meteorites, and so forth. George proposed to assess the anticipated carnage from the shade of a nearby tree, after which he would make statistical comparisons among the mortality rates of the three groups.

My friend has always maintained that had it not been for a few "bleeding hearts" on the University Human Subjects Committee, the world would by now know for sure whether God exists. George concedes that a few undergraduates might have lost their lives, but, as he so philosophically observes, "What kind of a life does an undergraduate have, anyway?"

Strangely enough, I now think that in some respects George was on the right track. While we cannot test for the existence of a supernatural power directly, we can do so indirectly if God is the sort of supernatural power who exerts particular kinds of effects upon the natural world. After all, if God really went in for divine retribution of the sort George's experiment assumed, his proposed study just might have worked (although in that case one wonders if that shade tree would have afforded him all the protection he might have needed).

We may not be able to see the "hand of God" directly, but perhaps we can see God's handiwork. For example, scientists know the force of gravity only indirectly through its effects on physical objects. If we consistently find that surprising, positive reversals of fortune occur whenever certain specifiable conditions are met, it would constitute indirect evidence of a supernatural power concerned about the well-being of humans.

This point of view appears to be gaining popularity. For example, according to Larry Dossey, M.D., even the traditionally conservative National Institutes of Health are now funding research on the effectiveness of prayer.[4] Like our investigation into deliverance, research on prayer is providing scientific evidence of divine intervention. In both cases, we are observing the conditions under which a supernatural power is *supposed* to intervene, and seeing that effects that seem "miraculous" do, in fact, manifest.

But How Can We Know if an Event Is of Supernatural Origin?

The problem is this: Even if we discover some pattern in our data that suggests the activity of a hitherto unknown influence, how can we be sure that it will not eventually turn out to be some previously undiscovered natural force? Historically, there have been many phenomena that seemed miraculous at the time but were readily explained by researchers of a later, more technologically advanced age.

I do not think that we will actually have much of a problem distinguishing natural from supernatural phenomena. Both naturalists and supernaturalists agree that natural forces tend to be random or probabalistic. They certainly do not display any evidence of conscious intention, or generate meaningfully organized chains of events in such a way as to fulfill an intelligible purpose.

In contrast, supernatural phenomena, if they exist, ought to be obviously purposeful. If we can document the activity of a disembodied force that produces high levels of meaningful organization in order to accomplish a desirable end, we would have good reason for supposing it to be supernatural rather than natural. At a minimum, a disembodied force that behaves like a benevolent, freely willing, all-knowing human mind would be unlike any natural force of which we are presently aware.

Take, for example, this story from Sophy Burnham's bestselling *A Book of Angels*.[5] It seems to me to reflect the activity of a benign intelligence that guided someone to respond appropriately to the needs of a total stranger. Many spiritually oriented individuals find that such chains of meaningful coincidences can be reliably set off by the prayer of their heart for some special sort of help. As you read this story, see if you agree that it suggests the activity of a loving higher power.

Elizabeth Paige

Writer Elizabeth Paige had been traveling alone in Greece. As she was preparing to leave the island of Páros for Crete, Ms. Paige was assailed by a sense of foreboding about her departure. So intense was her anxiety as she carried her belongings onto the ferry that she turned and pushed her way back off. She made arrangements to remain on Páros for another two days, although she had no idea how she would fill the time. Let me continue the story in Ms. Burnham's words.

That next morning, determined to stay out of the sun, she took a sketch pad to a shady street in the village and spent several hours sketching, thinking of nothing. At lunchtime she found herself wandering past each restaurant and then on, out of the village, and up along the road above the cliffs, her feet just moving her.

It was hot. She was alone. It was high noon and the sun beat down on her exactly as she had promised herself she would not permit, but she kept on walking. Off to her right was the ocean, to her left a kind of desert scrub. Soon she was thirsty. Not even a tree broke the glistening heat; and her feet kept taking her on.

In a few miles she saw a little house to her right, with a pine tree in front of it. The house, shuttered and closed up, had a sign on it with a telephone number. She stared at it a moment, wondering if the Greek meant "For Rent."

Then, because she was hot and tired and thirsty, she took the five or six stone steps down from the road to the house below and lay down gratefully in the shade of the tree.

She had not rested there five minutes when a motor scooter stopped on the road above. The two women on it looked at her curiously, then the older woman got off the scooter and the younger one drove off.

Suddenly Elizabeth guessed it was the owner. She rose to her feet, embarrassed at trespassing, and hesitated, wondering in which of her three languages to speak to the woman. For some reason, she chose her schoolgirl French: "Pardon, madame. I saw the shade of your tree . . . "

The woman looked at her sharply. It turned out she was French and spoke no English. Insistently she invited Elizabeth inside—would she like some water? And because Elizabeth was thirsty and also curious to see what a Greek house looked like inside, and because she liked the woman's looks, she accepted.

The woman, Nicole, was visiting her daughter on Páros. She told Elizabeth why she had been so startled to see her lying under the tree: because the day before, "we saw you on the beach with your sketchpad, and I said to my daughter, 'That woman, like me, is alone, but she looks so serene and content. I'd like to talk to her.' And then here you are right at my house. It's a miracle."

She had been in the Resistance during the war. She had married a Protestant minister, raised her children, and after thirty years of marriage been left by her husband for a younger woman. Ever since, she had lived in a state of anger, unable to forgive her husband or forget that the other woman had been her friend.

They talked. Elizabeth was surprised to discover how freely she spoke French. She didn't know she knew the language so well.

At a certain moment the woman turned to her: "Tell me—you know this—what is God?"

For some reason Elizabeth was hardly surprised.

"I cannot tell you what God is," she said, "but I can tell you how to find it." They spent the rest of the afternoon talking feverishly about meditation and the spiritual path, about forgiveness and prayer, and suffering, and love, about the writer Kazantzakis, the Buddha, Christ. Elizabeth says that she spoke with a passion that surprised her. She said things in French that she couldn't even say in English, and she listened in astonishment as the words rolled off her tongue, speaking of God.

Before she left, they knelt together and prayed. It was embarrassingly simple—two middle-aged women kneeling on the stone floor, praying for deliverance from pain and for the ability to love and trust again. Praying for knowledge of God. And then Elizabeth walked back to her hotel, marveling at the encounter. Was this why she had not been able to leave the day before? She was swept with humility at the goodness of God that gave her such words in French, that gave her the gift of serving as a channel for His words. For she knew it was not she, Elizabeth, who had been speaking so eloquently that afternoon.

50

The next day she left for Crete.

A year later she received a letter from Nicole. It was written in English, dictated from her hospital bed. She was dying of cancer, Nicole said, and she wanted Elizabeth to know how their meeting that afternoon in Greece had changed her life. She thought of it as a miracle, she said, for from that moment she had been released from her anger and had started to make her peace with God. She was dying, but wanted Elizabeth to know.[5]

A woman in torment longs for the advice of a particular stranger and somehow, despite all obstacles of language and logistics, the vital conversation is arranged. If this were only an isolated incident, one might be justified in writing it off as a lucky coincidence. But people like Ms. Paige who cultivate a relationship with their intuition find that meaningful "coincidences" like this occur with surprising regularity, making it hard to doubt that they are being guided by an invisible power that understands and responds to their deepest needs.

The vast majority of the world's people say that they believe in miracles and the power of prayer. It is my belief that they do so not out of ignorant superstition, but because—like the Frenchwoman in Ms. Paige's story—they have repeatedly seen their prayers answered. Each time a person in need asks God for help and pays attention to what happens next, it constitutes a small, private "experiment" on the reality of divine intervention.

Furthermore, in continually putting their beliefs to this sort of empirical test, religious people are behaving more "scientifically" than those scientists who refuse to look at the evidence. If we want to know whether or not divine intervention is real, we must carefully observe situations where supernatural theory predicts that God will intervene, and then see if any beneficial shift in the probabilities occurs. If, for example, we consistently find that endangered people who follow the recommended procedure for obtaining miracles wind up safe, it would strongly support the supernatural point of view. And that is precisely what we *do* find in the deliverance stories we will be considering in this book.

Perhaps out of a desire to avoid offending religious people, many scientists take the position that miracles are matters of faith to which scientific evidence is not even relevant. However, as an experimental psychologist, I tend to think that evidence is *always* relevant. The reality of divine intervention is ultimately an empirical question that must be answered through empirical observation.

Individuals who wish to be scientific are not at liberty to simply define God out of existence, as naturalists have attempted to do. This is reminiscent of the logic used by the French Academy of Sciences in the eighteenth century, when that august body declared that all reports of meteorites must be fraudulent, since it was obviously absurd to think that rocks could fall out of the sky. It is high time that we stopped pontificating about what *can* exist—and humbly took stock of reality to find out what *does* exist.

Although naturalists have long claimed that only physical things are real, it is now generally accepted that thoughts are not only "real," but capable of exerting powerful effects within the physical world. Further, as we shall see in the next chapter, there is good reason to believe that when people make sufficiently radical shifts in their thinking, outcomes that are arguably miraculous tend to occur. Before continuing with more deliverance stories, we will briefly survey some current lines of evidence that support the possibility that dramatic, positive changes in consciousness open the door to miracles.

4

Changing Your Mind Can Save Your Life

Everybody wants to change the world, but nobody wants to change his mind.

—Seaborn Blair

The explanation of miracles I am proposing links them to a particular kind of mental shift. By entering a peaceful, meditative state of consciousness, we make it possible for God to guide us in changing our physical reality. But this idea will not be convincing unless we first establish that thoughts are real, and that they can exert a potent influence over the things that happen in our world. As we have seen, the naturalistic view insists that thoughts are unreal and can have no real effects on anything at all.

For this reason, before we turn to the scientific research on miracles per se, we are going to explore the influence of the mind upon the body. After examining evidence that a shift into inner peace can "work miracles" upon our physical well-being, we will go on to see that mind is "non-local," which is to say that it is not limited by the body. Our thoughts can actually influence matter at a distance.

Inner Peace Heals the Mind

Psychologists have long known that our interpretation of a situation determines our emotional reaction to it. Cognitive psychotherapists say that people sometimes become emotionally disturbed because they entertain depressing thoughts that leave them feeling helpless and hopeless (for example, "I can't do anything right. Everyone would be better off if I were not here.").

It is also well known that when depressed individuals can be induced to question and reject such beliefs, their self-esteem improves, their personal effectiveness increases, and their behavior becomes more normal and adaptive. Thus, changing their thoughts exerts a profound effect upon both mood and behavior. Indeed, the antidepressant medications so widely used these days are designed to artificially simulate the neurochemical effects of positive thoughts. In this way, even people who are unwilling to question their basic assumptions about life can enjoy the physiological benefits of more adaptive thinking.

Negative Thoughts Stress the Body

Not only do negative thoughts produce undesirable effects upon mood and behavior, but emotional conflict can also take a serious toll on one's physical well-being. Sustained emotional stress often results in psychosomatic illnesses. Indeed, many physicians now believe that there may be an emotional component to *all* disease.

Medical research in the emerging field of psychoneuroimmunology traces the influence of thoughts—and the moods they produce—upon the immune system. Depression, for example, has been shown to have an immunosuppressive effect that makes it more difficult for the body to protect and heal itself. There is no longer any serious question that the negative mental states associated with constant anger, impatience, hopelessness, anxiety, fear, and guilt deplete the body's resources and jeopardize health.

But if psychological conflict is bad for the body, it is equally true that its opposite—inner peace—is good for it. Adopting a more serene, optimistic perspective triggers a cascade of neurochemical alterations in the brain that ultimately influences the behavior of every cell in the body. The healing and rejuvenating effects of such positive mental changes can be nothing short of astounding. A renewed sense of hope is often said to "work miracles" on seemingly intractable physical conditions.

Miracle Cures

Unexpected healings that could not have been caused by medical treatment alone are called *spontaneous remissions*. As cancer surgeon and writer Bernie Siegel facetiously observes, *spontaneous remission* is the accepted medical term for a miracle.[6]

Although these surprising healings seem at first glance to occur at random, many physicians have observed that they are often preceded by dramatic transformations in the individual's mental or spiritual outlook. Like people who experience deliverance from accidents and assaults, terminal patients who recover "spontaneously" appear, upon closer examination, to be doing something actively to produce their good fortune. As one woman who achieved a remission from lymphoma dryly observed, "It wasn't spontaneous — I worked my ass off for it."[7]

The Institute of Noetic Sciences — an organization established in 1973 by astronaut Edgar Mitchell and others to encourage consciousness research — has been trying to stimulate scientific interest in the healing power of the mind. When Noetic Sciences director of research Brendan O'Regan and his colleague Caryle Hirschberg began scanning the medical literature for information about mental influences in spontaneous remission, they found that there were only two books on the subject, both out of print. In an effort to rectify this situation, the institute has recently published the first compilation of abstracts on spontaneous remission, covering some three thousand articles from over 860 medical journals.[8] However, O'Regan noted that even with this new access to resource materials, it will still be difficult to tease out the influence of thought upon healing.[9]

Sad to say, O'Regan found that the medical reports collected generally omit all reference to the patient's state of mind. At most they might include a casual remark, such as this one about a woman considered beyond treatment with metastasized cervical cancer, "And her much hated husband suddenly died, whereupon she completely recovered."[9] A misguided allegiance to naturalism has too often led physicians to completely overlook the possibility that the patient's mental state *could* be affecting his or her health.

The Role of Inner Peace in Spontaneous Remission

Although little is known for certain about the causes of spontaneous remission, there is much anecdotal evidence indicating that inner peace plays a role. Some healings—like that of the woman with cervical cancer just mentioned—seem to occur because conditions in the sick individual's life have become more congenial. A source of conflict is eliminated. Needed physical and emotional support become available. It would appear that these are cases where circumstances surrounding the patient have changed in such a way as to foster inner peace.

However, while the restoration of inner peace sometimes occurs by accident, many other spontaneous remissions reflect a process of self-initiated mental change. Patients with terminal diagnoses sometimes set out to heal themselves by changing the beliefs and attitudes that produce negative emotions, such as fear, anger, depression, and guilt. There are even physicians who make the restoration of inner peace an integral part of their treatment.

For example, Dr. Gerald Jampolsky has founded the Center for Attitudinal Healing in Sausalito, California, an organization that provides support groups to catastrophically ill children and their families.[10] Patients there are encouraged to work at recovering emotional equilibrium through loving and forgiving themselves and others. We have already seen that inner peace may be a precondition for miracles of deliverance from accidents. Might it also be the key to spontaneous remission?

The Miracle-Prone Personality

Is there some particular mental state that predisposes one toward experiencing miracles of healing? Although rigorous scientific research on this issue is lacking, anecdotal evidence suggests that terminal patients who succeed in healing themselves do have some unusual attitudes. *New Age Journal* editor Marc Barasch proposes that there may actually be such a thing as a "miracle-prone personality."[7] Perhaps we can learn something about the mental state of miracle workers in general by exploring that of people who achieve spontaneous remissions.

First, many self-healers report that they went through some sort of *existential shift* or *psychosocial-emotional-spiritual about-face* before things began to improve. Sentenced to death, these individuals seem to search actively for the meaning of their existence. They take stock of their reasons for living and then reorganize their lives to focus upon what is really important to them.

For some, this inner shift leads to an abdication of onerous responsibilities in favor of *a more self-centered approach to life*. In the face of impending doom, self-healers seem to give themselves permission to change their focus radically and finally do what they *want*, rather than what they are "supposed" to do.

This rejection of other people's expectations seems often to free the individual to *become immersed in activities and projects that are personally meaningful*. Sometimes dying people become so engrossed in their new interests that they seem to forget all about being sick. The following story—possibly apocryphal but nonetheless amusing—serves to illustrate the way a fascinating new project can provide a reason for living.

Ann

A seriously depressed woman I'll call Ann was preparing to commit suicide. Her life no longer held any meaning for her, and she could see no reason to go on.

Ann began to write a final note explaining why she wanted to die. However, in order to make the reason clear, she found it necessary to allude to several painful incidents from her past. Then she realized that her loved ones would not understand what those experiences had really meant to her unless she explained them more fully. She went on to describe each one in detail, adding some of the actual dialogue and analyzing her own reactions to the things that had been said and done.

As she strove to articulate these pivotal events and explain their significance, connections started forming in Ann's mind. She began to see these incidents in a new light, and, for the first time, she began to understand why she had reacted the way she had. Caught up in the insights she was discovering, her last message grew longer and longer. Finally, it dawned on Ann that her suicide note was actually the beginning of the autobiography she had always dreamed of writing. She abandoned her plan to kill herself and penned a best-seller instead.

The attributes of self-healers who achieve remissions include a sense of surrender to reality. Miracle workers do not kid themselves about the trouble they are in. They *accept their diagnoses realistically and make necessary changes in their lifestyles.*

And, while self-healers *do not give up hope* for a cure, being cured is often not their primary objective. As in the case of others who experience deliverance, they seem to place their main emphasis upon *living in a way that is congruent with their inner values* for as long as they have left.

For some of those who walked the path of healing, disease seemed to have forced a moment . . . when life itself depended on becoming authoritatively, powerfully, even crazily, the person they were meant to be.
　　　　　　　　　　　　　　　　　　　　　　　　—Marc Barasch

From the point of view of our present inquiry into miracles, it is interesting that self-healers also frequently mention slipping into *altered states of consciousness.* They tend to be *intuitive, hypnotizable, fantasy-prone individuals* who find meaning in dreams and symbols and feel at home in their imaginations. In a later chapter, when we look more closely at the creative power of the mind, the significance of this will become apparent.

It is also interesting that long-term survivors of terminal diagnoses tend to be *rugged individualists* who are both *emotionally expressive and self-assertive.* They don't necessarily follow medical advice to the letter and, perhaps as a result, these argumentative, opinionated patients are often *perceived rather negatively by their physicians.* Medical descriptions of them frequently include terms such as *uncooperative, independent, bizarre, rebellious, anti-authoritarian,* and *nonconformist.*

If inner peace and positive expectations are essential to working miracles, it may be that only highly independent people *can* maintain the necessary emotional equilibrium when faced with a damning diagnosis. For example, a doctoral student in Idaho who was researching spontaneous remission found that many of her subjects flatly refused to put much stock in the medical experts who had pronounced their death sentences. The researcher asked one woman.

"How did you feel when the doctor told you that you had this terminal illness and that you'd be dead in six months?" "That was *his* opinion," was the reply. The interviewer said, "Would you like to say more about that?" She said, "Well, you know we're told all these things by all these experts. We live on a farm, and all these federal people come in and they look at the soil and they tell us that nothing will grow and we should put these fertilizers in and we should do all this stuff. We don't do it and hell, things grow there anyway. So why would I listen to an expert?"[9]

Given a choice between believing that she was doomed and believing that her doctor didn't have both oars in the water, this miracle worker opted for the latter possibility. Further, notice the *fearless* quality of her thinking. This is not a woman who is clinging to a physician as to a savior. She does not believe that medical science holds the key to her fate, and she is not afraid to make decisions for herself and go it alone if necessary.

An *"irrational" optimism in the face of a "hopeless" situation* is yet another characteristic that people who achieve spontaneous remissions appear to share with those who experience miracles of deliverance from accidents and assaults. Sadly, some self-healers find it necessary to insulate themselves against medical skepticism in order to salvage this optimism. For example, this reaction comes from a woman who had consented to be interviewed about her remission.

> "You're not a doctor, are you? I don't want to talk to a doctor!" The interviewer said, "No, I'm not. Really, honest." Then the woman replied, "Well, I just don't want to be put down and turned away again, like I was so many times. I'm going to keep my state of mind intact, no matter what."[9]

If optimism plays an important role in self-healing, we can readily understand how exposure to a physician's negative expectations might undermine a patient's inner peace, jeopardizing his or her remission. For example, O'Regan was told by many of the long-term survivors he interviewed that their physicians had actually been irritated by their refusal to accept the hopelessness of their situations.[9] Quite a few of these patients said that they had angrily walked out on their medical treatment. Their physicians never even knew that some of these "hopeless" cases recovered fully—much less why they did so.

However, even when patients with remissions do maintain medical contact, their doctors may be reluctant to credit their healings to something as intangible as a change of mental focus. In the case of my student Gino, for example, the attending physician did have an opportunity to learn that his patient had made an astonishing recovery, although, even then, he could not accept the idea that it could have resulted from the new thoughts Gino was entertaining.

Gino

At twenty-three, Gino nearly died of a serious illness. His condition was critical, but after weeks in the hospital and months in a convalescent facility, he was finally able to go home. However, it would be too much to say that he had recovered. His life would never be the same.

It seems that the infection had destroyed most of Gino's liver. His doctor had had the unpleasant task of explaining to him that it would not regenerate itself. Gino's health would always be fragile, and for the rest of his life he would have to be hooked up to a machine that would do for him what his devastated liver could not.

With the disability money he received from the state, Gino was able to rent a tiny apartment. His many friends pitched in to do his shopping and cooking and run his errands. Bedridden and permanently attached by tubes to a machine that had to be wheeled along with him on trips to the bathroom, this once-athletic young man tried to keep his spirits up despite the knowledge that he was going to spend the rest of his life as an invalid.

Gino had a lot of time on his hands. In an effort to relieve his boredom, one of his friends brought him the book *Creative Visualization* by Shakti Gawain.[11] In it, Gawain described an ancient spiritual technique for changing reality. She said that you could actually heal yourself by altering the way you pictured things in your mind. Glad to fill his tedious days and sleepless nights with some constructive activity, Gino began to visualize the healing of his liver.

"I used to lie there and work on my liver one cell at a time," Gino told me years later when he was attending the graduate school where I taught. "It was just too damned depressing to focus on the whole thing at once. My liver appeared in my mind's eye like this big, black blob—all discolored and flabby with just this one little area of healthy pink tissue.

"So I would lie in bed imagining myself with a teensy-weensy little toothbrush, scrubbing the crud off of a single cell, rinsing it carefully, and gently massaging in magical medicines. I don't know that I seriously thought it was going to help, but it was something to do. There is just so much television a person can watch."

As the months wore on, Gino became a little stronger. He could move about the apartment more easily and prepare meals for himself, but he continued to fill his idle hours by mentally tending his liver cells. Sometimes when he was alone, he would even croon to them like a loving father, urging the "little guys" to take heart and heal themselves. And each day the liver in his visualization looked slightly improved. Little by little, there got to be more pink, healthy cells and fewer crud-encrusted, black ones.

One day as he was stepping out of his tiny kitchen, Gino caught his tubing on the edge of the counter. A sudden move on his part, and he felt agonizing pain as the plastic umbilicus was ripped out of his body. His doctor had warned that such an eventuality could be fatal, and Gino lost no time in phoning the paramedics.

Gino's doctor met him in the emergency room, looking grim. "I'll have to operate, but I want to do some tests first so I know where we stand. The nurse is going to take you down for some X rays and stuff while I get scrubbed."

The tests were quickly completed, and Gino was prepped for surgery. After a short wait, however, the nurse returned and told him that something had gone wrong with his tests. They would have to be repeated.

Gino was put through another battery and again left to wait. This time it was his doctor who appeared with an apologetic expression. These tests were no good either. How about one more round?

However, after the third battery was complete, Gino's doctor strode into his room and eyed him with speculation. He waved the sheaf of results in the air and demanded, "Where the hell did you get this liver?"

"What?" Gino replied weakly.

"This isn't your liver! I know your liver, and this isn't it!"

Gino was nonplussed. "What do you mean? What's wrong?" he asked.

"That's just it!" his physician exclaimed. "Nothing is wrong! There isn't a damn thing wrong with this liver. You left here five months ago with almost no liver function, and now you show up with this perfectly good liver. And what I want to know is—how the hell did you do that?"

"You're not going to believe this, Doc," Gino replied, "but it must have been the visualization I've been doing. For hours every day I've been visualizing my liver healing. I guess it did."

Gino was right about one thing. His doctor never did believe that the visualization could have worked such a miracle. Not that he had any other theories to explain how it could have happened!

When I knew Gino ten years ago, he was a vital, energetic man in his thirties, with an unshakable belief in the power of mind over matter. This was what had led him to study psychology. As a psychotherapist, he hoped to help many people heal themselves by refocusing their thinking.

Mind Over Matter

It would appear, then, that thoughts are real and that changing them can have profound effects upon our bodies. However, for miracles to be possible, it would have to be true that thoughts could affect things *other than* one's own body. If the naturalistic perspective is correct, and mind is nothing more than an illusory sense of self produced by the activity of the brain, there would be no way for thought to directly influence the things that happen in the physical world.

63

According to Dr. Larry Dossey, co-chair of the newly established Panel on Mind/Body Interventions at the National Institutes of Health, the mind is non-local—which is to say that it
behaves in the laboratory as though it is omnipresent and exists
independent of the brain through which it operates.[4] That is why
the prayers of one person can profoundly affect the health of a distant
loved one who does not even know that prayers are being offered.

There is much parapsychological evidence that supports this
idea, although it has been difficult for mainstream culture to as-
similate it. When people demonstrate knowledge that could not
have come to them through their physical senses, this lends support to the supernatural view of an eternally living soul that operates through the body but can access information by intuitive
means. Miracles, near-death experiences, out-of-body experiences,
and evidence of memories that predate one's physical birth all fall
into the category of things that "cannot happen" if the naturalistic paradigm is true and complete.

Although many scientists continue to withhold judgment
about such phenomena, national polls indicate that the majority
of Americans have had personal experiences that convince them
that the mind does not depend upon the body for its existence.[12]
For example, my friend Hayden tells these stories about her daughter Leah's surprising psychic "hits." While they do not constitute
scientific proof, they are intriguing because they suggest that this
little girl may have been aware of certain things before her birth.

Leah

Hayden and Bill had never attempted to conceal from their
daughter Leah that she had been adopted. And there had been
no indication on Leah's part that she was at all troubled by the
circumstances of her birth until one day when she was about three.

"But, Mommy, why didn't *you* have me?" Leah demanded with
evident perplexity.

Hayden's thoughts flickered back a bit sadly over her four miscarriages and the hysterectomy that had followed. It had not been easy getting Leah! When they had been forced to give up the idea of having a child of their own, Hayden and Bill had tried to adopt but had found that path also filled with heartbreaking obstacles and frustrations. They put themselves on the list at an adoption agency and settled down to wait for years until a baby would become available to them.

Then suddenly their luck had changed. A pregnant woman Hayden had encountered casually in a boutique tracked her down and announced that she would allow no one but Hayden to adopt her baby. It had all seemed so strange.

Before she had run into the girl in the shop, this unwed mother-to-be was adamant about keeping her child. However, an hour after meeting Hayden, she had sought her out and insisted, "This is *your* baby. I just know it is. It has never felt like mine, and now that I've met you I know that it's meant for you. If you won't adopt it, I won't let anyone else have it." The adoption had been arranged in an atmosphere of celebration on all sides, and once the baby had arrived, there had been no question in Hayden and Bill's minds that the birth mother had been right. Leah had always felt like "their" child.

However, Hayden was certainly not going to try to explain all of that to her preschool-age daughter.

"It just wasn't possible, honey," she replied lightly.

Leah reacted to this facile reply with indignation. Hands on hips like someone who has been put to a great deal of unnecessary trouble, Leah admonished her mother, "You know, I *tried* to come to you *four times*, Mommy!"

Hayden was electrified by the realization that each of those four miscarriages might have represented one of Leah's attempts to take her place in their family. Once that avenue had been closed, her daughter had had to try a different strategy to get where she was determined to be.

A year after this incident, this same little girl noticed a picture among a pile of photos her now-divorced mother had tossed into a box. Examining the snapshot more carefully, Leah pointed to a particular man standing among several others.

"I know this man, Mommy," she announced.

"Which one?" Hayden asked absently, as she put on her makeup at the mirror. Leah brought the picture over and pointed to a man Hayden had met at a conference. Stephen had been one of the speakers, and the two of them had hit it off with each other at a reception that same afternoon. However, that had been months ago, and she had not seen or heard from him since.

"You don't know that man, sweetie," she told her daughter. "I met him at a conference, but you've never seen any of those people."

"I do too know this one!" Leah insisted.

"Those people all live in California, honey. That's very far away. You've never been there, and you've never met any of them," Hayden tried again.

"I *do so* know him!" the little girl repeated in frustration. Then, with the air of someone playing the winning ace, she announced, "I knew him in heaven!"

Well, Hayden reflected with secret amusement, there isn't much you can say to something like that. This was one argument she could see she wasn't going to win. "That's nice, Leah."

But her daughter's parting shot took her by surprise. As Leah flounced triumphantly out of the room, she called back over her shoulder, "and God's going to send him to *you* as a *special treat!*"

Hayden married the man in the photo a few months later.

Incidents such as these do not, of course, constitute scientific evidence that the mind does not begin and end with the body, but they are nevertheless strongly persuasive to the individuals who experience them. There appears to be a great deal of anecdotal evidence that people sometimes possess knowledge that would have been unavailable from the point of view of their physical senses. Reports of reincarnation fall into this category as well.

Reincarnation

The idea that people live more than one life is often thought to be peculiar to Eastern religions, but it has always been a tenet of Judaism and was accepted by the early Christians for some four hundred years. It is also found in African and Native American religions and seems to crop up in the thinking of cultures throughout the world, from the Australian Aboriginal to the Eskimo. As psychiatrist Brian Weiss is discovering, memories of what appear to be past lives sometimes occur even to people who do not even believe in reincarnation.[13]

Now, even assuming that they can be authenticated, the presence of such memories does not necessarily prove that someone has lived before. Perhaps the person is simply in mental contact with the soul of the individual who lived the life he or she appears to know so much about. But at a minimum, such "past-life memories" suggest that *some* aspect of consciousness survives the death of the physical body and that there is an intuitive mechanism for gaining knowledge to which one does not have physical access.

Only a few qualified scientists have systematically explored past-life memories, and when the media have attempted to do so—as for instance, in the famous "Bridey Murphey" case—the results have often been slipshod and misleading. But when professor Ian Stevenson carefully investigated a number of such claims, he found considerable reason to believe some of them authentic, including the case of Shanti Dev summarized here.[14]

Shanti Dev

From the time that she first began to talk, a little girl in India named Shanti Dev claimed that she had had a former life as a wife and mother in a distant village. Shanti said she had died in childbirth, and she would often weep inconsolably for her beloved husband and the children she had left motherless.

Eventually, Shanti's parents decided to see if any such person as this former husband existed. They addressed a letter to a man of that name in a village of the name Shanti gave, describing their daughter's peculiar obsession. Shortly thereafter, a stranger came to their door. The moment she saw the visitor, Shanti rushed up and joyfully embraced him, identifying him as her husband's brother.

The visitor was indeed the brother of the man to whom they had written. Since he lived in the same city as Shanti's family, he had been delegated the task of trying to get to the bottom of this strange situation. As it turned out, the man Shanti claimed had been her husband had had a wife of the name she had given, who had died in childbirth some years earlier. His circumstances were just as Shanti had described them. At this point, scientists from the local university were called in to investigate.

The researchers questioned Shanti extensively and eventually conducted her to the village where she claimed to have lived in a former life. She was able to pick her husband and the children who had been living during the other woman's lifetime out of the crowd at the train station without difficulty, although she did not recognize the son to whom she had supposedly died giving birth. Shanti was transported with joy at being "reunited" with her family, and witnesses were moved to laughter by the spectacle of this little girl lavishing maternal affection and concern upon her strapping "sons" who were so much older than she.

The child was able to lead the investigators through the village to the house where she claimed to have once lived, although the family had since moved elsewhere. She also told about some valuables she had hidden there, and the man who was supposed to have been her husband confirmed that he had found them before moving. Altogether, Shanti was able to accurately relate hundreds of intimate details regarding the personal life of the woman she claimed to have been. She passed all of the scientists' tests, and they were entirely satisfied that this small child had demonstrated knowledge she could not have obtained by any normal means.

Out-of-Body and Near-Death Experiences

If past-life memories provide some reason to suspect that the mind is not identical with, and limited to, the life of the brain, so do out-of-body experiences. These include instances where a person who was either close to death or actually clinically dead reports experiencing events elsewhere in the world, or in another dimension, prior to resuscitation. Such stories often include contact with angels, deceased loved ones, and/or a loving being with whom the nearly dead individual reviews his or her life before determining that it is not yet time to die.

While one may be tempted to write off tales of other dimensions as dreams or hallucinations, many of these individuals also say that at some point they found themselves outside their bodies, often looking down upon them from above. In this disembodied state, they report being able to move through walls. There are many documented cases where resuscitated individuals have brought back accurate knowledge of things seen or heard in one part of the hospital while their unconscious bodies were undergoing treatment in another.

Thoughts Affect Physical Things

If naturalism has prevented scientists from considering the possibility that the mind exists independent of the brain and that it can *know about* things we have not encountered with our senses, it has also denied the possibility that thoughts can *affect* physical things independent of the body. However, there is growing scientific evidence that this is so.

For example, more than a decade of experimentation at Princeton University's PEAR (Princeton Engineering Anomalies Research) Program has led scientists to the conclusion that there is unmistakable statistical evidence that people can influence physical processes at a distance through the intention to do so.[15] *There is now scientific evidence that some individuals can use the power of their minds to make things happen the way they want them to.*

When someone uses mental power to influence the behavior of physical objects (such as dice, a random number generator, etc.), this is called psychokinesis. When the emphasis is upon making things turn out well for others, this is called intentional healing of the sort found in connection with prayer, the laying on of hands, and visualization. Numerous controlled experiments have shown that people recover more quickly from injuries and surgical trauma when they become the objects of the healing intentions of others.[4] This means that the thoughts of one person can affect the health of another. That this is not merely a matter of suggestion is shown by blind research and a growing body of evidence that plants, animals, and even microorganisms heal more quickly when prayed for.

It is difficult to avoid the conclusion that the mind is real and can know and affect material things independent of the body. In a later chapter, we will see that some modern physicists now believe that the mind actually brings the material world into manifestation. Once we acknowledge the power of thoughts to influence physical processes at a distance, *it is a short step to the recognition that particular shifts in mental activity may produce the corresponding shifts in physical circumstances that have traditionally been called "miracles."*

Now let us turn to some more of the deliverance stories—ones where the danger resulted from an assault. Keeping in mind the possibility that people's thoughts may very well influence what happens to them, consider whether these folks may have kept themselves safe through their own mental behavior.

5

Assaults, Part I:
The Disarming Power of Love

*No one walks so safely as one who walks humbly and
harmlessly with great love and great faith. For such a
person gets through to the good in others (and there is
good in everyone), and therefore cannot be harmed.
This works between individuals, it works between groups
and it would work between nations if nations had the
courage to try it.*

— Peace Pilgrim

So far we have focused upon danger through accidents and
illnesses, but in many of the stories I have collected, danger comes
from assault. These cases suggest that inner peace has the power
to keep us safe even when someone else is determined to harm us.

The assault stories I have been told seem to fall naturally into
two categories. The first includes cases where a potentially dangerous situation was completely defused after the individual slipped
into a peaceful altered state of consciousness. The second contains stories where lives were saved by the inner shift, although
property was lost and, in some cases, the individual was injured.
In this chapter, we will consider the first category.

Let me begin by acknowledging that cases where frightening situations simply evaporate inevitably raise questions about
whether the danger was real to begin with. Since nothing bad
actually happened to the person telling the story, it is reasonable

to wonder whether anything would have happened if he or she had not shifted consciousness.

Perhaps these folks simply misread the cues. Perhaps their alleged assailants never seriously intended to hurt them, and the "danger" was only a product of their own overworked imaginations. How can we conclude that a miracle of deliverance may have occurred when we have only a single individual's subjective opinion about what would have happened otherwise?

I would simply ask you to suspend judgment on this issue for the time being. In all of these cases, the people who shared these accounts with me believed that someone meant to harm them. Nevertheless, they responded to this threat with peace, love, self-confidence, and even humor. Later, when we discuss cases where there was injury and loss, we will see the same principles operating in a context where it is no longer reasonable to doubt the seriousness of the threat. I believe that the stories in the present chapter demonstrate the way in which a shift in consciousness can deflect undesirable possibilities. The ones we will explore later make a strong case for the idea that the shift in consciousness can actually turn aside mortal danger.

As you read these accounts, try to put yourself in the position of the person going through the experience. How would you expect to feel if the same thing were happening to you? Does the individual's response seem ordinary and natural in the circumstances, or is it surprising? Would you expect to feel relaxed, loving, and utterly confident that the threat was imaginary, or might you be afraid? Let's begin with Phil's narrow escape.

Phil

Phil had spent several months as a member of a spiritual community in the San Francisco Bay Area, where he was trained to work with homeless street people. It was understood that those dealing with this population often encountered irrationality and aggression. Alcohol, drug addiction, and mental illness were common. Great emphasis was placed upon preparing Phil and the other brothers for this work by teaching them always to meet hostility with love. Phil learned that no matter what the question, love must always be the answer.

Late one night, Phil and a few others were in the Fillmore district, handing out free sandwiches and coffee on the street. An enormous drunk with the build of a heavyweight boxer lurched up and grabbed him by the front of his shirt, roaring, "You mothafucker! We don't want your kind around here! I'll teach you to come around where you ain't wanted! I'm going to knock your fuckin' teeth down your throat!"

With his left hand, the drunk lifted Phil almost off his feet while he pulled back a huge right fist and took aim. Phil realized that he was physically helpless, but he did not forget his training. Instead of struggling or becoming fearful, he relaxed, gazed into the man's eyes, and poured out love upon him. When the fist came flying at his face, he just kept radiating love with all the power of his being.

His assailant pulled the punch when it was a fraction of an inch from Phil's nose. Phil doesn't think he even flinched. He was so focused upon loving this man that nothing else seemed to exist in the world.

The drunk was deeply impressed. He continued to hold Phil for another few moments, staring at him in surprise. "You one brave mother!" the drunk said, releasing Phil. There was real respect in his voice. "Ain't you scared of nothin'?"

Phil just kept pouring on the love. He began to talk about God, and the drunk listened. His former antagonist hung around the rest of the time Phil was there, asking him questions and verbally defending him from the hostility of other street people.

"This guy's all right!" the drunk told them. "You best listen to what he has to say. He ain't afraid of nothin'!"

Phil is convinced that the drunk fully intended to hit him but that the love he was sending back prevented him from doing so. Since then, he has felt that the power of love has kept him safe in many dangerous situations.

Phil says that his unusually loving and fearless mental state somehow disarmed his assailant's hostility and created a bond between them. The urge to commit violence seemed to wither in the face of it. Dona, below, believes that she thwarted a potential rapist by actively holding her mind in fearlessness. While many of the people who told me their stories entered the peaceful altered state spontaneously, Dona was very conscious of rejecting the fearful victim role her assailant was trying to force on her.

Dona

Dona, then in her early twenties, noticed a well-dressed man she later described as "built like a football player" entering a grocery store she was leaving. She was dimly aware that he had given her a glance as they passed, but nothing further occurred. Continuing on her way without a second thought, Dona walked several blocks to the laundry building behind her Los Angeles apartment house and went inside to begin her wash. When she heard the garden gate creak, she looked out the window and discovered with a sinking feeling that the man she had seen in the market had followed her home.

Before Dona could get to the only door, the stranger planted himself in it, blocking her exit. Dona described him as "obviously working himself up" for some sort of action. He was flushed and breathing hard, and his nostrils were flaring. She felt that he was watching her gloatingly, the way a cat watches a mouse before pouncing on it.

Dona remembered then that there had been a series of rapes in her neighborhood and saw that this man fit the sketches and descriptions published in the papers. It dawned on her that she was cornered in this isolated building by the so-called Mid-Wilshire Rapist.

With this realization came a momentary sense of panic that reminded her of the way she had felt as a child when she was being beaten by her stepfather. This memory was followed by a surge of determination never to be anyone's victim again. "I just thought, 'I'll be damned if I'll let any man terrorize me again!'"

Suddenly Dona found herself becoming oddly peaceful and self-confident. She coolly met the man's gloating gaze, and it was her impression that a psychic message passed between them through their eyes. "His eyes invited me to recognize his power over me and be afraid. I calmly but firmly sent him the psychic message back, 'This isn't for me. You've got the wrong person.'

"It was like being in an altered state," Dona continued. "I felt that our minds were communicating with each other. The man was trying to persuade me to enter a state of consciousness that would be complementary to his so that we could act out a drama together. He would be the powerful aggressor, and I would be the terrified victim. All he needed in order to attack me was for me to get scared. He was waiting to see that I was afraid—that's what rape victims are supposed to do. And I saw that he could not carry out his plan if I refused to match energy with him. I just flatly declined the invitation to go into fear or to credit him with the power to hurt me. And I could see that it really confused him."

Having refused the "invitation," Dona experienced herself becoming enormously large and powerful. "This guy was over six feet tall and easily twice my weight, but in my mind I suddenly began to feel as though I was twelve feet tall, and he was just some puny little creature that could not possibly imagine itself strong enough to interfere with me.

"I knew that I had to get out of there, so I just locked onto his mind with this sense of being enormous and powerful, and I walked straight at him where he was blocking the door. He looked surprised when I just kept coming, but at the last minute he backed out of my way and let me pass. As I went by him, I saw him hold up his hands defensively, the way people do when they are trying to ward off something powerful and dangerous. I know that in his mind, too, I was big and strong while he was little and weak."

Dona walked to her apartment and locked herself in. The man

made no attempt to follow her. "It sounds crazy, but I know that I kept him from attacking me by not matching his expectations of how I was supposed to behave. If he had detected any fear in my mind, he would have been on me in a second."

Dona learned from the newspapers that the Mid-Wilshire Rapist went on to murder his next victim. She is uncomfortably aware of how close she came to being that next victim.

Here we see Dona briefly consider responding to a physical threat with fear or anger and then change her mind. Disgusted with men who used their strength to intimidate women, Dona decided that she would not give this one the satisfaction of believing that he could frighten her. This single-minded determination appears to have provided the motivation for the leap into peace.

The situation reminded Dona of her childhood powerlessness and frustration, but she fought the temptation to see herself as a helpless victim again. Although she did not mention becoming parental in relation to the man who menaced her, the size and power difference she mentally projected reminds me of a parent-child relationship, with Dona in the adult role. Perhaps Dona convinced the would-be rapist that she was an unsuitable victim partly by evoking parental associations.

There is an important recurring theme to these stories that we will discuss in greater detail later. *Participants in an interaction must establish some sort of unspoken consensus about what kind of a situation it is.* If one person simply refuses to accept the other's interpretation, it is difficult (if not actually impossible) for the other to continue as planned. How can a rapist satisfy his lust for power with a woman who is neither frightened nor angry? How do you conquer someone who is not opposing you? How do you act out your fantasy with someone who utterly refuses to play a complementary role?

Dona's story was only one of several I heard where women felt that they had protected themselves from rape by refusing to go into the fearful or angry state of consciousness appropriate to a victim. While it is possible to dismiss their claims and attribute their escapes to luck, all of these women were personally convinced that they had effectively blocked the rapist's next move by redefining the situation. Consider the following case.

Jeanne

Jeanne was living in Tempe while she attended the University of Arizona. Like many students, she had no car and mostly got around on foot, although she occasionally hitchhiked.

This particular day, she was hitching home from her part-time job and was picked up by a man in his thirties, driving a beat-up old car. An outgoing nineteen-year-old, Jeanne responded cheerfully when the driver struck up a conversation. Driving past the place she had asked to be dropped off, the man insisted that he wanted to show her a particularly beautiful place nearby in the desert. Jeanne realized that she didn't really have a choice, so she consented to a brief drive in the desert, merely stipulating that they would have to come back soon as she only had half an hour to spare.

The man drove to an isolated spot and suggested that they get out to enjoy the natural beauty of the landscape. Jeanne expressed delight about the view and strolled around with him for a few minutes, chatting happily. Then the driver started trying to put his arm around her and kiss her, but Jeanne laughed and pushed him away. She joked with him in a friendly fashion and treated his behavior as a foolish flirtation, "Come on, now, don't go getting all mushy on me!"

Jeanne was fully aware of the situation she was in. Now that she was standing outside the car, she could see that the backseat was strewn with pornographic magazines and that there were ropes and kinky-looking leather bondage equipment there, too. Jeanne says that she is very intuitive, and she strongly suspected that the driver had raped other women and that he wanted to rape her. Nevertheless, she pushed that possibility out of her mind.

77

"I just refused to be in that reality. In my reality, we were friendly people who had recently met and enjoyed each other's company. He had graciously taken me for a beautiful drive in the desert, for which I was grateful, and now it was time for us to be getting back. That's all.

"I could see that he had some other scenario in mind, but I just refused to understand what he meant. I kept treating him like a buddy and laughing and kidding with him the way I do with my brother. I acted real dense about his intentions, and it just made it impossible for him to get tough with me. He would have been ashamed to hurt me when we were having such a good time and I obviously liked him so much. He would have had to sacrifice my good opinion, and I knew that he would not be willing to do that. He probably had had few people in his life who responded to him very positively.

"I can't explain it to anyone, but I just knew that I was deciding what my reality was going to be and that it didn't include rape. I have never thought of myself as the sort of person who could be raped, and he seemed to finally grasp that. I kept on chatting and joking with him in a very asexual way, and eventually he just gave up. We drove back to town, and he dropped me where I asked him to. We said good-bye as the best of friends.

"My girlfriends all told me I was nuts when they heard about it. They think I must have been crazy to get into a car with this guy and go out to the desert with him. Maybe I was a little naive at first, but I felt in complete control the whole time. My friends say I was just lucky, but I know that I protected myself by dictating what was going to be the reality he and I shared. The poor guy just really picked the wrong person for what he had in mind."

Here again we see an intended victim communicating to a potential rapist that she was the wrong person—that she was not prepared to undertake the victim role. Like Dona, Jeanne believed that her refusal to share her assailant's interpretation of the situation, or get on the same wavelength with him, blocked him from going any further. Tina had a very similar experience, which she understood in the same way.

Tina

Tina was hitchhiking up the coast highway north of San Francisco when she was picked up by a young man in a pickup truck. They chatted in a friendly manner, but when he left the highway and headed up into the hills, Tina could see that she had a problem on her hands. She asked him to drop her off if he was taking another route, but he mumbled some excuse for the detour and said that it wouldn't take long. She was not surprised when he parked in a remote, wooded area and started behaving in an amorous fashion.

"Why don't we just sit here and get to know each other better?" he said in a suggestive way, reaching out to pull Tina to him. Tina slipped out of his grasp with a laugh and got out of the truck, saying, "I have an even better idea. Why don't you take me back to the highway! I've gotta get going."

The driver got out, too, and came around to her side of the truck to pursue the point further. He grabbed her forcefully and tried to kiss her, but Tina, who continued to laugh and treat the situation as a minor nuisance, squirmed away from his embraces saying, "Hey, knock it off, will you? This is all very flattering, but I've got to get to Mendocino before dark. Maybe when I come back through we can get together, but I don't have time for this now. Now why don't you be a pal and start up that truck?"

Tina says that she knew very well that the driver had brought her out there with rape in mind, but she also knew that she wasn't going to be raped. "He might be able to intimidate some girls, but I just figured he'd met his match. I'd be darned if I'd let some Neanderthal pull this kind of crap on me.

"I knew that he was a lot stronger than I was and that I wouldn't have a chance if it came down to physical force, so I just made up my mind that it wasn't going to come to that. He wasn't a really dangerous character—just some creep who thought he saw a chance to get away with something. But even rape has some social amenities, and I wasn't going to make it easy for him by recognizing what he had in mind and playing my assigned role.

"He expected me to get the picture and then get scared or mad. He'd know how to play it from there. My guess is that if I had acted scared he would have enjoyed it and felt powerful. He probably would have promised to go easy on me and felt like a big man raping me. If I'd gotten hostile, he would have enjoyed overpowering me, and he could have justified the rape as teaching me a lesson.

"So instead of doing either, I just kept missing the point. I kept treating him casually and even kind of flirting with him. I acted like I thought he was a nice guy and appealed to his gallantry to help me out by getting me back to the highway. And in the face of that, he just didn't know what to do. What was he going to say, 'Uh, excuse me, but I'm going to rape you now'? He didn't say that, but if he had I would have laughed that off, too.

"My complete inability to understand what he had in mind created a very awkward situation for him. I came off very sweet, naive, and innocent, and it would have taken a bigger jerk than he was to assault me in the face of that. By the way he grabbed me, I knew that he would have been willing to use force, but what he wasn't willing to do was to look into my trusting, innocent eyes and explain what he had in mind.

"I know that this routine wouldn't have worked with every rapist. But I knew it would work with him. He wasn't too bright, and was just looking for something easy. My reaction didn't fit his picture of how a rape victim was supposed to behave, and he couldn't figure out what to do about it. He didn't know how to go about raping someone who trusted him. It would have been too embarrassing, and when I kept smiling back at him he couldn't seem to get started. Finally he just gave up and drove me back to the highway. I said good-bye as if I still had no idea what he'd been planning to do to me."

Like Dona and Jeanne, Tina believed that she faced a serious threat of rape but that she blocked it mentally by acting as if no such possibility existed. However, a skeptic might say that these women had only imagined that these men had rape in mind. No specific threats were made. Perhaps these men had only meant to romance them. Maybe cornering them in isolated places was just intended to permit private conversation or promote voluntary intimacy.

These subjects are all known to me personally, and I consider their judgment good. They are sophisticated women who are not strangers to male attention, and I would credit them with the ability to accurately judge the intentions of the men they were with. However, I think the degree of threat is clearer in the following stories.

Cynthia

Cynthia was returning to her Venice Beach apartment after attending a party in L.A. that had lasted into the early hours of the morning. She parked her car and was crossing the deserted lot when two men emerged from the shadows and seized her roughly.

"Hi, honey!" said one suggestively. "You're just in time to provide us with a little entertainment. Get those panties off, and let's go!" One man grabbed at her breast while the other maneuvered around behind her. Both made a variety of vulgar comments related to her physical endowments and the things they were planning to do to her.

The beach where Cynthia's apartment was located was always teeming with homeless men who made the area very dangerous at night. These two were shabbily dressed and had obviously been drinking. Cynthia knew that she wasn't going to be able to outrun them in her spike heels even if she could get free, and, although there were undoubtedly people sleeping in nearby apartments, the embattled residents would know better than to get involved in her problems if she screamed. Violence was a common nighttime occurrence in Venice, and Cynthia was about to become the next victim.

"I became very calm. I could see that I was going to be raped—there was nothing I could realistically hope to do about that. It just seemed like there was no point in getting upset about something that was inevitable," Cynthia told me.

"And when I accepted that, my mind moved on to the next thing—which was that as bad as it was going to be to be raped by these two creeps, it was even worse to think of it happening here on the gravel in the parking lot. Not only would I be raped, I would also wind up scraped and filthy, and my beautiful new dress would be ruined! So I said, 'Hey! If you're going to rape me, get it over with! But let's not do it here. My apartment is right over there. You can at least have the decency to rape me somewhere clean and comfortable!'

"That really threw those guys for a loop. They both burst out laughing, and one of them said, 'Boy! You've really got balls, lady!'

"'Hey, this is a new dress and it cost beaucoup bucks!' I said truculently. 'Anything happens to this dress, and you guys'll wish you'd never been born! Got that?'

"'Got it, lady. We sure wouldn't want to get you mad at us. No sirree. You're one tough mama. Lead the way.'"

As they walked to her apartment, Cynthia began to banter with the men. They were obviously tickled by her self-assertiveness. The idea of a rape victim calling the shots was clearly a new experience for them. Cynthia has a wonderful, biting wit, and as she exchanged humorous barbs with her assailants, ideas of rape seemed to recede into the background. By the time they reached her door, the atmosphere was downright friendly.

"It was like they were buddies of mine walking me home," Cynthia recalls. "One of them was still laughing about me being such a ballsy chick, and the other was giving me a brotherly warning to be more careful next time. A pretty woman like me ought not to be out alone after dark in this neighborhood. Didn't I know there were a lot of dangerous characters hanging around? All I can tell you is that it was really bizarre!"

Cynthia unlocked her door. "So, are you guys coming in?" she asked.

"Naw," one replied. "I guess we'll just be getting along. You have a good night now. And be a little more careful next time. Not everybody out here is as nice as us."

Once again we find a potential victim declining the victim role. Cynthia bypassed fear and anger after realizing that there was nothing she could realistically hope to do to protect herself. In the peaceful altered state, she seems to have read her attackers correctly and found their vulnerability. These men were obviously not beyond a sense of shame about what they were doing, and she showed them a courage that they had to respect and admire. By kidding with them as she did, Cynthia treated them like friends, and they were unable to resist the impulse to be friendly in return.

It is my belief that all of the people who shared their stories with me called upon their higher power for help, either explicitly or tacitly by releasing fear and anger and turning within for help. Each of them seemed to tune into the highest and best part of his or her own mind, and this may be what consulting one's higher power comes down to in practice. However, in the case of Dennis below, we see someone who prayed for divine assistance quite explicitly.

Dennis

While making his living as a clown, Dennis was hired to entertain at a fair in Norfolk, Virginia. In addition to performing himself, he was also responsible for the ten other clowns whose services he had contracted to provide.

One of the highlights of the day was a concert by a famous Motown group. After they had completed their set and left the stage to thunderous applause, Dennis got up there to do a parody of their act.

This six-foot-tall man was dressed as a baby clown, sporting enormous elephant feet, pink longjohns covered with red hearts, a huge, baggy diaper, bib, and baby bonnet. Sucking on a giant pacifier, he facetiously mimed the routines of the recent singers, and his comic antics were a tremendous hit with the crowd. High on his success, Dennis left the stage and went off to see how the clowns he had hired were making out entertaining the fairgoers around the rides and concessions on the midway.

The shortest route to the midway took Dennis through a large concrete parking structure. As he clomped ponderously through the dark, echoing building in his gigantic clown shoes, he had the misfortune to attract the attention of a gang that had been hanging out down there.

"What say we kick that honkey motherfucker's ass?" one of the young gangbangers proposed. This suggestion was taken up enthusiastically by others. Some twenty hostile youths began to close in on Dennis from his left.

Nervously casting his eyes to the right, Dennis discovered that a gang of teenage girls was bearing down on him from that direction. "I say we get into that honkey's diaper!" proposed one of the girls, flipping open a switchblade knife with a salacious grin. The others, many of them similarly armed, joined in with blood-curdling threats of a sexual nature. Dennis was completely surrounded. All that remained were a few seconds while the two gangs vied with each other about which would do the honors.

"I could see that there was no way out," Dennis reports, "but I didn't panic. Actually, my first reaction was anger. I figured to take a few of them down with me.

"But then I realized that violence wasn't the answer, and I decided to call upon the Holy Spirit instead. Inwardly I said, 'Help me, please.'

"The next thing I knew, I was behaving in a way I would never have thought of in a million years. It wasn't as if I planned it or anything. I just suddenly went into action, and what I did surprised me as much as anybody else.

"Acting in character as a baby clown, I threw my arms wide

like an infant asking for a hug. With a big grin, I toddled merrily up to the leader of the male gang and reached to embrace him, burbling, 'Da-da! Goo-goo! Da-da!'

"The guy looked stunned and backed away, saying, 'Man, you must be fuckin' crazy!'

"Then everybody got real quiet and drew back as if I had the plague. I swear, the crowd just parted like the Red Sea! Remaining in character as a baby clown, I toddled off toward the midway, and no one made the slightest attempt to interfere with me. I guess they thought I was really crazy or retarded or something. One way or another, they no longer saw me as someone it would be fun to hurt. I just whispered, 'Thank you, Father,' under my breath and toddled out of that parking structure as fast as I could!"

Dennis believes that his would-be assailants were put off by what appeared to be his mental deficiency. However, having viewed so many similar cases, my focus is slightly different. Again and again I have seen people set free after they somehow reminded an attacker of the existence of love. Here we find Dennis trustingly approaching the gang leader in the manner of a child greeting his father. As we shall see when we consider deliverances from murder, many of the people who told me their stories mentioned addressing their assailant in a tone of voice they habitually used with a relative.

I believe that each of these individuals met an "enemy" with an open heart. Instead of accepting the role of "adversary" or "victim" that was being thrust upon them, they recast themselves as a friend and responded from that position. By completely ignoring their assailants' hostile intent, they seemed to redefine the situation as a silly misunderstanding and induce their would-be attackers to see it that way, too. Could this shift in perception be the basis of miracles?

In the next chapter we will consider what some of the experts on miraculous phenomena have to say about them. We have seen that there are no good scientific or philosophical reasons for believing that supernatural phenomena *cannot* exist. However, saying that something could exist in theory is not the same as saying that it actually does occur. In the next chapter, we'll consider some of the scientific evidence that things really do happen that cannot be explained on the basis of naturalistic causes.

6

What the "Experts" Say About Miracles

We know very little and can achieve very little; but we are at liberty, if we so choose, to cooperate with a greater power and a completer knowledge. If we cooperate, we shall be all right even if the worst should happen. If we refuse to cooperate, we shall be all wrong even in the most propitious of circumstances.

—Aldous Huxley

Since miracles cannot be accommodated within the naturalistic paradigm, Western scientists have generally been content to assume without evidence that people who report them are either lying or mistaken. Confident that the laws of probability can comfortably account for any unusual events that actually did occur, few scientists have bothered to examine the evidence.

However, one notable exception is the research that has been carried out at the Shrine of the Virgin at Lourdes, France, where a spring is said to have emerged from the spot on which the Virgin Mary allegedly appeared in 1858. The water flowing from the spring is reputed to have miraculous powers. Every year, hundreds of thousands of people from around the world make the pilgrimage to Lourdes, hoping for miraculous healing. Large numbers of them assert that they have received the help they sought.

An international medical team has been investigating claims

of miraculous healing connected with the waters at Lourdes since 1947. This twenty-five member commission includes four surgeons, three orthopedists, two psychiatrists, a radiologist, a neuropsychiatrist, a dermatologist, an opthalmologist, a pediatrician, a cardiologist, an oncologist, a neurologist, and a biochemist, along with a number of physicians in general practice. Ten members hold chairs in their respective medical schools. All are practicing Catholics.[16]

Of more than six thousand cases where miracles have been alleged, some sixty-four have survived rigorous investigation and been accepted by the commission as legitimate. The question the commission asks is: "Does the cure of this person constitute a phenomenon which is contrary to the observations and expectations of medical knowledge and scientifically inexplicable?" Aware of the power of suggestion, the investigators refuse to even consider any recovery, however spectacular, that could be an example of spontaneous remission. This excludes even complete and instantaneous healings from diseases such as cancer, lupus, multiple sclerosis, tuberculosis, and so forth.

The committee is not interested in cures that are merely unexpected, but only in the documentation of those that are *physically impossible.* Cases are only accepted as miraculous if it can be established beyond any reasonable doubt that something occurred for which there is no possibility of naturalistic explanation. One example is that of Vittorio.

Vittorio Michelli

Vittorio Michelli had had his hip joint completely destroyed by a fusiform cell carcinoma (cancer). The pelvis was disintegrated, and the leg was nearly separated. He was treated in the Military Hospital at Trente, Italy, where the destructive progress of the disease was charted with radiological evidence.

A year after his initial diagnosis, Michelli went to Lourdes and was bathed in the waters in the plaster cast that was holding his hip together. He reported sudden sensations of heat moving through his body while he was in the water, and when he emerged from the spring his appetite and energy returned immediately. A month later, his doctors finally consented to remove the cast and take another X ray. When they did so, they determined that the tumor was regressing.

The tumor soon disappeared completely, at which point the bone began to regrow and eventually completely reconstructed the hip. *Michelli was walking two months after his return from Lourdes.* Brendan O'Regan quotes the commission report to this effect, "A completely destroyed articulation was completely reconstructed without any surgical intervention. The lower limb which was useless became sound, the prognosis is indisputable, the patient is alive and in a flourishing state of health nine years after his return from Lourdes."[17]

Miracles Elsewhere

Medjugorje in former Yugoslavia has become a new pilgrimage site where an apparition of the Virgin Mary has been appearing daily since June 24, 1981. The apparition is seen every evening by six children—two boys and four girls—who report that Mary has come to encourage peace and to remind us of the need to become aware of God, *in our own way.*

The Catholic Church has not acknowledged the legitimacy of the reported visions and miracles from Medjugorje, possibly because the apparition of the Virgin is not suggesting that it is necessary to become a Catholic or, indeed, a Christian. Brendan O'Regan of the Institute of Noetic Sciences reported that there was considerable consternation within the church when a Muslim boy was miraculously healed.[9] Father Slavko, a Franciscan monk with a Ph.D. in psychology who is the children's spiritual director, has been sending reports of miraculous cures at Medjugorje to the medical commission at Lourdes, but as yet no effort has been made to investigate them.

The government has also been very uncomfortable with the Medjugorje phenomenon and has made numerous attempts to put a stop to it. The children have been interrogated repeatedly by the police, and Father Slavko was jailed for eighteen months as a result of his participation. Police roadblocks have been used to discourage pilgrims. The combined indifference of the world scientific community, the Catholic Church, and the government has so far prevented any effort to evaluate the many reports of miracles occurring there.

Aside from the considerable body of research on the efficacy of prayer, Lourdes is the only place where spontaneously occurring miracles have been investigated using the standards of Western science. But they are reported in all cultures. For example, there are numerous reports of miracles performed in India by Sai Baba, a holy man who routinely materializes objects bearing the likenesses of the saints and avatars of many religions for those who come daily to receive his blessing. There are also accounts of miraculous healings attributed to Sai Baba, some of which have been observed and documented by Western physicians. But then there are miracles being reported in every inhabited area of the globe.

Evaluating Miracles

Miracles can be evaluated in two ways: scientifically or personally. The medical commission at Lourdes represents an attempt at scientific validation by experts. But even when such events are attested to by credible authorities, their findings are not necessarily convincing. Experts can be mistaken, and we can, and should, question the things they tell us. After all, science progresses by disproving yesterday's "truths."

Nevertheless, despite the inherent limitations of expert opinion, it would be of enormous benefit to humankind if an independent international commission could be established to evaluate reports of miracles. The findings of such a commission would be even more convincing if its makeup included experimental psychologists, physicists, professional illusionists, and representatives of many faiths, as well as open-minded atheists and agnostics. At the present time, such phenómena tend to be investigated, when they are investigated at all, by groups and individuals with a vested interest in finding for or against them. No matter how reputable the medical commission that authenticates miracles at Lourdes, there may always be something unconvincing about Catholic physicians ruling upon the legitimacy of miracles at a Catholic shrine.

At the other extreme are those committed to "debunking" claims of miraculous phenomena. For example, James Randi, aka "The Amazing Randi," is a popular stage illusionist who has done a great deal to demystify apparently miraculous phenomena by showing how trickery has been used to intentionally mislead people. He recently exposed a prominent faith healer whose seeming omniscience about the personal affairs of members of his audience was based upon information gleaned by confederates in the auditorium and radioed to him through a hidden microphone in his ear.

In his book *Flim-Flam! Psychics, ESP, Unicorns and Other Delusions*, Randi explains many ways in which miracles have been simulated to fool the unwary.[18] For example, one common ploy used by faith healers is to have assistants offer to place people who walk with difficulty in wheelchairs when they enter the tent or auditorium. The solicitous confederate then wheels the individual to an area near the stage. Later, when the revivalist "heals" them and they rise and walk, it creates a very impressive spectacle for those who do not realize that these people had come in under their own power.

While there is no question that unscrupulous people throughout history have simulated miracles in order to gain power and enrich themselves, we must remember that just because something *could* be simulated by trickery doesn't mean that it was actually done that way. In their enthusiasm for exposing fakery, some "debunkers" present a picture unfairly slanted in the opposite direction.

For example, a California-based organization that lists many prominent scientists among its supporters purports to provide unbiased evaluations of claims of the paranormal. However, their first director resigned when he concluded that his colleagues were not so much objectively investigating such claims as actively distorting the data in order to refute them. The Catholic physicians who investigate miracles at Lourdes may be suspected of a vested interest in finding them genuine, while people like James Randi, who make their living by exposing trickery, have a clear motive for invalidating them. If we wish to know the true status of supernatural phenomena, we must approach them without bias.

One investigator who did just that was the great stage illusionist and escape artist Harry Houdini. He spent many years investigating spiritualists, exposing numerous charlatans whose apparently miraculous powers were faked. However, since Houdini is often cited as an authority by those who wish to establish that supernatural phenomena are *always* the result of trickery, it is worth taking a few minutes here to set the record straight.

"Debunkers" of the supernatural who use Houdini's experience to prove their point invariably focus upon some parts of his story while carefully avoiding others. For example, it is seldom mentioned that Houdini's interest in the supernatural was initially sparked by the following personal experience.

Houdini

During one of his famous escapes, Houdini arranged to be dropped through a hole in the ice on a frozen river while shackled and sealed in a padlocked trunk. The brilliant escape artist quickly freed himself and shot to the surface, only to discover that a strong current had carried him away from the hole. He was trapped beneath the frozen river with only seconds to live and no clue as to where the opening in the ice might be.

Houdini began to swim around frantically but quickly realized that, in his panic, he was as likely to be moving away from the hole as toward it. He forced himself to calm down and found that he could buy some time by snatching partial breaths from air pockets trapped under bubbles in the ice. But it was clear that he would freeze to death if he did not locate the hole very quickly, and this he was unable to do. It began to dawn upon him that this just might be the time he was not going to make it.

Suddenly Houdini heard his mother calling him. Without hesitation, he used the last of his strength to swim in the direction of her voice, and it led him to the hole. He was dragged out of the freezing water half-dead, to the thunderous applause of a crowd that had no idea how badly wrong his stunt had gone. However, his mother was not among those present. As he was shortly to learn, she had died at home in bed at precisely the time he had been trapped beneath the ice.

This profound personal experience of communication with his dead mother instilled in Houdini a lifelong curiosity about spiritual realities. His interest was not fueled by skepticism, as is often suggested, but by his personal conviction that his mother had indeed reached out to him after death to save his life. Since there were many mediums who claimed to communicate with those who had "passed over," Houdini eagerly began to seek them out in the hope of reestablishing communication with his mother.

However, this did not turn out to be as simple as he at first imagined. As a master of illusion himself, Houdini was quick to discover that the dramatic effects produced in seances were usually nothing more than trickery. He did encounter sincere mediums who were not trying to fool the public, but even in these cases it was difficult to say with certainty whether or not the information they brought through was really the result of communication with departed souls.

First of all, Houdini was well aware of how easy it is to generate plausible hypotheses about a person from astute analysis of his or her physical appearance, vocabulary, manner, and so forth. Any clever magician can amaze an audience with intimate knowledge of their affairs, and as an expert at the same game, Houdini was in a better position than most to detect fraud. However, he realized that even an honest medium might be employing such information unconsciously, despite a sincere conviction that he or she was receiving communications from the dead.

Houdini realized that in his case, the only way to verify conclusively that a communication was coming from his mother would be for the medium to relate information that he could be sure was known only to his mother and himself. But what would that be? So much had been written about Houdini in the papers that many things about him were common knowledge or could be easily researched. Other pieces of personal information might have been confided to a friend by his mother without his knowledge, or overheard by a neighbor thirty years earlier. See for yourself whether you can think of any piece of information that you know beyond all possibility of doubt was known *only* to you and a deceased loved one.

Because of the incident beneath the frozen river, Houdini suspected that dead people did live on in spirit and could communicate with the living. However, he was continually frustrated in his efforts to verify this possibility. He did receive mediumistic messages that *might have* come from his mother, but none that *could only have* done so. Unfortunately, the things you would expect your dead mother to say are precisely the same things that a fraudulent medium would expect her to say.

In order to resolve the issue once and for all, Houdini arranged an experiment with his wife. It involved a secret code that he was absolutely confident was known only to the two of them. They agreed that whichever of them died first would attempt to transmit the code to the other through a medium. When Houdini passed away, a substantial monetary reward was advertised to anyone who could bring his widow conclusive proof of his continued existence.

Naturally she was deluged with communications from people who said that Houdini had sent her a message through them: "Your husband says he is alive and well and loves you very much."

"Houdini is very concerned about your finances and warns you to be careful of your money." All such communications were patently false, since there would be only one message her husband would be sending.

However, eventually the prominent Washington, D.C., psychic Arthur Ford received an unintelligible message that he was instructed to pass along to Mrs. Houdini. Upon receiving it, she dropped everything and rushed off to attend a seance with him. Ford had correctly delivered the first part of the code, and now it was up to Mrs. Houdini to decide how to reply.

In her session with him, Mrs. Houdini found that Arthur Ford was able to make the correct response to every one of her conversational gambits. She joyously announced to the press that Ford had met all of Houdini's rigorous requirements, and he was awarded the prize money amid a flurry of excited media coverage.

However, there was a sequel. Years later, when Mrs. Houdini had fallen upon hard times, a Hollywood production company approached her with the idea of making a movie about her husband's life. If they decided to go ahead with the project, they explained, they would hire her as a consultant at a very handsome salary. However, because of all the strangeness surrounding Houdini's flirtation with the supernatural, they were not sure they wanted to make the movie. In their opinion, American audiences were not ready for the idea that the dead could communicate with the living.

What it came down to was this: If Mrs. Houdini sincerely believed that her husband had really communicated from beyond the grave, they would reluctantly be forced to shelve the project. However, if she had any doubt in her mind—if, for instance, she might possibly have mentioned the code to another person, or if there was any chance that someone could have overheard Houdini talking with her about it—then they could legitimately disregard the whole issue and make the movie the way they wanted to.

Under these conditions, Mrs. Houdini found that she now for the first time remembered that someone *could* have overheard her talking about the code with her husband. So it was just barely possible that Arthur Ford *might* have gotten the code some other way. The movie was made, and Mrs. Houdini's financial picture improved dramatically.

It seems extraordinary, but skeptics frequently use Houdini's story to prove that mediumship—and by extension, other supernatural phenomena—is all fakery. They ignore his personal experience of communication with his dead mother and the fact that Arthur Ford's performance had completely satisfied Mrs. Houdini until years later, when financial considerations made it expedient to cast doubt upon it.

In fact, I think that this story provides a wonderful illustration of the point I will be making throughout this book—that "reality" is an individual construct. People determined to disbelieve in spiritual realities can and do take from Houdini's experiences the parts that support their point of view, ignoring the aspects that point in the opposite direction. The simple truth is that no amount of evidence will convince people against their will, and closed minds will always find their prejudices vindicated by whatever "facts" they allow to be facts.

No one is truly convinced by mere facts in any case, and herein lies the folly of relying exclusively upon "experts." I think we should all be like Houdini and place our greatest faith in that which we know from our own experience. If miracles are not a reality in your own life, what does it matter whether others believe in them?

But if miracles are really possible, why are they so rare? Before we go on to explore more deliverance stories, let us consider why miracles remain outside many people's frame of reference.

7

Why Are Miracles So Rare?

It is through solving problems correctly that we grow spiritually.

— Peace Pilgrim

If miracles really are possible, why are there so few individuals who actually experience them? Surely with so many religious people praying for divine intervention, miracles ought to be commonplace. Yet you almost never hear of anyone claiming to have had a miracle, and on the rare occasions when you do, there always seems to be reason to question either their veracity or their discrimination. If miracles are real, why don't we experience them ourselves, or meet credible people who have experienced them?

First, there may be many more instances of miracles than we ordinarily recognize. Because they fall outside the framework of our cultural thinking, miracles are not reported as such by mainstream news media. As a matter of fact, in the current intellectual climate, the mere fact that someone claims to have experienced a miracle is often enough to make people write him or her off as a religious fanatic. Under these conditions, it should not be surprising if people do not always call public attention to their unusual experiences.

An analogous case might be that of near-death experiences. When psychiatrist Raymond Moody first began to hear about near-death experiences from his patients, he was skeptical.[19] However, he found that whenever he mentioned these odd reports with

97

open-minded interest in his lectures, someone from the audience would generally sidle up afterward and whisper, "You know, the same thing happened to me." Moody was amazed to discover not only how many people had had dramatic near-death experiences that changed their lives, but also that *most had never told anyone about them* for fear of being regarded as some kind of a nut. In our culture, people tend to hush up spiritual experiences.

Such is the prejudice against miracles that even the individuals to whom they occur may not identify them as such. For example, if a person diagnosed with an "incurable" illness recovers, everyone concerned may be much more likely to conclude that the initial diagnosis was wrong than to recognize that their prayers have been answered. Because we ordinarily think of miracles as signs of special favor from God, even religious people often feel foolish and grandiose attributing a piece of "luck" to divine intervention.

So, one answer to the question of why miracles appear to be so rare is that they may not really be rare at all—simply under-recognized and underreported. Few of the people who told me about their experiences of deliverance claimed to have experienced a miracle, yet I believe that they may have done so. Think of how often our fears prove groundless—our lost car keys turn up in time to make our appointment; we find the mortgage money after all; someone who has been making our lives miserable suddenly decides to be "reasonable." These may *all* be unrecognized instances of divine assistance.

For example, I believe that Sam's experience recounted below illustrates miraculous healing from an illness, yet it is only the coincidence of the offer of healing with Sam's peaceful altered state that even hints that a supernatural influence might have been involved. As is often the case, the remission itself was a gradual process, and many events occurred along the way, any one of which could have been responsible for the result. In the story below, however, it is at least clear that the healing was *initiated* following Sam's shift in consciousness.

Sam and Jim

Sam was just completing his doctorate in psychology when he discovered that the rare autoimmune disease that had nearly killed him ten years earlier had come back. After extensive tests, he was informed one morning by his physician that his only chance for survival was to enter the hospital immediately for intensive chemotherapy.

Sam had spent six months in the hospital the last time, and the prospect of further agonizing treatment was more than he could face. Meditating upon his choices, Sam's initial reaction, "Why is God doing this terrible thing to me?," gave way to acceptance and surrender. After all, it was God's universe, and who was Sam to tell the Creator how to run it? Sam concluded that it was ultimately up to God whether he would live or die—not to some doctor. He informed his physician that he would not be seeking further treatment.

Having made the decision to leave his fate in God's hands, Sam felt oddly peaceful. He awaited developments with a sense of calm detachment. His young son was visiting that day, and Sam found that he was able to put aside his personal concerns and cheerfully devote himself to the Indian dish they had looked forward to preparing together.

That evening, Sam received a phone call from a man he knew slightly through a mutual friend. The caller, a psychologist named Jim, said that he had heard some time ago that Sam was seriously ill, and that for weeks he had been hearing a voice in his head instructing him to call Sam and offer to try to heal him.

Jim said that he was a student of *A Course in Miracles,* and that he assumed that he was hearing the voice of the Holy Spirit. He explained that he had not called sooner because there had seemed to be little point, knowing as he did that Sam was intensely skeptical about the possibility of spiritual healing. However, the voice had been so insistent today that Jim had decided to make the call just to get it to leave him alone.

Sam was astonished by the coincidence of his decision to leave his life or death up to God and the immediate offer of spiritual healing. He had briefly examined *A Course in Miracles* when someone had given him a set of the books years earlier, and he had not thought much of it. As a Jew, he had found it difficult to relate to the Christian terminology. As a scientist, its promise to teach people to perform miracles seemed preposterous.

Nevertheless, in the present instance Sam couldn't see that he had anything to lose by meeting with the caller, and just maybe he would have something to gain. Why the Holy Spirit (assuming that it existed) would be going out of its way to help a Jew who didn't even believe in it, Sam couldn't imagine, but he felt he might as well look into it.

Sam and Jim set up a series of meetings that went on for months. Sam found his would-be healer to be a brilliant but stubborn man. Although Jim did some energy work on him, much of their time together was spent in heated debate over Jim's contention that Sam himself must be creating the illness at an unconscious level. As Sam began to realize the influence his habitual negative thoughts were having on his health, his thinking changed and the illness remitted. A few months later he was well again.

Notice that while the *offer* of healing is suggestive of help from some supernatural source, the healing itself depended upon Sam's change of mind. If Sam had steadfastly maintained his original skepticism or been unable to understand his own role in creating his illness, it is likely that no actual healing would have occurred. Jim encouraged Sam to think about his problem in a different way, and by doing so, Sam probably healed himself. The only supernatural element may have been the inner voice that prompted Jim to offer help.

Creating the Right Conditions for a Miracle

Our deliverance stories shed light upon the reasons a lot of people who ask for miracles don't receive them. First, there is the matter of the detached and peaceful altered state. Like Sam, all of the people who experienced miracles seemed to give up at some level and acknowledge that the outcome was not in their hands. They didn't kid themselves that their efforts alone would be able to change things. There is an element of personal surrender in these stories that differentiates them from the average adventure tale.

This sense of surrender seemed to take people who experienced miracles beyond fear, and inner peace would also appear to be a necessary condition for a miracle. We have already seen, and shall see again, examples of deliverance in cases where people had to struggle against their fear. Although strongly tempted to panic, these individuals fought for clarity and concentrated upon their inner guidance. However, so far I have not heard any stories about people who experienced deliverance after giving way to fear or investing in the belief that their anger was justified. Those who are unable to get past their emotional turmoil and reach a detached and peaceful mental state do not seem to access miracles.

Further, miracles seem to require people to change their perception of the problem. Sam initially thought he was being threatened by a disease, but Jim helped him understand that he was really being assaulted by his own critical thoughts. As we shall see when we explore the procedure for creating miracles in greater detail, our thoughts may be influencing the events we experience, and our personal contribution to a situation may lie in our interpretation of it.

Accessing Miracles May Be an Acquired Skill

In considering the prevalence of miracles, it is also important to remember that many things exist as human potentials that are not realized in a given person. As a human being, I am theoretically capable of doing most things that other humans can do, but in actuality I can only do the things that I personally have learned and am able to do. I cannot run a four-minute mile, hot-wire a car, or—if my husband is to be believed—even make a decent cup of coffee. But this is not evidence that such accomplishments are beyond the reach of everyone. And the fact that a given person is not aware of being able to perform miracles is not evidence that miracles do not exist.

Notice that most of the people who told me their stories had had some spiritual training. They had invested time and effort in developing a relationship with their higher power, and this may have made it easier for them to access help when the need arose. Attaining the mental state necessary for miracles may simply be a skill that some people cultivate and others do not.

Miracles Are Not Always Welcome

In understanding why miracles are not more common, it is also important to recognize that many troubled people do not truly *want* help, miraculous or otherwise. As a psychologist, I am convinced that people create certain problems in their lives for a reason. Difficult situations force us to learn important lessons and, from a certain point of view, ultimately turn out to have been worth the trouble they cost us.

For example, many people look back upon a painful chapter in their lives with a sense that going through it helped make them the men and women they are today. It wasn't pleasant, but in retrospect, they would not wish to have missed out on the growth it promoted. The agonizing social rejection experienced by a teenager may make him better able to empathize with others as an adult. The child of a severely dysfunctional family may learn an inner strength and self-reliance that her peers lack. The unwillingly divorced wife may eventually find herself happier with her freedom than she had believed possible.

There will be pain in your spiritual growth until you will do God's will and no longer need to be pushed into it. When you are out of harmony with God's will, problems come. Their purpose is to push you into harmony. If you would willingly do God's will, you could avoid the problems.

—Peace Pilgrim

If a problem were artificially removed before it had served its purpose, it might interfere with lessons we ourselves had chosen to learn. For example, I frequently see clients in my psychotherapy practice who complain bitterly about a painful situation in which they find themselves, only to discover later why they needed it. Only at the point of insight are they ready to really release the situation, and then their seemingly insoluble problem often clears up with amazing speed.

Let me illustrate this point with a case of nonmiraculous non-healing.

Alice

A friend of mine I'll call Alice constantly gets herself into awful financial trouble. Her credit cards are always maxed out, and she is perpetually plagued by dunning phone calls from people to whom she owes money. Life for Alice is a scramble to keep food on the table and the rent just current enough to avoid eviction.

Alice is a bright woman who makes good money when she works. However, she usually has an "excellent" reason why she cannot work. Sometimes it is health, but more often it is some important project that she considers a good long-term investment of her time and effort, but which never seems to pay off.

Living the way Alice does would drive me crazy, and I assumed that she felt the same way about it. She certainly complained about her life as though she did. In my anxiety for her, I would lend her money, find her jobs, and offer advice constantly. My efforts were always very much appreciated, but somehow they never improved Alice's situation for long. Whenever her income was augmented in any way, the increase was quickly offset by some important new expense that just had to be incurred immediately.

I began to find myself resenting Alice. It upset me to see her continually living on the edge of disaster, and I began to be very critical of the way she handled her financial affairs. Needless to say, this put a strain upon our friendship. Alice always had an airtight explanation of why things had to be done exactly the way she was doing them.

One day it dawned on me that Alice was creating her financial problems intentionally—not that the intention was conscious, but there was something about the situation of financial insecurity that she seemed to need. I realized that there must be some lesson she hoped to learn that could only be learned in the laboratory of financial chaos.

Perhaps it had to do with living by her wits, or coping with anxiety, or eliciting friendly support from others. Maybe she was symbolically recreating some early trauma in an effort to process it. The reason was unclear to me and was really none of my business. However, it clarified things enormously when I finally understood that she needed her financial problems and was not prepared to give them up.

I had been feeling like a lifeguard who repeatedly pulls a drowning swimmer out of the surf only to have her offer sincere thanks and then go back in for another quick dip. The more I urged Alice to "stay away from the water," the more she resented my interference and made it clear that I was not going to tell her how to run her life. I finally realized that what had looked to me like drowning was really a unique form of swimming-under-adverse-conditions, which my friend was determined to perfect. My attempts at rescue merely put her to the additional trouble of recreating her financial dilemma so that she could get on with the education she had planned for herself. When I finally stopped interfering and just kept her company in her struggles, we got along much better.

If it is true, as I am suggesting, that our thoughts influence our physical circumstances, then it must also be true that the unconscious aspects of mind also exert an influence. When we discover why we might unconsciously "need" a painful situation, our conscious mind may be able to find a different and less distressing way to accomplish the same goal.

This is where psychotherapy comes in. No one consciously desires illness, financial problems, personal rejection, and such. Nevertheless, we may have mental habits that create such experiences, or hidden reasons for thinking that we deserve them. Good psychotherapy might have helped Alice understand her reasons for creating the financial problems that continually seemed to befall her, as it helped Sam understand the effects his thoughts were having on his autoimmune disease.

While psychotherapy can be very helpful, I believe that it is also possible to receive information from our higher power directly, as my deliverance subjects did. However, this direct approach requires practice in meditation.

My Cold Sores

I went through a period of many years when I was plagued by painful and ugly cold sores. They invariably became large and infected, and no sooner would one clear up than another would begin. I felt very much a victim of the herpes virus that creates these disgusting blisters.

One day as a new sore blossomed on my lip, I decided that it couldn't hurt to at least see whether these painful blisters were being generated with my own unconscious complicity. The whole idea seemed utterly ridiculous, but I decided to go into meditation and say, "If there is a reason why I would unconsciously want cold sores, I would like to know what it is."

The response astounded me. I was shown that I was living under incredible stress (teaching seven days a week for three different universities in four different cities) and that I generally took no care at all of my health. I knew that my eating habits were terrible and that I never got enough sleep. Add to that a great deal of emotional turmoil over finances and the stress of my on-again, off-again relationship with a current boyfriend, and I had a recipe for disaster.

In the past, I had often been sick with persistent respiratory infections that were exhausting and sometimes stopped me cold. When they resulted in missed work, my stress was doubled, since I didn't have the kind of job where someone else could take over for a few days. I was reminded that since I had developed cold sores, these illnesses had become less frequent. This was because I knew that the only way to get the cold sore to heal was to rest, take vitamins, and eat better.

I was shown that I was unconsciously using the cold sores as an early warning system. Every time one appeared, I would finally slow down and take better care of myself. In this fashion many of the debilitating respiratory illnesses were prevented.

I was awed by the realization that the herpes virus had actually been my friend rather than my enemy. And I was also determined to mend my ways. Although I might not be able to eliminate all stress, I could at least eat better, rest more, and take vitamins regularly. I thanked the herpes virus for its help and began a regime that was at least marginally more sane.

From that day on, cold sores became a very rare event in my life. When one began to appear, I would thank it silently and use it as a signal to take better care of myself. I found that under these conditions, the sore would often quietly disappear within a few hours, its mission accomplished.

Because of my own experiences, and those of clients and friends, I have come to believe that *all illnesses and accidents are unconsciously intended to serve a purpose.* As the examples above indicate, the reasons for creating a painful situation may be surprising and are usually not at all obvious to the sufferer. However, as long as a problem is unconsciously regarded as the solution to an even bigger problem, the individual will not be open to permitting a cure, miraculous or otherwise.

Many physicians would agree that all healing depends upon the patient's inner decision to release the problem to solution. A medication that heals one person may be ineffective for another, while a third is allergic to it, and a fourth gets well without treatment. Our unconscious ambivalence may interfere with our ability to accept miracles in the same way that it limits our response to the healing efforts of physicians.

Miracles Await Welcome

Even if we are prepared to accept help with a painful condition, it does not follow that we are prepared to accept *miraculous* help. The whole idea of miracles is disturbing to many people—probably because it implies the existence of a God who may judge us. The Judeo-Christian thinking that has been most influential in the West has often depicted God as a vengeful punisher of sin. I suspect that fear of divine retribution makes some people shy away from the idea of God altogether, and this may make non-miraculous help far more acceptable than the miraculous kind. In a culture where evidence of a supernatural power may be deeply frightening, it should not be surprising if most healings are attributable to traditional medicine and most dangers are averted in ways that can be written off as "luck."

Remember that if everyone has free will, no one can "inflict" miraculous healing upon someone who is not prepared to accept it. My research suggests that miracles do not necessarily require conscious faith in God, but they do presuppose some degree of open-minded optimism about a positive outcome on the part of the recipient. Not even great spiritual masters can work wonders for the stubbornly skeptical.

For example, the New Testament tells us that Jesus was unable to perform many miracles when he revisited Nazareth, the town where he had grown up (Matthew 13:53–58). His old acquaintances were simply not prepared to accept help from the little boy who used to run around their village, and their steadfast refusal to entertain the possibility that Jesus *could* heal them made it impossible for him to work miracles on their behalf.

Miracles arise from a mind that is ready for them. By being united this mind goes out to everyone, even without the awareness of the miracle worker himself.

—*A Course in Miracles*

All of this is to say that miracles may go unrecognized or may fail to occur at all because they are unwelcome. *Divine intervention occurs only to people who are ready, willing, and able to accept it.* As we explore deliverances from rape and murder in the next chapter, try to get a feel for the unusual state of consciousness that is associated with miracle readiness.

8

Assaults, Part II:
Saving Grace

The truly helpful are invulnerable, because they are not
protecting their egos and so nothing can hurt them.
— *A Course in Miracles*

The cases in this chapter involve deliverance from assault, and here I don't think there can be any reasonable doubt about the danger the people who related them were facing. In each story, the assailant's intentions are unambiguous and, in many, the person telling it does actually suffer some injury or loss. As you read these accounts, keep your eye on the unusual state of consciousness that always seems to precede deliverance.

Rae

Rae checked into an Athens hotel the night before she was scheduled to fly back to the United States. She had spent several weeks vacationing with friends in the Greek Isles and was on her way home by herself.

A fellow American named Victor struck up a conversation with her in the hotel lobby and invited her out for a night on the town, but Rae wasn't interested. However, when he insisted that she at least have dinner with him in the hotel, she saw no reason to refuse. After all, she had to eat.

Dinner with Vic was reasonably enjoyable. He explained that

he was in Greece doing engineering work for an American company, and he talked about his wife and two children back in the States. They chatted about their experiences in Europe as travelers will. Nothing at all remarkable occurred, and after dinner Rae announced that she was going to bed since her flight would be leaving early the next morning.

Vic urged her to stay and have a drink, but she declined. He then insisted upon walking her to her room. It was obvious to Rae that he wanted to be invited in, but she was not about to do that. When he would not give up, she politely thanked him for dinner and firmly told him, "Good night!" She pushed him out of the way and closed the door more or less in his face, reflecting wryly, "Some men just won't take 'no' for an answer!"

In the middle of the night, Rae was awakened by a loud crashing and thumping. It sounded like a large pane of glass breaking close at hand. As she sat up in bed, she was horrified to see Victor looming over her. The dim light that filtered through the curtains revealed that he was completely naked and bleeding from many cuts.

Startled, Rae screamed, but Victor leaped upon her and began choking her. Pinned beneath his weight and unable to breathe, she could only claw ineffectually at his powerful hands.

As the hopelessness of her situation became increasingly apparent and consciousness began to slip away, Rae found herself in a strangely peaceful mental state. "I became very calm and detached," Rae reported. "Somehow whether I lived or died didn't seem to matter very much. I can't explain it. It was as though it was all happening to someone else." Rae stopped struggling, and a few moments later, Victor relaxed his grip on her throat. She could breathe again.

Rae remembers that it was as if a loving presence came over her. She began talking to this man who had just been strangling her, and her words and voice were compassionate and tender. Rae says that she had no idea what she was going to say—the words just poured out. Strangely enough, she was aware of being filled with great love for Victor—an impersonal sort of goodwill that made her deeply sad that he would degrade himself by behaving this way. It was as though he were someone she knew well and cared about deeply.

Despite the obvious danger she was in, Rae was not aware of any concern for herself. All she wanted was for Victor to love and respect himself enough to see that this sort of desperate and cruel behavior was unworthy of him. There was no fear in her.

Rae remembers assuring Victor that he was really a good person and that he could still mend his ways and have a good life. In retrospect, she feels that it was as though some spiritual force was talking to him through her. The loving words that poured forth were as surprising to her as they obviously were to him.

Rae talked to Victor for what seemed like a long time, sitting beside him on the bed as he wept with shame. She held him and tenderly caressed his face as he cried. Finally, he leaped up and, after jumping the short distance from her balcony to the ground, ran off naked into the night. She never saw him again.

When she looked into the bathroom, Rae found broken glass all over the floor. She summoned the hotel manager and learned that Victor had rented the room next to hers after she had gone to bed. There was a small crawl space that connected the bathrooms of the two rooms, but it was closed off at each end by a mirrored panel. Victor had removed the panel on his own side, wriggled through the space and broken through the mirror into her bathroom, cutting himself badly in the process. There was blood everywhere.

When she returned home the following day, friends and relatives were appalled by the deep bruises on her throat and horrified to learn of the terrible experience she had been through. They expected her to be badly shaken, but she laughed the whole thing off and was surprised to realize that she sincerely meant it when she assured them, "I'm fine. Really! It was no big deal."

111

In Rae's case, it is impossible to argue that Victor intended only an innocent flirtation. It seems clear that he had something violent and sexual in mind, but again we find that a peaceful, loving state of consciousness seems to turn things around.

Miracles for Self-Defense

The story Elizabeth shared has many points of similarity with that of Rae. Notice in particular the strangely fearless and compassionate mental state that came to her rescue. See whether you agree that it transformed the way her would-be assailant thought about her.

Elizabeth

On her way back to her car after a ballet class in Hollywood, Elizabeth remembers passing a tall, rough-looking man who sought eye contact with her. An experienced city dweller, she quickly averted her gaze and hurried on.

Upon reaching her vehicle in a dark, deserted lot, Elizabeth warily paused a moment to make sure no one was hiding in or around it. Reassured, she unlocked the door, and that was when she was silently seized from behind. Her assailant forced an expert hand under her tongue to keep her from screaming. He shoved her into the car and followed her inside, brandishing a knife. Despite the dim light, Elizabeth had no trouble recognizing the man she had seen a few moments earlier on the street.

Although she was terrified, Elizabeth says that she felt oddly comforted by the fact that the weapon the man was holding at her throat was only a serrated steak knife. Not that it wouldn't have done the trick, she knew, but somehow it suggested to her that her attacker was not an experienced criminal. Someone who had done this many times, she thought, would have had a different kind of weapon.

"Just calm down and keep quiet," the man ordered, seizing her keys and starting the car. "I'm not going to hurt you."

"Well, that's pretty hard to believe with that knife in my face," Elizabeth gasped. "You'd better get out of my car. I've got to get home. My little boy is waiting for me. He'll be worried to death." Ignoring her protests, the man drove off, although he repeated his assurance that he was not going to hurt her.

Elizabeth doesn't remember exactly how it happened, but somehow her mention of her son started him talking. The man seemed to *need* to talk. He said he had been a commando in Vietnam and that he had seen many children weeping over the bodies of their dead mothers. Elizabeth sensed that the idea of those motherless children still got to him, so she continued to emphasize that she was a single parent with a helpless child waiting at home. Perhaps he would hesitate to be responsible for another grieving orphan.

The man drove them to his own car and ordered her to get into it. Elizabeth balked.

"What are you going to do to me?" she demanded apprehensively.

"Why does every white woman think a black man wants to fuck her?" the kidnapper snapped bitterly. "I told you I wasn't going to hurt you. Just shut up and get into the car! I'll have you back here in twenty minutes."

Elizabeth did as she was told, and her assailant drove into the Watts ghetto of L.A. He finally pulled to the curb on a semi-deserted business district. By now it was about ten or eleven at night. A few incurious pedestrians hurried by on the sidewalk, but Elizabeth knew better than to anticipate any help from that quarter. Suddenly, her kidnapper reached over and stuck his hands down her pants. Apparently he was planning to molest her right there in the car.

"Well, isn't this just great!" Elizabeth snapped indignantly. "You tell me you aren't going to rape me, and then the first thing you do is make a grab for me! This is exactly what you said you weren't going to do! I can see now that you are not a man of your word!

How am I supposed to believe anything you say when you lie to me this way?"

Her assailant froze, stunned by her angry outburst. But Elizabeth had plenty more to say. "I suppose it was all a lie that you weren't going to hurt me, too!" she continued contemptuously. "You should be ashamed of yourself, a big man like you, taking advantage of a woman! And not only that, but lying to me after I trusted you! And besides, what time is it?"

Her captor appeared confused by her assertive behavior and the question she had fired at him. "Why? What do you mean?"

"You said you'd have me back to my car in twenty minutes. That's what you promised. But is that what you're doing? No! It's more than twenty minutes already, and here you are behaving this way! You should be ashamed of yourself, treating a woman like this!"

Her captor seemed taken aback by the authority with which she berated him. Her manner was that of a parent who is not about to tolerate any "funny business" from a wayward child. Despite the similarity of their ages, her indignant tone said, "If you think for a minute that I'm going to put up with this, young man, you'd better think again!"

Elizabeth said that she was surprised to find that she was now absolutely fearless and self-confident to the point of truculence. The shock and terror she had felt earlier were magically gone. As far as she was concerned, she was completely in charge. I asked Elizabeth what she had imagined herself to be doing.

"I think I was trying to get through to his higher self," she replied. "I sensed that this was basically a decent guy who had taken a wrong turn that night, out of some personal desperation. He'd been trained as a killer in Vietnam and had probably seen and done some pretty revolting things. My guess is that civilian life wasn't working out very well, and he was wondering why he shouldn't just take whatever he wanted by force.

"In a way, I guess you could say I was telling him 'why not.' Because it was dishonorable. Because it hurt innocent people. Because it made children suffer. My intuitive sense of him was that he was in a lot of conflict about taking advantage of a woman this way. I think that he was a man who normally took pride in living up to his word."

Whatever fantasy this man had had of how the assault would go, it probably did not involve a woman looking him in the eye and indignantly reminding him of his responsibilities as a man. Elizabeth's speech had taken the wind out of his sails. Her assailant yanked away from her with a baffled and aggrieved look and sat staring at her in perplexity. He seemed uncertain how to proceed.

"How much money do you have?" he finally demanded.

"I don't have much," Elizabeth replied. "About fifteen dollars. How about if I give you half?"

The man shook his head, stunned. "Jesus Christ! I don't believe you!" he burst out, pounding the steering wheel in frustration. This was not the way victims were supposed to behave.

"Well, you can't blame me for trying," replied Elizabeth coolly. "This is all the money I have. I've got a three-year-old son to support, you know. You're not the only one with problems."

"Give me the money!" the man ordered angrily. He seemed utterly flummoxed, and it struck Elizabeth that he was backing down from whatever he had planned to do to her and was settling for the cash. She handed it over without further comment, and he quickly started the engine and wrenched the vehicle back into traffic. On the way back to her car, he held the knife against her ribs and said menacingly, "If you make a sound, you'll be sorry!"

"I won't make a sound," Elizabeth agreed meekly.

"He had to act like he was in charge," she told me, "but at that point, I think we both knew that it was over. He was just saving face. He couldn't bring himself to hurt me."

Pulling up a block or so from her car, the man angrily shouted, "Get out of here!" But before she could open the door, he added in impotent fury, "Look at me! *You* did this to me!"

Elizabeth looked over and saw that his face was a mask of anguish and that it was streaming with perspiration. He was obviously in a state of powerful emotional turmoil, and his distress touched her heart. Turning back to him, she reached over and tenderly cradled his face in her hands. Looking deep into his eyes, she found herself quietly saying, "The next time you feel this way, I hope you'll realize that what you really need is to reach out and touch someone. This is about communication. There are a lot of ways to make contact with people, and I hope that next time you'll pick a different one from the one you chose tonight. You don't need to act this way. You're a good man. This isn't who you are."

As Elizabeth gazed into the man's eyes, she suddenly felt his defenses fall away. He seemed to open to her and become vulnerable. It was a moment of incredible intimacy. A current of pure love passed between them that was so intoxicating that Elizabeth says it made her feel as if she was high on a drug.

So caught up was she in the compassion she felt for her would-be assailant that she experienced an overwhelming desire to help him. "You're not going to believe this," she told me ruefully, "but I actually had to restrain myself from giving him my phone number so that he could call me if he ever needed someone to talk to! I realized that that would be absolutely insane, and I didn't actually do it. But in that moment I loved him so much. I just wanted to show him that someone cared about him and that he didn't have to try to get affection from people by force." Suppressing the impulse, she got out of his car and hurried to her own.

Elizabeth was still in that exalted state as she drove to her house. She said that it was as if she had undergone a "spiritual revelation." She felt giddy and invincible. When she finally arrived home much later than expected, her boyfriend, who had been babysitting her son, met her at the door with evident concern.

"Where on earth have you *been?*" he demanded anxiously.

At these words, Elizabeth felt herself crumble. Although she had been supremely self-confident during and after the incident itself, she suddenly fell back into ordinary consciousness and quite literally went into shock. She began to shake uncontrollably. Her teeth chattered, and her friend had to wrap her in a blanket and hold her tight for a long time before she could pull herself together enough to tell him what had happened. Now that it was over, she could scarcely believe the masterful way she had handled herself only a short time before.

Today, Elizabeth remembers her assailant with affection. "I still think about that guy all the time and wonder what happened to him. I hope he's okay. I was really lucky. What I did wouldn't have worked with everyone. He was really a good man. I like to think that he was as deeply affected by our encounter as I was and that he never did anything like that again."

When a brother behaves insanely, you can heal him only by perceiving the sanity in him.
—A Course in Miracles

Elizabeth seemed to lock onto an image of her assailant as a good man and then insist that he live up to it. When he attempted to assault her sexually, she coldly reminded him that this was not an appropriate way for a decent person like him to behave. Was he, or was he not, an honorable man?

Indeed, I am left with the impression that Elizabeth overcame her assailant in some sort of contest of wills. He had the knife, the strong physique, and the commando training, yet by the end of their encounter he was a broken man, rebuking Elizabeth for what she had done to him. There is something both pathetic and ludicrous about his final accusation: "Look at me! *You* did this to me!"

How does an unarmed ballerina make a highly trained, knife-wielding commando beg for mercy? As we shall see in a later chapter, Elizabeth was unwittingly practicing a martial art. Her degree of mastery speaks for itself.

The Disarming Power of Love

The dynamics of miraculous self-defense become even clearer in the case of Kathleen. Some miracle workers, like Elizabeth, just

117

seemed to slip imperceptibly over the border between terror and the "peace that passeth understanding." Others, like Kathleen, had to struggle continually to keep fear at bay. Unlike most of the people who told me their deliverance stories, Kathleen was aware of metaphysical realities and the creative power of consciousness. She understood exactly what she would have to do to save her life, and her only uncertainty seemed to be about her ability to do it.

Kathleen

At age twenty-three, Kathleen was returning home from a waitressing job at 2:00 A.M. when she realized that a car was following hers. It was still there after stops at a gas station and an all-night market, so Kathleen took evasive action, making a series of sudden turns through the deserted San Francisco streets. Thinking she had lost the tail, she drove on to her apartment.

When she got out of her car, however, Kathleen saw that the man who'd been following her had caught up. He intercepted her on foot as she crossed the street, but Kathleen remembers that even then she was not particularly worried. She was right outside her house, and he was a rather small man. She was used to dealing with guys who couldn't take a hint and did not anticipate that this was going to be a particularly difficult situation. The man attempted to start a conversation, but Kathleen brushed him off in a friendly way and started to walk on by. At that point, he pulled a gun out of his pocket.

Kathleen said that when she saw the gun, she instantly burst into tears. "All I can tell you is that at that moment, I realized that all of the rules of the universe had changed—that nothing was the way I had thought it was, or ever would be again. I can't tell you how completely disorienting it is to realize that something like this could happen to *you!*"

The gunman ordered her to get back into her car, and he drove to a nearby park. All the way there, Kathleen felt as though she were in shock. She wondered numbly if she should try to jump out of the moving vehicle, but he had the gun trained on her the whole way, and she couldn't see that she could get far on the deserted streets even if she was not badly injured in the fall.

When they reached the park, it clicked into place that the police had been finding women's bodies there regularly. It had been the talk of the neighborhood for a long time now. Her assailant ordered her out of the car and into the woods. Kathleen offered him the money in her purse, but he was not interested. Instead, he told her that he was going to rape and murder her. He said that he regretted having to kill her—he never enjoyed doing it—but that there was just no other way now that she had seen his face.

It was then that Kathleen found herself going into an unusual state of consciousness. Her senses felt heightened, and the smells and sounds of the woods were deeply etched in her mind. At the same time, she was completely unaware of the cold. She said that there was a strange lightness about her and that she suddenly went from revulsion and fear to feeling completely peaceful and loving toward her captor.

"It's hard to explain, and I feel really embarrassed about it now. I felt detached about what was going on. It just seemed like it was going to be all right. At the same time, I felt like I loved this guy. It was so bizarre! I went into a peculiar state of mind where I was just like an angel in my body, radiating love and compassion to this man who wanted to kill me!"

Her assailant ordered her to walk through some heavy underbrush and continued to wave the gun around and talk graphically about the things he was going to do to her. Every time he mentioned killing her, Kathleen mentally brushed it aside, resolutely thinking instead, "No, you won't do that."

In retrospect, Kathleen said that she felt that her previous experimentation with psychedelic drugs like LSD and mescaline helped her by giving her an inner experience of the way reality is created by the thoughts held in consciousness. It was very clear to her that she must not become fearful or in any way entertain the possibility that the man would kill her.

Kathleen emphasized that her refusal to do so was based upon her own choice, not on her reading of the man she was with. It was clear to her that he had murdered other women and seriously intended to do the same to her. Nevertheless, she invested totally in the conviction that he could not possibly kill her. She said that she structured her personal reality in such a way as to cast him as a person who would see that she was someone who deserved kindness.

As they blundered through the undergrowth in the dark, Kathleen began to talk to her assailant in a casual, friendly way. She said that it was hard for her to walk and asked if it would be all right to take his arm. He agreed, and she clung to him for support, aware that she was creating in every way possible the atmosphere of two people on a date.

Years later, Kathleen laughed in embarrassment and perplexity as she told this part. "I kept acting dependent and trying to get him to take care of me. Like I was a lady in distress and he was a kind gentleman I was relying upon for help. It was as though I was trying to get him to play Rhett Butler to my Scarlet O'Hara!"

When they came to a clearing, Kathleen kept talking in a relaxed, chatty manner from the peaceful altered state she had fallen into. She talked about herself, trying to help him recognize her as a real person with feelings like his own, and she asked him questions about his life, some of which he answered. They sat together on the ground for a long time just talking, as Kathleen radiated angelic compassion to this man who planned to rape and murder her.

When he waved the gun around, Kathleen confided that just seeing it made her afraid, and she asked if he would mind very much just putting it out of sight so she would not have to look at it. He did so. Kathleen said that he pulled it out a number of times, obviously getting off on the macho display, but each time she very sweetly asked him to put it away and he did. Her feminine dependence upon his kindness probably gave him an alternative way to feel powerful by being gallant instead of by hurting her.

Finally, he did rape her. With a gun to her head, Kathleen did not resist. Although it was an awful experience, she remained in the peaceful, loving altered state throughout, and treated him with kindness and compassion despite what was happening. "I actually apologized to him for the fact that my body wasn't producing any lubrication. Did you ever hear anything so sick?! I have always been so ashamed of myself for acting that way, but at the time I was only concerned with being kind to him."

Kathleen emphasizes that, as strange as it sounds even to her, it was not an act. She really felt detached and loving and absolutely confident that there was kindness in this man that would keep him from killing her. By focusing totally upon that goodness, she felt she could bring it to the surface.

When he was through raping her, he said that he had changed his mind. Maybe he would not kill her after all. But she must never tell anyone about what had happened. Kathleen promised without hesitation and thanked him sincerely for sparing her life. They drove back to Kathleen's apartment, and he told her to sit in her car until he passed her in his. She did so, although she again had to resist the fear that he would shoot her as he drove by. However, he went on his way without further incident.

Kathleen reported the rape to the police immediately, but they were unable to find her assailant. Soon afterward she bought a gun and carried it with her for several years. Despite her peaceful, loving altered state at the time, she experienced tremendous rage about the incident when it was over and is convinced that she could easily kill anyone who threatened her that way again.

Kathleen also felt much shame. In retrospect, she thought that she had behaved in a cowardly fashion, being so nice to someone who was putting her through an experience like this. Now a Marriage, Family and Child Counselor, Kathleen is aware of concepts like "identification with the aggressor," and this was her in-

121

terpretation of what she had done. She felt that her life had been threatened and to save herself she had behaved in a servile manner. Kathleen said that it was very difficult for her to integrate the detached, compassionate consciousness of that night with her normal one, or with the vengeful rage she felt for years afterward.

"It was like being an angel for a little while. That's all I can tell you. I didn't feel as though I was pretending to care deeply about him—I really felt that way. Every time he threatened me, I knew he meant it, and I had to work to keep the fear from coming in. I was very aware of using the power of my mind to make the situation turn out okay. Not that rape is okay, but it's a lot better than murder!

"I knew that if I let the possibility of his killing me into my mind, it could manifest in physical reality and that I had just better not do that! Every time he threatened me, I would think, 'Oh, no. That isn't really what's going to happen. You think you mean it, but you wouldn't really do that to me.' I know how nutty this sounds, but the fact is I feel sure even now that if I had allowed the possibility of his murdering me to exist in my reality, it would have happened."

"Perfect Love Casteth Out Fear"

As these stories pile up, it becomes increasingly difficult to dismiss the idea that the peaceful, loving state of consciousness was instrumental in turning around a bad situation. Clearly, the people in jeopardy believed that it was. Kathleen's assailant was a self-confessed serial murderer as well as a rapist and there is little reason to doubt that he was ready to carry out his threat to kill her. Somehow, by becoming "an angel in my body," she persuaded him to spare her life.

Fate often saves an undoomed warrior when his courage endures.

—Beowulf

Notice that Kathleen was prepared to believe that her assailant would rape her but steadfastly refused to believe that he would kill her. If belief is playing a role in the outcome, this is precisely what we would anticipate. We would predict that a person who believes she can be raped can be, and that one who does not believe she can be killed cannot be.

Remember Jeanne who said, "I have never thought of myself as the sort of person who could be raped"? Remember Dona, who initially thought of herself as someone who could be victimized by men, and then decided that she was no longer that kind of person? Even my informants who believed that they were about to die were active in trying for a better outcome, as if they did not really accept the inevitability of their deaths.

Is it simply a coincidence that nothing happened to any of these women that they refused to believe inevitable, or could it be that the belief that some person or situation can hurt you constitutes acknowledgment of their power to do so? Do we, in fact, make possibilities real for ourselves by believing in them? Is it conceivable that by focusing upon better outcomes, the people who shared their stories with me brought them into physical manifestation?

The Love of "Last Resort"

In the next story, Debra understood very well the probability that she and her husband would be murdered. However, like Elizabeth, Kathleen, and Rae, she mentally set that possibility aside in order to concentrate all of her attention upon the good in her attackers, lovingly reaching out to contact some deeply hidden kindness within them.

Debra

Debra entered her Beverly Hills home one afternoon to be confronted by two masked men with automatic weapons. She turned and ran for the door but was roughly tackled from behind, dragged into the bedroom, and tied hand and foot on the bed. The men, speaking with heavy Middle-Eastern accents, demanded that Debra open the safe for them, but she explained that she did not know the combination. They taped a mask over her face so that she could neither see nor speak and told her that they would wait for Debra's husband to come home, force him to open the safe with the threat that they would kill her otherwise, and then murder them both.

These Arab terrorists had picked Debra's house because she and her husband were wealthy Jews. Throughout the afternoon, while one of the men ransacked her home, the other held an automatic rifle to Debra's head. Despite the conviction that death was imminent, Debra was surprised to find that she was not afraid.

"It was as though I was out of my body, and I know I must have been in some sort of altered state," she told me. "You know how when you have your nails done you can't go to the bathroom for a while because it would mess them up? Well, I was just returning from a manicure when I came home that day. I was racing for the bathroom—maybe if I hadn't been in such a hurry, I would have noticed that something was wrong sooner.

"Anyway, they threw me on the bed on my stomach and tied my hands to my feet behind my back. I know I was in an altered state because it was three hours later before I got free but I don't remember the slightest discomfort, either from the ropes or my bladder."

Debra found her mind poised in a place of perfect inner peace. Despite the tape over her mouth, she eventually worked open a small gap through which she could talk, and she began to converse with the man holding her at gunpoint. Debra is a friendly, outgoing person, but it was bizarre hearing her account of a very ordinary chat in such extraordinary circumstances.

Debra got her assailant talking about his hometown in Lebanon and his family. As the afternoon wore on, he spoke to her very openly about missing his son, about jobs he had held in the

ASSAULTS, PART II: SAVING GRACE

United States, and about terrorist activities he had taken part in, including the murder of witnesses like herself. He detailed his grievances against the Jews, and Debra found herself deeply moved by the suffering he and his people had experienced.

In her altered state, Debra felt a compassion for this man and his partner, which she finds hard to explain. They seemed to her to be precious souls, and her heart ached for the pain that had driven them to lives of violence. She found herself encouraging and comforting the one who held the gun to her head, and she was unaware of any fear, although she did not doubt that he would kill her.

In the course of the long afternoon, the other terrorist finished searching the house and decided to rape Debra. However, his partner, with whom she had developed a relationship, would not permit it. The two argued heatedly for a long time.

After three hours, Debra's husband arrived. The men forced him to open the safe and then tied him up in the bed next to her.

"Do you love your wife?" the man with whom she had been speaking unexpectedly demanded of her husband.

"Yes," he replied.

"Tell her so now!" the terrorist ordered.

As her husband said, "I love you, Debra," both of them were convinced that these would be the last words they would ever hear on Earth. But then the men silently stole away. They moved so quietly that neither she nor her husband heard them go, but Debra said that she could *feel* them withdraw, as though she were lovingly connected to them in some way.

When the two finally got free and called the police, the authorities were astonished that Debra had not been raped and that both had not been murdered. The police readily identified their assailants as the ones who had committed other, similar crimes, and they had never before left a witness alive. Further, it seemed strange that they would have confided personal information to Debra unless they fully expected that she would not live to repeat it.

Since she had not seen her attackers' faces, Debra could see little point in looking at mug shots. However, the police were pretty sure they knew who the men were from their M.O. and were anxious for her to take a look on the chance that she had seen them in the neighborhood casing the house beforehand.

When eventually prevailed upon to go through the books of photographs, Debra confidently picked out the pictures of both men the police had in mind from among hundreds of others. She was astonished by her sense of knowing the people in those shots, despite having no recollection of ever having seen their faces before. While she cannot discount the police hypothesis that she may have seen them in the neighborhood, she is personally convinced that she did not. Instead, she feels that she somehow recognized their inner being from intimate acquaintance.

Debra says that she was so focused on the goodness that seemed to be in these men just below the surface that she felt nothing for them but unconditional love. It seemed to her as though she left her body and some loving presence took over for her. Even now when she tells the story, she feels as though it happened to someone else. It is difficult for her to refer to the men as "terrorists" because it sounds so violent, and she experienced them as precious and gentle. She has long felt that she will never adequately explain that state to anyone else.

Fail not in your function of loving in a loveless place made out of darkness and deceit, for thus are darkness and deceit undone.
                                                    —A Course in Miracles

Debra's story represents a truly astonishing victory of love over fear. The hostility in the terrorists' minds met with no similar emotion in her. Like a number of my informants, Debra felt as though some infinitely loving higher power took over and spoke and acted in her place. Somehow, the unconditional love she was expressing elicited a corresponding compassion from these violent men.

Is it possible that by overlooking their errors and focusing totally upon their basic goodness, Debra brought that goodness into manifestation? Or is it only a coincidence that that peaceful, unconditionally loving mental state keeps cropping up in the experience of people who escape death at the last minute? To decide, we will need to have a clearer idea of what the concepts of *coincidence* and *luck* will cover.

9

Fat Chance!

Chance is perhaps the pseudonym of God when he does not wish to sign.

—Anatole France

Let me begin this discussion of coincidence by acknowledging that no matter how many endangered people enter an oddly peaceful mental state and then find their way to safety, there will always be some possibility that the relationship between these events is merely coincidental. This is because in theory, *any* relationship *could be* coincidental. This possibility has led naturalists to suppose that purely random factors can account for anything and everything.

For example, it has been said that if a troop of monkeys were locked in a room for all eternity with a typewriter and enough paper, they would eventually produce all of the great English novels. According to this logic, there are no circumstances that cannot be explained by the mindless interaction of random factors. The naturalist philosophy holds that even the most highly skillful expressions of human intelligence and creativity are actually the result of blind evolutionary processes.

But, despite the fact that so many of us pay lip service to the naturalist view, *we don't behave in practice as though we really believe it.* The fact is that while many things are *possible,* some are so *improbable* that we are simply unprepared to believe that they have really occurred. The same person who insists that in theory a monkey could write *Pride and Prejudice* will laugh at you if you try

128

to prove that a monkey actually *did* accidentally type an intelligible sentence.

Using Our Common Sense

Let's make this point a bit more concrete with an example offered by the distinguished physical chemist and philosopher of science Michael Polanyi.[20] Imagine that we look out of a train window and observe that there are rocks on a nearby hillside arranged in such a way as to spell out the name of the town through which we are passing. We instantly assume that they were placed there intentionally by human agency. We know that it is *theoretically possible* for rocks to roll down a hillside and accidentally arrange themselves in such a way as to spell out an English word—and not just *any* English word, but the name of the town through which we are passing. However, we also recognize that it is *astronomically improbable* that this is the true explanation for the phenomenon.

We might readily accept the idea that falling rocks had accidentally formed a single letter, but not the precise sequence of letters that just happens to spell the name of the town. While coincidence is undeniably a *possible* explanation, there is a far simpler one available that experience tells us is also infinitely more probable—that the rocks were placed as they were by someone with an intelligible purpose in mind. The obvious purpose is to inform travelers regarding their present location so that they can make a decision about getting off the train.

If a traveling companion remarked upon the "incredible coincidence" of the rocks accidentally spelling out the name of the town, we would assume that he or she was joking. Indeed, we would expect any child old enough to read the word to realize that it *could not* be the product of coincidence. *The meaningfulness of the result constitutes convincing evidence that it was created intentionally with some intelligible purpose in mind.*

Meaningful Versus Meaningless Coincidences

Coincidence properly refers to an unusual constellation of events, some of which accidentally share some common feature. The common element gives coincidences an intriguing, superficial resemblance to meaningful, intentionally organized events. They look as though they might mean something, but—being only random occurrences—they don't.

For example, if I am on my way to a particular store in my car just when a commercial for that store plays on my radio, I might deem it a coincidence. Two events which have something in common, and both of which are fairly rare, happened to coincide quite by accident. What does it mean that I happened to hear the commercial while on the way to the store? Probably nothing. That is why we tend to call coincidences "mere."

Psychiatrist Carl Jung coined the term *synchronous experiences* to designate a subset of seemingly random events with common elements that are too profoundly meaningful to be written off as mere coincidences. The fact is that when coincidences are *too* appropriate to the needs of those involved, we tend to abandon the idea that they *are* coincidences, and suspect instead that some hidden intention is directing the outcome. Take Alana's situation, for example.

Alana

Alana says that when she was a starving student she became very ill with a serious throat infection. The doctor at the student health clinic wrote her a prescription for antibiotics but she discovered that filling it would cost three dollars. She didn't even have one dollar, so she started wearily home without the medicine. However, something caught her eye in the snow beside the walkway as she left the clinic. When she investigated, she found three crisp dollar bills.

To think about three dollars and then encounter three dollars might be a "mere coincidence," but for Alana to "accidentally" find three dollars just when she so badly needed exactly that amount qualifies as a synchronous experience. Circumstances appear to be arranging themselves with an intelligible purpose in mind. It is difficult to avoid the impression that events in the physical world are behaving the way we ourselves might behave if we wanted to help Alana.

Here's another example of synchronicity.

Harvey

I was chatting one day with a faculty colleague named Harvey over lunch in his office. We were talking of this and that when the concept of synchronicity came up, and Harvey expressed complete skepticism. We debated the point with much good-humored kidding back and forth.

Harvey eventually remarked that he hadn't enjoyed a good argument about synchronicity in years. In fact, the last time was with a young woman who was a friend of his daughter's. Her name was Penny, and as Harvey traveled back in memory he got a faraway look. "You know, I don't think I've thought about Penny in the last fifteen years. It's funny how people can be important in your life at one point and then just pass out of it without a trace. I wonder whatever happened to her?"

My friend and I went back to our discussion of synchronicity, but it was soon interrupted by a phone call. Harvey froze as he listened to the voice on the other end. He stammered a reply and then covered the mouthpiece with his hand and croaked, "It's Penny!"

When the call was over, Harvey looked dazed. He reported that Penny had said she just happened to be thinking about the old days and had had an urge to see if he was still at the same number.

"I suppose you're going to say this is evidence for synchronicity," Harvey laughed nervously.

"I suppose I am," I agreed.

131

Jung's synchronous experiences would appear to represent divine intervention in less dire situations than those where deliverance is required. Alana's case occupies the border between synchronous and deliverance experiences, since finding the money did "rescue" her from further anxiety and illness. The example in Harvey's office, on the other hand, is purely synchronous. It seemed more intended to open his mind to the possibility of supernatural influence than to save anyone from danger. Neither can properly be called coincidental.

To say that a circumstance is meaningful and fulfills an intelligible purpose is to suggest that it is not really a coincidence — not really a random event. In synchronous experiences, it is as if a larger mind that is aware of our thoughts and needs is arranging events in the physical world so as to accomplish some goal or make some point. When a person or an animal arranges the physical environment so as to accomplish a desirable end, we conclude that it is acting intelligently. When the universe behaves in the same way, is it unreasonable to wonder if it too may be intelligent?

Distinguishing Miracles From Coincidences

But how do we know whether a particular coincidence is "mere" or meaningful? Do these deliverance stories represent the workings of blind chance, or might they reflect an intention in the mind of God?

Psychologists usually try to distinguish coincidences from nonrandom events by estimating how likely it is that the result they received *could have* occurred by chance. If the odds against its random occurrence are less than, say, five in a hundred, they tentatively conclude that it was probably not due to chance.

However, while this strategy is feasible in the laboratory, it is seldom so in real life. How can we estimate the odds against Alana finding three dollars in the snow precisely when she needed them? What are the chances of Penny's call coming during a discussion of synchronicity, and right after Harvey was speaking about her for the first time in fifteen years? Common sense tells us that the odds against such things are humongous, but "humongous" is not a statistical term with which scientists can work in a rigorous fashion.

The fact is that some events are so rare, and so extraordinarily meaningful, that we cannot even begin to estimate how improbable they actually are. Naturalists will be content to assume that any event must have had *some* probability of occurring by chance and let it go at that. However, those rocks on the hillside also have some probability of chance occurrence, and I, for one, would not be satisfied to attribute them to chance even if they had been found on the lunar surface by the first astronauts to reach the moon!

Distinguishing Coincidences From Instances of Divine Intervention

I think that there are three criteria that can be used to distinguish miracles from coincidences. First, in our deliverance experiences the peaceful altered state coincides with a beneficial reversal of fortune far more often than coincidence allows. It has been my experience that many people have only to hear a few of these stories to realize that the same thing has happened to them. Being random by definition, true coincidences should be rare. If the relationship between inner peace and deliverance is as common as it appears to be, it cannot legitimately be written off as an unusual, chance occurrence.

Second, we do not attribute an event to random factors if its occurrence is predictable. For example, most of us do not deem it a coincidence if our car starts when we turn the key in the ignition. This is precisely what we expected would happen. And, as we shall see, mystical theories from throughout the world predict that miracles will occur whenever someone goes into a peaceful, meditative state of consciousness and follows inner guidance. These positive reversals of fortune cannot be coincidental if they are predicted by supernatural theory.

And finally, these outcomes are so meaningful, and so uniquely appropriate to the needs of the people involved, that it is difficult to resist the conclusion that they were intentionally arranged by a loving consciousness not unlike our own. Miracles of deliverance and synchronous experiences represent organized, goal-directed behavior on the part of the Universe itself. Logic rebels against the idea that such perfectly timed, and extraordinarily significant, circumstances could be the product of blind chance. Consider Louise's experience.

Louise

My student Louise told me that she had been shopping for food one day in 1969 when she suddenly "saw" her husband, a navy pilot in Vietnam, going down in flames. She heard him call her name, and a moment later knew that he had died.

Louise left her partially filled market basket in the aisle and fled from the store in tears. She drove home and called her mother, saying, "Please come over right away. Ralph is dead."

When the chaplain from Miramar Naval Air Station came up her front walk early the next morning to deliver the bad news, Louise and her mother met him at the door. "I know—Ralph's dead," Louise said flatly before he could speak. She later found out that when the time difference was taken into account, Ralph's plane had gone down the previous day at precisely the time she had been in the store.

A skeptic could certainly say that Louise just happened to imagine that her husband was dying at the precise time when he actually was dying. Wives of men engaged in dangerous duty *do* sometimes imagine that their husbands are in danger or have been killed. Perhaps this was truly a coincidence, rather than a psychic event that shows that minds are connected and that distance is not an insurmountable barrier to communication between loving hearts.

How can we even begin to assess the probabilities in a situation such as this? It is possible to estimate the likelihood of a given pilot being shot down on a given mission, but it is not possible to establish the frequency with which Louise vividly pictured her husband's death, because this was the only time that such a thing had ever occurred. Louise emphasizes that this incident in the supermarket was completely discontinuous with her ordinary worry about her husband. She did not wonder if he was all right or fear that he might be in danger. She *knew* that he was dying at the precise time that he actually was dying.

Let's look at another case where the probability of chance occurrence is impossible to estimate, but which is so meaningful that it seems absurd to attribute it to coincidence.

Mel

Mel was walking back from town to the children's camp where he was working as a counselor one dark, moonless night. The visibility along this little country road was so poor that he found it necessary to walk with one foot on the gravel shoulder and the other on the pavement, just to keep track of the turnings. He walked facing oncoming traffic so he would be sure to see the headlights of approaching vehicles in time to get out of their way.

As he strolled along thinking of this and that, Mel suddenly heard a voice in his mind say, "Move to the left!" Mel was surprised but did nothing. The voice came again. "Move to the left, now!"

Mel had never heard a voice in his head before, and he didn't know what to make of this one, except that he wasn't about to be ordered around by it.

"No. Why should I?" he demanded.

"Just do it!" the voice responded.

"No!" Mel said again. "This is silly."

"'The problem with you is that no one can tell you anything!'" the voice came back. "You always think you know better, and you never listen. You've been stubborn all your life. Are you completely incapable of accepting advice? No one is watching. You will not be embarrassed. Just move off the road!"

Mel's obstinacy had often been criticized by others, and he had to admit that this indictment was not entirely without basis. It was true that he was a very stubborn person and that he usually preferred to follow his own counsel. But to say that he was *totally incapable* of accepting advice was going too far.

In order to show the voice how wrong it was, Mel made a comical balletic leap to his left. After all, he was alone in the dark, and there was no one there to observe his irrational behavior. At the moment his feet touched the ground, he felt a powerful blast of air accompanied by a swooshing sound on his right. A silent automobile, traveling without lights on the wrong side of the road, had just swept over the patch of pavement he had occupied a moment before. Had he not leaped to the left when he did, Mel would have been run over.

Once again, while we can readily estimate the likelihood of a person being hit by a car on a dark country road, there is no conceivable basis for establishing the probability of the voice that spoke to Mel. This was the only time in his life that Mel ever heard a voice in his head telling him to move to the left, and it was also the only time in his life that he needed such advice. To call this a mere "coincidence" seems absurd and does violence to what we ordinarily mean by the word.

In Mel's case, it is difficult to avoid the conclusion that some voice in his consciousness was aware of the impending danger and took action to direct him through it. Whether this voice is best thought of as some higher part of his own mind, God, an angel, a spirit guide, or something else remains to be seen. But the voice was clearly responding appropriately to a need that Mel did not even recognize that he had.

Notice that this experience also seems like a test of some sort. The voice could presumably have told Mel that there was a car coming, but instead it told him to move left and declined to explain further. Mel saved his own life by accepting and acting upon a form of inner guidance that seemed to make no sense. Is it possible that his higher power was trying to teach him to follow his intuition rather than his intellect?

Liz's case also seems to involve an intuitive warning, although it did not come in verbal form.

Liz

Driving through the Mojave Desert late at night, Liz found herself drifting into fantasy. In her imagination she saw herself coming upon the scene of some sort of accident. A car was stopped on the shoulder at an odd angle, its doors standing open. A female figure was sprawled immobile on the ground beside it. A man in shirtsleeves frantically signaled Liz to stop and help.

In her fantasy, Liz pulled over onto the shoulder. The man ran up and yanked open the passenger-side door. His head appeared in the opening, and then Liz was jolted by the realization that there was a gun in his hand, pointed at her. The woman who had appeared to be unconscious was right behind him as he leaped into Liz's front seat.

This surprising turn of events startled her back to reality instantly. What a weird thing to imagine! Liz could not remember ever having had such a bizarre train of thought before.

Some fifteen minutes later, the scene she had imagined took shape before her in physical reality. There was the car, the inert woman's body, and the man in shirtsleeves silhouetted in her headlights, frantically waving her down. Every detail of the setting was just as it had been a few minutes earlier in her waking dream. Slowing her car, Liz stared at the scene in disbelief. The thing she had imagined was now actually happening!

Liz is a tenderhearted person, and in a situation like this one she would ordinarily do precisely what she had done in her fantasy. This time, although it was hard for her, she swerved past the waving man without stopping.

Laughing guiltily at the memory, she said, "For all I know, they were perfectly nice people who really needed help. To this day, they are probably still talking about what a bitch I was for not stopping! But I just couldn't do it. It was too eerie after that fantasy I'd just had. Once I saw the whole scene starting all over again, I knew it was a warning, and there was just no way I was going to make the same mistake twice."

In many of the deliverance stories, we see people intuitively guided to do something they would not ordinarily consider, and their unusual behavior winds up saving them. This raises the fascinating possibility that these brushes with death were orchestrated at a higher level in order to force the individuals to choose between their conscious grasp of the situation and their intuition. Perhaps there are some problems that cannot be handled successfully using only our own intellect, experience, and skill. It is as if a larger mind reaches through to us to provide helpful advice and information. The fact that these messages are often anonymous should not lead us to conclude that they are the result of random factors rather than meaningful communications.

The following synchronous experience is one that happened to me. See if you think it constitutes anecdotal evidence that there is a higher power that intervenes in our affairs when invited to do so.

Carolyn

Several years ago, I was driving alone from Los Angeles to Sedona, Arizona. As I sped through the high desert, I began to experience symptoms of severe anxiety. I felt agitated, and I had a recurring fantasy of my car skidding off the road.

Why would I suddenly be having an anxiety attack when I

had never had one before? As I tried to sort things out, I realized that the altitude and the thin air had something to do with it. I was able to associate thin air with mountains, and I remembered the experience I recounted in the Introduction when my car had almost skidded over a cliff after a blowout on black ice. Although I had not been upset about the experience as it happened, I realized that my body must have developed a phobic response to driving under conditions that reminded me of it.

Anxiety made the drive across the desert miserable, and this was a disappointment because I usually love long car trips. I stopped for the night and the next morning drove into real mountains. The anxiety was still present, but it was tolerable. I could comfort myself that it was late spring, and at least there would not be any snow or ice. I knew that I could just wear the anxiety out eventually if I didn't let it stop me.

Soon I began to notice snow on approaching vehicles, and I realized that there must be some up ahead. My anxiety intensified, but I kept going as driving conditions became worse. Before long, the road was rutted with ice and snow and I was in a full-blown panic. I pulled to the side and consulted a map.

Before me lay a ten-mile stretch with a single lane in each direction. At the end of that stretch, I could connect with the freeway, which would be clear of snow. My lane, I could already see, wound along the outside edge of the mountain with a cliff dropping away only a few feet from the pavement. There were no safety guards to catch a skidding vehicle, and the twisting road was completely choked with thick snow and ice. My worst fears were realized.

I sat there staring at the map for probably ten minutes. Perhaps I should just turn around and go back? It would take most of the day to retrace my path and come around the long way, but that would be better than facing that ten-mile stretch to the freeway.

In the end, I decided that I just had to go on. I love the mountains, and I knew that if I ran away now, the fear would only be worse the next time. I could not face giving up the mountains for the rest of my life out of fear. I would ask my higher power for help and somehow get through the next ten miles.

I started off slowly. Overwhelmed by fear, I clutched the wheel convulsively, panting with anxiety. The fantasy of sliding over the edge just a few feet away intensified like a nightmare in a horror movie. It was the most terrifying experience I have ever had.

I think of my higher power as Jesus, so I began repeating his name over and over. If only I could feel his presence and know that he was with me, I could relax a little and get through this somehow. However, after repeating "Jesus Christ, Jesus Christ" over and over for several minutes, I had to admit that it was doing no good at all. My panic was increasing, as if that were possible!

"Okay," I told myself, "Let's think about this logically. If I am calling on Jesus, then he must be with me. It can't be that he could be unaware of my situation or ignoring it. So he must be here. But that is not helping because I can't feel his presence. I can't prevent the panic until I feel his presence, but the panic is preventing me from being aware of his presence. What the hell do I do now?"

About then, I began to have an idea that Jesus had a message for me on the radio. Now I generally consider hospitalizing my clients when they start having thoughts like this, so I quickly brushed it aside. However, it kept coming back. "Turn on the radio. I have a message for you."

"That's ridiculous," I thought. "I must really be desperate if I'm coming up with things like that!" I had turned off the radio forty-five minutes earlier because it was impossible to get a station here in the mountains in any case. And turning it back on would require me to remove a hand from the wheel, just when it seemed as though only unceasing vigilance could get me through this alive.

But the idea wouldn't go away, and eventually I realized I'd have to turn on the radio just to get rid of it. It was distracting me from my driving. At this point, I was in first gear, going about five miles per hour.

I switched on the radio, and to my astonishment it was tuned to a station with perfect reception. The voice of Neil Diamond came booming through in the middle of a familiar refrain: "reaching out, touching you, touching meeeeee . . . Sweet Caroline!"

I was initially startled by the excellent reception. Then I remembered that it was supposed to be a message to me from Jesus, so I examined the words. I had been complaining that I couldn't receive the assurance that he was with me and here were words—along with a variant of my name—confirming that we were in contact. I was shocked and confused. "Is that song there for me?" I asked in wonder.

My body answered the question. Tears poured down my face, and energy blasted up my spine. There was absolutely no doubt in my mind that the answer was "Yes!" Unable to reach my consciousness directly, my higher power had arranged for that particular song to be played on the station my radio was tuned to and had gotten me to turn it on at exactly the right moment to hear Jesus' words from the singer's mouth.

Laughing with relief, I confidently accelerated to a normal speed. It seemed ridiculous that I had ever been afraid of a little snow and ice. At the end of the ten-mile stretch to the freeway, I had already decided to continue on the secondary road through the mountains, but the authorities had closed the route over the pass due to heavy snow. I remember thinking a bit scornfully that they were probably being unnecessarily conservative. I was quite sure that I could have gotten through with no trouble if they would only let me try!

I can't speak for you, but I find the idea that the appearance of that particular phrase on my radio at that time was merely coincidental utterly preposterous. I don't know what the odds are against a person named Carolyn who is desperately asking for reassurance about her higher power's presence imagining that there might be a helpful message on the radio, and then switching on the radio to a station playing the exact words she wants most to hear, including even a variant of her own name. However, I'm quite

141

certain that something like this would occur fewer than five times out of a hundred by chance!

Should we dismiss the relationship between the altered state and the beneficial outcomes in the deliverance stories as pure coincidence? I don't think so. We would not conclude that such a relationship was coincidental if it occurred in any other area of scientific inquiry. An experimental psychologist would not ignore a pattern like this if it pertained to, say, discrimination learning in rats. It is only our ingrained prejudice against the possibility of miracles that makes us assume without evidence that there *could not* be a causal relationship between inner peace and positive outcomes.

But if the continual appearance of the peaceful altered state was not just a coincidence, might it have been related to precognition or luck? In the next chapter, we will consider these possibilities.

10
Getting Lucky

That the universe was formed by a fortuitous concourse
of the atoms, I will no more believe than that the
accidental jumblings of the alphabet should fall into a
most ingenious treatis on Philosophy.

—Jonathan Swift

In the previous chapter, we cast doubt upon the possibility that the relationship between inner peace and escape from difficulties could be dismissed as coincidental. The fact is that while in theory any relationship *could* be due to coincidence, we do not ordinarily attribute circumstances to random factors when they are (1) regularly occurring, (2) predicted by theory, and (3) deeply meaningful. The people who told me their stories desperately needed help and they did precisely the things that mystics say will lead to a miracle. The outcome looks purposeful and is precisely what we would anticipate on the basis of a supernatural worldview.

But might the state of inner peace actually be nothing more than the result of positive, if irrational, expectations? Perhaps these people suspected that the outcome would not really be as negative as might appear, and this was the reason they were not more upset. Perhaps inner peace was the *result* of the expectation of a happy outcome, rather than the *cause* of that outcome.

It should be clear by now that these people did not *consciously* anticipate deliverance. Many of them believed they were about to die and were extremely surprised when this did not occur. Although they were at peace with the situation and felt that "everything was going to be all right," this acceptance somehow coexisted with their expectation that they were probably going to be badly injured or killed.

However, it could be argued that this sense of "all rightness" was based upon *unconscious* foreknowledge. While the conscious mind believed that disaster was likely, some other part of the mind may have foreseen the actual outcome and recognized that the danger was only apparent. Let us consider this possibility.

Precognition

Precognition is generally thought of as the ability to foresee the future. Like Liz, who had a premonition that warned her not to stop for the couple in the desert, many people have isolated episodes in their lives where they feel that they know how something is going to turn out before it does. The familiar déjà vu experience is an example of this. A much smaller number of people cultivate this ability to foresee the future and develop a talent for "reading" others. These "psychics" sometimes earn a living through their precognitive abilities.

There is disagreement within the scientific community about whether or not precognition is possible. On the one hand, reputable research scientists at Princeton University and elsewhere have found "unmistakable statistical evidence" that it does occur.[15] On the other, no body of research is beyond criticism.

The concept of foretelling the future appears to contradict our intuitive ideas about the nature of time. And although the relativistic view of time of modern physics is itself paradoxical and counterintuitive, it is difficult for most people to see how someone can know about things that have not yet happened.

When psychics talk about what they do, however, they do not claim to speak with certainty about the future. Instead, they usually regard themselves as reading a person's *probable* future, based upon his or her current conscious and unconscious intentions. Thus,

a person with an unconscious self-destructive urge may be creating a future that involves accidents, illnesses, and so forth. A psychic senses this intention and the ways it is likely to manifest. A psychic prediction, then, is a statement of probabilities. If the future were inevitable, there would be little point in prophecy. The whole object of the enterprise is to make people aware of what *may* happen so that they can change things if they wish. One psychic named Diane put it this way.

Diane

"If I can see that you are right now passing the Santa Monica Boulevard exit, driving south on the 405 freeway at fifty-five miles per hour, it is not too difficult to estimate where you might be an hour from now. But it's really only an estimate. You could pull off at the next exit or encounter a traffic snarl that holds you up for hours. Still, if you continue on your present course, it is very likely that you'll pass through San Diego within the next few hours. If you don't want to pass through San Diego, you'd be wise to make some changes.

"In the same way, I can tune in and see where someone is in their life right now. I can also see what they are creating for their immediate future. But the whole picture changes completely if the person changes his or her mind.

"I feel as though what I do is give people a choice. I can show them where their intentions are leading, and I can help them understand why things are happening the way they are. Then they can make their own decision about whether they want to continue on their present course or make a change."

Let me illustrate this process of elucidating a person's probable future with a story told to me by a friend.

Eileen

Eileen had had a very successful career as a popular singer, which took her on several triumphant world tours. Talented, beautiful, and famous, Eileen was one of those women who "can have any guy she wants." She dated a succession of rich, sophisticated, and powerful men, most of whom also "looked like Greek gods."

Eileen longed for true love, but somehow it always eluded her. One day, she went to see a prominent psychic. "When will I find someone to love and marry?" she asked him.

"You never will!" he announced dramatically.

Eileen was shocked. That was absurd! She certainly didn't lack male attention, and she was eager to find a husband. How could this man suggest that she would never succeed?

"Just look at the men you are attracted to," the psychic continued. "How could you find love with any of them? How could anyone? They are all totally selfish, self-absorbed, and crazy. These characters aren't capable of loving you or anyone else!"

Eileen thought dismally back over the rogues' gallery of men with whom she'd attempted relationships, and she had to admit that it was a depressing spectacle. Fascinating, romantic, and "drop-dead gorgeous" they had been. But the psychic was quite right. Each one of them had turned out to be a predator of some sort who was utterly incapable of loving or respecting a woman.

Some were merely narcissistic and emotionally unavailable, but it got a lot worse than that. Eileen thought back with embarrassment over her brief flirtation with a South American president who she later learned was responsible for the torture and murder of thousands. And one of her lost loves was now serving time in prison for having murdered another of her ex-boyfriends to whom she had introduced him. Although Eileen had not been aware that either of them even used drugs, it turned out that they had gotten involved in a big cocaine deal that had gone bad. Why did she always wind up with attractive losers? Eileen wondered miserably.

Deeply shocked by the reading she had received, Eileen got into psychotherapy. She began to understand the ways her taste in men had been influenced in the process of growing up with an emotionally unbalanced mother and no father. Slowly, old wounds began to heal.

Today, Eileen has been happily married for fourteen years to a man who is quite different from the ones she used to date. So different, in fact, that when she first went out with him she thought she'd made a terrible mistake! It took a lot of hard work for Eileen to become comfortable with a loving relationship, but she will be forever grateful that she put in the effort.

The fact that she did succeed in finding a wonderful husband does not seem to Eileen to be proof that the psychic was wrong. Instead, she believes that he made her good fortune possible by confronting her with her mistakes.

"If he hadn't woken me up, I might have spent the rest of my life brushing off terrific guys in favor of glamorous jerks. It wasn't that there weren't any good men out there. I just couldn't see them until psychotherapy helped me fill in my blind spot."

Creating Your Future

The theory behind precognition, then, implies that our future is being created by us in each moment. Long-standing conscious and unconscious intentions take shape in the physical world to allow us to have experiences that hold some interest for us. In Eileen's case, a lack of appropriate role models had left her with a legacy of mistaken ideas about what makes a man "wonderful." These ideas condemned her to repeatedly seek out attractive men who were arrogant and insensitive. The first part of her fairy-tale romance fantasy would come true, but it never led to "happily ever after."

Eileen eventually changed her luck by correcting the idea that she needed a man who was godlike and looking instead for an ordinary mortal who was genuinely kind, loving, and fun. As long as she perceived cruel, selfish men as desirable, her probable future was a succession of disappointments. When she worked out her own relationship issues, she found herself attracted to a man who was capable of loving her back. This is a small but important miracle of the sort that frequently occurs in psychotherapy.

Because I suspect that all of the events in our lives are created in precisely this way, I do not think that the people who told me their deliverance stories felt peaceful in the face of danger because of precognition. There was no fixed outcome to be foreseen, and it seems clear that the most probable of their possible futures was tragic.

We have already pointed out that in such situations it is impossible to assess *objectively* the probability of the actual positive outcome in the absence of any hypothetical supernatural intervention. Nevertheless, these deliverance stories are surprising precisely because we all *know* what is most likely to occur when you drive off a cliff, lose control of your car on the freeway, or find yourself at the mercy of a rapist or murderer. Our sense of surprise at the way things turned out indicates a subjective conviction that the probability of a positive outcome was very low indeed.

Luck

But what about the argument that the people who experienced deliverance were simply lucky? While miracles are commonly associated with an aura of superstition, grandiosity, and spiritual pride, the assertion that one is lucky strikes most people as acceptably humble and realistic. Individuals who would never dream of saying that they had experienced a miracle would cheerfully assert that they had had a "lucky break."

However, it may be that the exact opposite is true—that it is grandiose to think that one is lucky and realistic to believe that one is occasionally the recipient of a miracle. This is because I believe that the only qualifications for having a miracle are that one returns one's mind to peace and follows inner guidance. *This means that ordinary people can expect miracles if they take the required action.* The concept of being lucky, on the other hand, is often tied up with narcissistic fantasies in which the individual unconsciously regards himself or herself as God's special favorite.

Like coincidence, the term *luck* is used in more than one sense.

149

In some usages, it is almost synonymous with randomness, as is the case when one speaks philosophically of "the luck of the draw." One is "lucky" on those rare occasions when a desirable outcome of low probability happens to manifest. If this is all that is meant by having been "lucky," then our earlier discussion of coincidence applies equally well to it.

However, there are usages where something other than randomness is intended. Certain people are superstitious about luck. Compulsive gamblers, for example, often suppose that winning is the evidence that they are somehow special and superior to losers. If you are lucky, "something" will make the dice fall the way you want them to. If you are lucky, "something" will provide intuitive direction in the form of hunches: "I just knew that red was going to keep coming up," or "Something told me the number six horse was going to win."

Who or what is this "something" that makes things happen in accord with our requirements or gives us valuable tips that enable us to beat the odds? Doesn't "luck" in this sense sound suspiciously like an oblique reference to some invisible supernatural agent with ultimate power over the affairs of humans? Doesn't it seem as though some gamblers are actually courting divine intervention of the sort that tipped off Mel and Liz?

In thinking reminiscent of Greek and Roman mythology, compulsive gambling seems to be the sacrament of a strange religion where people seek special favor in the eyes of a god or goddess who will sponsor their cause. "Dame Fortune" is wooed through rituals reminiscent of religious observances, as though a "lucky" (holy) object, article of clothing, ritual, or phrase could confer power and be used to call up and command unseen forces. In ancient times, this hidden power was personified as the goddess Fortuna, whose likeness is still to be seen in the Tarot deck. Today she is more likely to be referred to as "Lady Luck."

Is it possible that compulsive gamblers are actually amateur sorcerers? A winning streak means to them that they have supernatural power at their command, while to be unlucky is to be punished by one's god. However, either outcome gives the individual a gratifying sense of his or her own importance to the universe. If Fortune (God) singles someone out for special love or special hate, that person must be very special indeed!

It seems to me that to attribute miracles to luck in the sense of being Fortune's favorite is basically misguided. It involves the assumption that there is a supernatual power that created all of us but which can be won over through flattery and induced to favor the interests of one individual at the expense of another.

Of course, this is really no different from the way many religious people think—praying that their nation win in battle, and assuming that they are entitled to special favor from God. Their opponents, naturally, think exactly the same thing.

Clergyman to Abraham Lincoln during the American Civil War: "Let us pray that the Lord may be on our side."

Lincoln: "I don't worry about that. The Lord is always on the side of justice. Let us pray that we may be on the side of the Lord."

The deliverance stories suggest that people access miracles precisely because they *do not* feel self-righteous and *do not* will personal victory. Instead, they "love their enemies," empathizing with their pain and willing a solution that is fair to everyone.

According to the mystical perspective, miracles are not signs of special favor from God. Quite the contrary, *A Course in Miracles* defines them as "signs of love among equals."[21] In this view, we open ourselves to the possibility of divine intervention whenever we adopt a larger perspective in which the interests of others—including our so-called "enemies"—are as important to us as our own. When we recognize our antagonists as people like ourselves who make mistakes but nevertheless deserve kindness, we adopt

a genuinely constructive attitude. As a result, we seek, and therefore find, miraculous solutions that work for everyone.

Aren't Religious People Special to God?

I have mentioned that most or all of the people who told me
their deliverance stories were spiritually oriented individuals and
that this may have had something to do with their success in obtaining miracles. The reader may be wondering if this is a claim
to special virtue that entitled them to special favor from God. I
believe that the answer is no. There are no special people.

As we shall see in the next chapter, individuals who experience miracles may actually be utilizing their intuition to connect
with their higher power in a state of deep meditation. If a meditative state is a prerequisite for miracles, it should not be surprising
that people who have practiced stilling their minds and listening
within for guidance access them more easily. A child who has
been trained to dial 911 in an emergency is more likely to do so
than one who has never been taught this solution. Yet such a child
is not special or better than other children—just more likely to
obtain quick access to emergency services. And it is my belief that
people who cultivate their ability to listen within for guidance
are not better than other people or more loved by God—just more
likely to access a miracle.

In summary then, precognition does not appear to be an ade-
quate explanation for the peaceful altered state. As we shall see
even more clearly in Chapter 12, there was no predetermined outcome to be foreseen. Further, these are cases where one need not
be psychic to know that the most probable result was disastrous.
I believe that these miracle workers intentionally set out to actualize a highly improbable outcome.

And, although some people really do seem "lucky" in the sense
that things habitually work out for them better than one would
expect, I believe that this is because they have learned to connect
intuitively with their higher power, rather than because they are

Fortune's favorites. In the next chapter, we'll take a closer look at that peaceful, loving, and detached consciousness and see that it bears a remarkable resemblance to the kinds of meditative states that creative people throughout history have employed as a means of accessing "intuitive" guidance.

Part Two
Creating
Miraculous Solutions

11

Cultivating Intuition

Thus we see that meditation in the wider sense of the word is the advanced form of concentration in any field of investigation, whether science, art or philosophy. It is the power of the concentrated mind to enter into the essential structure of an object, resulting in a sense of intimate rapport or identity. Eventually their uninterrupted flow of thought may result in a sudden flash of intuition.

—Haridas Chaudhuri

I am suggesting that people who experience miracles may escape danger by following divine guidance and that the oddly peaceful and detached awareness they describe may actually be a state of meditation. But is it realistic to suppose that these ordinary people were meditating in the midst of life-threatening emergencies? What exactly is meditation, and how might it have helped?

It is often said that *prayer* is talking to God, while *meditation* is listening to God. Many people use the term *prayer* to refer to both activities, but I believe that the distinction is valuable. In prayer, we bring our troubles to the divine presence within, asking for help. Meditation, on the other hand, is a deeply focused mental state in which we quiet the mind to commune with the deepest levels of our being.

Some 75 percent of Americans say that they pray regularly.[12] However, I suspect that many fewer have trained themselves to

157

listen for a response, and this may be one of the reasons people so often seem to ask for miracles without receiving them. If meditation *and* prayer are both necessary for miracles, then petition by itself is not guaranteed to produce results. This would be a little like calling a hot line for help but hanging up before the expert you have reached can offer any advice.

If, as mystics say, you are unwittingly creating the problems that plague you through your attitudes and beliefs, then the only way your higher power *could* help would be to encourage you to change your mind. God could not undo circumstances that you are holding in place without violating your free will. Like a loving parent who will give advice if asked but will not otherwise interfere, our higher power lets us decide whether we want to listen and learn.

Learning to Meditate

This suggests that people who want miracles should study meditation. Although learning to meditate usually involves a certain amount of practice and patience, many adepts say that meditation is actually a very natural state and one we all go into from time to time throughout the day. Everyone enjoys moments of detachment and inner peace. The effort involved in meditation training revolves around the difficulty of *sustaining* a peaceful and detached mental attitude. The ego is constantly coming up with distractions and most people find it all too easy to climb aboard an irrelevant train of thought and ride it to the end of the line.

Once we acquire the knack of focusing the mind in peace, however, we can meditate at will without resorting to chants, rituals, mantras, and so forth. Indeed, advanced spiritual seekers attempt to live in a state of continual meditation—maintaining uninterrupted communion with a higher reality. It is actually quite reasonable to suppose that a person could enter this state quickly in an emergency.

Hearing the Voice of God

Meditation, then, is a loving, peaceful, and detached, state of consciousness in which people often say that they can metaphorically "hear" the "voice of God." However, since "hearing voices" is associated in the popular mind with madness, many people are reluctant to acknowledge that they do so.

Further, the idea that the "Lord of the Universe" would deign to communicate with us personally strikes many people as dangerously grandiose. For example, there is an old joke among psychotherapists that holds that it is perfectly sane and normal to talk to God. However, when you start hearing God talk back—then you're in *big* trouble!

Yet, if we are prepared to make the assumption that there is a supernatural Being that created all of us, it is surely reasonable to make the further assumption that our Creator would wish to communicate with its offspring. To pray *without* any expectation that God hears you and might respond—that would *really* be crazy!

Despite the fact that psychotic individuals are sometimes tormented by bizarre, persecutory voices in their heads, hearing inner voices is actually an everyday experience for perfectly normal people. For example, in his entertaining autobiography *Surely You're Joking, Mr. Feynman,* Nobel Prize–winning physicist Richard Feynman tells an amusing story about the time he was given a psychiatric deferment from the army because he "heard voices."[22]

Richard Feynman

Richard Feynman had spent most of World War II at Los Alamos working on the Manhattan Project and had only just returned home at the war's end, when he received a draft notice. Since he was a man with a hearty appetite for absurdity, he did not immediately call attention to the fact that he should have been ineligible for the draft. Curious to see what would happen, the young genius reported as ordered.

Feynman sailed through the physical examination without difficulty, but he failed the psychiatric interview simply by being strictly honest. Asked if he ever heard voices in his head, Feynman assured the psychiatrist that he heard them constantly. Asked if he had ever had a sense of mentally communicating with his recently deceased wife, Feynman acknowledged that he frequently went off by himself and had long talks with her. Apparently, that was all the army doctor needed to know in order to conclude that Feynman was mentally unbalanced and totally unfit to serve his country!

Most psychotherapists today recognize that we all have internal voices that keep up a constant inner dialogue. Our egos (personalities) are made up of many subpersonalities (sometimes called "archetypes" or "ego states"), each with a unique point of view, and each inclined to vigorously argue the merits of its own perspective.

Psychotherapists often mediate disputes within the personality by facilitating dialogue between subpersonalities with conflicting agendas. These individual "voices" are sometimes identified with colorful labels, such as the *inner child,* the *critical parent,* the *rebel, top dog, underdog,* and so forth. So intense can the conflicts between these subpersonalities become that perfectly normal people sometimes feel as though their heads are resounding with the shouts of an argumentative committee!

Perhaps lost amid the many, clamoring voices of the ego there really is another that speaks on behalf of God. Perhaps, as mystics suggest, we all hear it without realizing its significance. But what exactly is this "voice of God?" and is it ever heard by people who are neither saints nor lunatics?

Conscience

If it is true that God's voice is familiar to everyone but not recognized as such, then it is likely that we would know it by other names. The "voice of conscience" is one such label. Conscience is often called, "the still, small voice that teaches right from wrong." It has traditionally been regarded as a divine source of moral inspiration, available to each person within the privacy of his or her own mind.

Conscience is God's presence in man.

—Emanuel Swedenborg

Spiritually oriented individuals use conscience as an internal compass to remind them "which way is up" when they begin to lose their bearings—a higher court to which they can appeal when other people accuse them of being in the wrong. For example, it was conscience that prompted many of psychologist Abraham Maslow's self-actualizing subjects to take issue with culturally accepted forms of immorality, such as racism and slavery.[23]

Maslow found that extraordinary humanitarians, such as Mohandas Gandhi and Abraham Lincoln, invariably acknowledged a sense of responsibility to some power greater than themselves. They often felt "called" by God to perform some service for humanity, and divinely directed in their efforts to fulfill this moral obligation.

Say nothing of my religion. It is known to God and myself alone. Its evidence before the world is to be sought in my life: if it has been honest and dutiful to society the religion which has regulated it cannot be a bad one.

—Thomas Jefferson

That naturalists do not see anything supernatural about conscience goes without saying. For them, it is just another ego voice patterned after our parents' moral values. "Right" and "wrong" are simply a matter of what people in a given time and place have been conditioned to regard as appropriate.

If conscience is only an artifact of upbringing, it has no legitimate claim to universal moral authority. In that case, charitable love could be "right" for one person, while sadism, or cannibalism, is equally "right" for someone else. Because naturalism has been so influential in this century, we are presently living in a climate of moral relativism, where it is considered both ignorant and arrogant to suppose—as did such persons as Gandhi, Lincoln, Jefferson, and Martin Luther King, Jr.—that we have a moral responsibility to discover, and adhere to, an absolute, God-given standard of goodness.

Intuition

While morality has a political dimension that makes conscience a touchy issue, *intuition* is a term for the voice of God that currently enjoys considerable credibility. This probably reflects the fact that while we don't want God telling us what to do, most of us don't object to the occasional helpful suggestion.

The word *intuition* means *inner teaching*. Throughout history, creative people have recognized that there is an internal voice that responds brilliantly to our requests for information and guidance, although it is easily drowned out by mental chatter. Intuition is discernible only when we still our egos, relax deeply, and take some psychological distance on our problems—that is to say, when we meditate. We ordinarily think of people who have cultivated their access to intuition as lucky, imaginative, visionary, and highly creative.

Because of its supernatural connotations, the status of intuition is ultimately as controversial as that of conscience. Naturalists cannot really allow it to represent anything more than the odd lucky hunch. In their view, an intuitive insight is only a vague and unreliable intimation of truth arising out of haphazard associations within the memory, the nervous system, or the unconscious mind.

Yet Jeffrey Mishlove, director of the Global Intuition Network, points out that there have always been important thinkers who believed that intuition reflects a human capacity for extrasensory attunement to some abstract field of information at large in the universe.[24] Geniuses from Socrates to Einstein have recognized that in moments of deep mental relaxation, the solutions to puzzling problems seem to slip into the receptive mind unbidden.

Intuition in Art, Music, and Literature

Artists of all kinds have always relied upon intuitive promptings for inspiration. The ancient Greeks, for example, attributed artistic creativity to the "muses," nine minor deities said to mentor receptive humans by implanting ideas in their minds. Great artists right up to the present, claim that it is as if brilliant new concepts are worked out elsewhere and then handed over to them for execution.

For example, Wolfgang Amadeus Mozart was a child prodigy who wrote music the way another person might take dictation. From early childhood on, he was able to relax deeply and tune in to exquisite orchestral arrangements playing in his mind. He would then simply jot them down without alteration. He put it as follows.

> When I am in particularly good condition, perhaps riding in a carriage, or on a walk after a good meal, and in a sleepless night, then the thoughts come in to me in a rush, and best of all. Whence and how—that I do not know and cannot learn.[25]

As a result of his inner atunement, Mozart could write "divine" music of astonishing complexity in the midst of many distractions. He did not so much *create* music as *channel* it from some source beyond himself. We very properly think of him as an "inspired" composer.

The nineteenth-century philosopher Friedrich Nietzsche main-

163

tained that he wrote his masterpiece *Thus Spake Zarathustra* under the influence of just such an inspiration.

One hears, one does not seek; one takes, one does not ask who it is that gives; like lightning a thought flashes out, out of necessity, complete in form—I have never needed to choose. It is a rapture, the enormous excitement of which sometimes finds relief in a storm of tears; a state of being entirely outside oneself with the clearest consciousness. Everything happens in the highest degree involuntarily, as in a storm of feeling of freedom, of power, of divinity.[26]

Intuition in Science

Nor is the vital role of intuitive guidance confined to the realms of music, art, and literature. Scientists rely upon it, too. For instance, Michael Polanyi—a brilliant physical chemist who trained two Nobel Prize winners—pointed out that mediocre scientists typically attempt to make discoveries by applying the trial-and-error method to hypotheses generated by logical thought. They utilize rational and empirical methods but slight intuition.[20]

Polanyi emphasized that the truly great scientists throughout history have arrived at important theoretical insights intuitively. Certainly outstanding researchers also do empirical research and think rationally about their problem. However, the solution, when it comes, almost invariably takes the form of a sudden intuitive flash that allows them to simply "see" how things work. They then design research to verify the answer their inner vision has already revealed.

That such scientific insights cannot be the gift of our rational egos is underscored by the fact that they sometimes arrive in symbolic forms or even in dreams. For example, the structure of the carbon ring was discovered by a chemist who dreamed of a serpent biting its own tail. And the sewing machine was invented by Elias Howe after he dreamed of a knight holding a lance with a hole at its tip. All previous efforts to develop such a machine had failed because they utilized ordinary sewing needles with the hole for thread *opposite* the end that pierced the cloth.

Intuition in Psychotherapy

It is also widely recognized that the best psychotherapists, from Freud on, have always relied upon intuition. They relax, attune themselves to their client, and feel guided to the right intervention. The contrast between this intuitive approach and one that is more rational and empirical was apparent when two researchers decided to study the methods of several outstanding counselors. Among their subjects was the brilliant hypnotherapist Milton Erickson.

The researchers found that they were able to identify a number of behaviors that all of the great therapists shared. For example, they tended to sit in a posture that mirrored that of the client. They employed words and metaphors uniquely suited to the mentality of the person they were trying to help. From such empirical observations, the investigators deduced principles of good psychotherapy related to posture, choice of vocabulary, eye movements, and so forth.

However, it is said that when Erickson viewed their conclusions he burst out laughing. "They think they have me in a nutshell," he said, "but what they have is the shell and not the nut."[27] The nut was, of course, intuition. Erickson did not monitor his behavior. Had he been conscious of such things he would not have been truly present with the client. Instead, he simply relaxed and did what he was inspired to do in each moment—with magical effect.

Intuition in Business

Intuition also plays a vital role in business and finance. For example, the Newark College of Engineering PSI Communications

Project explored the precognitive abilities of over five thousand executives.[28] They discovered that company presidents who had doubled their organization's profits during the preceding five years scored much higher on tests of precognition than did their less successful counterparts. Further, some 80 percent of these phenomenally successful businesspeople said that they believed in extrasensory perception from their own experience. By utilizing their intuitive abilities, these "winners" found a way to anticipate trends and developed a knack for being in the right place at the right time.

Intuition, then, would appear to be an essential aspect of creativity in all fields. For example, the distinguished Russian-born sociologist and philosopher Pitirim Sorokin, emphasized that empirical, rational, and intuitive ways of knowing naturally complement one another. By using each appropriately, we can hope to arrive at an apprehension of "integral truth."[29]

Like Polanyi, Sorokin believed that contemporary Western science had mistakenly glorified empiricism and rationalism at the expense of intuition. He saw us as poised on the brink of a cultural shift in emphasis that will carry us back into a deep appreciation for intuitive ways of apprehending reality.

Intuitive Premonitions

Intuition not only provides creative insights and guides people out of perilous situations; as we have already seen, many individuals use their intuition to avoid trouble in the first place. "Something" warns them to stop before it is too late. Take the story Brett told me about his mother's sudden panic in an airport.

Brett

When Brett was a teenager, he and his mother and brother were returning home after a visit to family friends in another city. They were at the airport, seated at the gate, when Brett's mother had a premonition of disaster. According to Brett, she just suddenly "went ballistic."

"One minute we were quietly waiting to board our flight, and the next she was not only refusing to let any of us get on the plane—she even became frantic about our bags. Mom demanded that the airport personnel transfer our luggage to another flight immediately.

"Well, by then the plane was loading. The people at the gate insisted that while they could switch our reservations, there was no way they could get our baggage off at that point.

"Now, my mom is ordinarily a rather reserved, polite person, but suddenly she was screaming at these people, and carrying on like a maniac. My brother and I were really embarrassed. It will give you some idea of how completely deranged she was acting when I tell you that they actually did hold up the flight to unload our stuff.

"After this buildup, I guess you won't be surprised to learn that the plane crashed. There were only a few fatalities, but some of the people who died had been using our seats.

"You see, because of my father's disability, and his difficulty in getting in and out of airline seats, our family always flies in the first row of the first-class section. Even though my father wasn't with us on that trip, his travel agent had booked us those places as a matter of course. Since they were choice seats, I guess some of the other passengers had moved into them during the flight. They had all been killed.

"The crash and the fatalities were reported on the television before we could get through to my father about our change of plans. When he heard which flight it was and what part of the plane had received the most damage, he assumed that we were the ones who had been killed. But thanks to my mother's intuition, we were still wandering around the airport when our plane went down."

Skeptics will say that Brett's mother was acting irrationally, and that it was pure chance that her behavior later appeared to be justified. "What about all of the people who are afraid to fly, despite the fact that their planes do not go down?" they will ask. "Statistically, it is inevitable that some neurotic people will occasionally be booked on flights that do experience problems."

While this is undoubtedly true, it is not really to the point. Brett's mother was not someone who had a chronic fear of flying. She was suddenly afraid to let her family fly on that particular plane, although she was perfectly comfortable with the idea of their boarding another, immediately afterward. And her concern extended to her possessions, which is not typical of people who are simply phobic about air travel. This woman had an intuition that flying on that particular plane would be disastrous for her family, and she turned out to be right.

In the same vein is another story told me by a former psychology student.

Rachel

On her way home from work one afternoon, Rachel was suddenly overcome with dread. Her apartment had always seemed like a safe haven, but now the thought of going there filled her with an inexplicable terror. The closer she drove to it, the more her panic increased. She pulled to the curb to think things through, while she was still several blocks away.

Rachel had never before experienced anything like this. She told herself she was being ridiculous, but every time she tried to restart her car to continue home, she began to pant, perspire, and tremble. After a twenty-minute struggle, she realized that she simply couldn't do it. She could not go home.

Having grown up in the same city, Rachel had many friends and relatives she could have gone to visit. Any one of them would have been happy to give her a bed for the night, but she would have had to explain why she wanted it. How could she let anyone know that she was in the grip of an irrational fear? They would think she was nuts!

In the end, Rachel decided to go to a motel. She hated to spend the money, but it was preferable to having anyone know how silly she was being. When she woke up in the morning, the sense of dread had disappeared completely. What an idiot she had been! At least no one would ever know.

Rachel checked out and drove home to shower and change. When she pulled into her parking slot, a vigilant neighbor ran over and handed her the number of a police officer she was supposed to call. It seemed that her apartment had been robbed the previous afternoon. Piecing together the accounts of neighbors, the police concluded that the burglary had been in progress at the time Rachel was driving home.

"It's a good thing you didn't come straight back from work!" the officer she contacted told her. "We know that these guys were professionals—they must have gotten their timing badly screwed up to still be there at a time when you might come back. I can't tell you how many citizens get killed every year walking in on a burglary and seeing things they shouldn't. If you'd gone strolling into that apartment at 5:30, I wouldn't give a nickel for your chances of being here now!"

You will never convince Rachel, or Brett's mother, that it was just a coincidence that their sudden, irrational dread saved them from injury or death. They will go to their graves believing that "something" warned them away from danger. But what is this "something" that alerts us to a robbery taking place miles away, or a plane crash that will not occur for another hour? What is it that shows the Mozarts of this world how to create a great work of art and the Einsteins where the solution to their problems lie? Might it not be divine guidance?

Intuition and Meditation

It is difficult to avoid the conclusion that unusually lucky and creative people are turning within for inspiration. These individuals all seem to relax, release their preconceptions about a problem, and tune in to their intuition to see what is really going on, and what to do about it. Is it just a coincidence that this attitude of emotional neutrality and inner attunement is so similar to what spiritually oriented individuals call *meditation?* And, is it only a further coincidence that it so closely resembles the inner process of those who experience miracles of deliverance?

Religious persons say that "God guides" them, while successful scientists report that, in moments of relaxation, they "glimpse the true state of affairs" through some as yet poorly understood intuitive faculty. Prosperous gamblers and businesspeople "play their hunches," while fine artists poetically claim to have been "inspired by their muse." And those who experience what I have been calling miracles of deliverance say that they just detached emotionally and then "something" came over them, causing them to behave in a fashion they would never otherwise have considered.

Faced with problems they cannot solve, highly successful people the world over calm down, turn within, and then find themselves directed to a surprising solution. And notice that it does not seem to matter whether or not they regard the source of their inspiration as "divine." As Mozart put it, "Whence and how — that I do not know and cannot learn."

It is perhaps the ultimate irony that one need not even believe in God in order to receive the benefits of divine guidance. If *conscience* and *intuition* are indeed just other names for the voice of God, committed atheists may be equally, or more, responsive to divine promptings than are people who pride themselves on being religious. Where spiritually oriented people "pray," or "meditate," or "consult their conscience," in order to receive direction, ethical nonreligious people "ponder the ramifications of their choices," or "try to see what will be best for everyone in the long run." The language is different, but the activity would appear to be the same. Agnostics and atheists may be listening to the voice of God without even realizing it.

If you are not guided toward a faith (or even if you are)
seek God in the silence—seek within.

— Peace Pilgrim

But what can we say about the mysterious source of wisdom people access through intuition? And in what sense might it be considered "supernatural"? In the next chapter, we will attempt to answer these questions as we explore the growing convergence of scientific and spiritual thinking.

12

Groping the Cosmic Elephant

The general notions about human understanding which are illustrated by discoveries in atomic physics are not in the nature of things wholly unfamiliar, wholly unheard of, or new. Even in our own culture they have a history, and in Buddhist and Hindu thought a more considerable and central place. What we shall find is an exemplification, an encouragement, and a refinement of old wisdom.
—Julius Robert Oppenheimer

There is a well-known Sufi parable about four blind men who are introduced to an elephant for the first time. They approach the enormous animal with lively curiosity and grope whatever part of it they can reach.

"Oh," says the first, attempting to encircle a huge leg with his arms, "I understand now. An elephant is very much like a tree."

"No," the second corrects him while reaching up to feel the vast expanse of the elephant's side. "An elephant is very much like a wall."

"You are both mistaken," declares the third as he tries to hang onto the great beast's probing trunk. "An elephant is very much like a snake."

GROPING THE COSMIC ELEPHANT

"I cannot imagine where you get such ideas!" exclaims the fourth, holding up the tail. "It is perfectly obvious that an elephant is just like a rope!"

This story has been used for centuries to illustrate the discrepancies between the findings of science and mysticism. It underscores the fact that scientific observations are always made from some limited point of view and focused upon a restricted field of study. The conclusions arrived at by this method may all be correct enough as far as they go, but they may nevertheless fail to capture the essence of the entire phenomenon.

Through intuition, mystics attempt to catch a glimpse of the cosmic "elephant" as an integrated being engaged in purposeful activities. Scientists, on the other hand, have usually tried to get it to hold still for a minute, so that they could meticulously analyze a handy patch of trunk, leg, torso, or tail. Small wonder that they did not seem to be talking about the same thing!

As a result of this difference in approach, nineteenth-century physicists arrived at conclusions about the nature of the universe that appeared to be hopelessly incompatible with the intuitive perceptions of mystics. How could the cosmos that had mindlessly evolved out of inanimate matter be the intelligent, divinely purposeful, living entity spiritually oriented people thought it?

However, the Sufi parable also suggests that if the blind men were to continue exploring the elephant long enough—sharing information with each other along the way—they would eventually derive a more integrated understanding of their subject. When their observations had encompassed the entire living entity and its habitual activities, you would expect that their descriptions would begin to sound very much like those of sighted persons.

And this is precisely what has happened to twentieth-century physicists. They have finally gathered enough information about the universe to realize that, taken as a whole, it is actually very much the way mystics described it. Relativity and quantum theory have opened a window on a mysterious, and arguably "supernatural,"

173

dimension of reality. As Fritjof Capra and others have pointed out, these days it is sometimes difficult to tell the difference between statements made by modern physicists and those of ancient spiritual masters.[30]

While the naturalistic science most of us learned in school seemed to completely foreclose the possibility of miracles, some contemporary physicists are themselves offering plausible explanations of the way miracles might work. Our groping scientists are not yet in *perfect* agreement with mystics about the nature of the cosmic elephant, but the "tree, wall, rope" days are long gone. As the quotation from physicist Julius Oppenheimer that opens this chapter indicates, the revolutionary new quantum universe is neither "new" nor "revolutionary" to students of sacred knowledge. Let us see what light contemporary science has to shed upon our investigation of miracles.

The Existence of Mind

As we have already seen, naturalists have long assumed that thought would eventually be reduced to the activity of neurons in the brain. However, many contemporary scientists feel compelled to discard this idea. By the middle of the twentieth century, a "consciousness revolution" was gaining strength within physics and spilling over into other disciplines. The theory that mental phenomena could be dispensed with was simply no longer tenable.

For one thing, the role of an observing consciousness is central to relativity theory. At the quantum level, physical things cannot be said to exist at all until they are observed. In his book *Bridging Science and Spirit,* Norman Friedman explains:

> The paradox is this: we need particles of matter to make up the objects of our everyday world (including us), and we need an object in that very everyday world (us) to define and observe those particles. Observation implies consciousness.

Any construct that purports to describe reality in terms of contemporary physics clearly must include a role for consciousness.[31]

Today, in the wake of the consciousness revolution, the majority of scientists in all fields accept the idea that mental phenomena are real. As Nobel Prize–winning psychologist Roger Sperry put it, it is now known that thoughts direct the activity of the brain's neurons in the same way that a television script directs the activity of electrons on a TV screen.[32] The naturalist view that only physical things are real has been soundly trounced. Indeed, nowadays there is serious question about whether *physical* things really exist.

"Oh Dear, What Can the Matter Be?"

It is ironic that as mind has become "real" for modern scientists, the status of matter has grown increasingly problematic. Danish physicist Niels Bohr, for example, insisted that there is no such thing as "objective reality" at the subatomic level. This means that there is no "real" world out there. We know from Heisenberg's Uncertainty Principle that the perceiver inevitably influences the perception, and this suggests to some scientists that we are actually living in a vast perceptual illusion generated within our own minds. As physicist John Wheeler put it, "Useful as it is under everyday circumstances to say that the world exists 'out there' independent of us, that view can no longer be upheld."[33]

The Existence of Free Will

In place of the objective, billiard ball universe of nineteenth-century physics, modern scientists speak of living particles that embody meaning and respond intelligently to the information encoded within their energy fields. According to physicist Freeman Dyson, "Every particle in the universe is an active agent making choices between random processes."[34]

175

So, contrary to what naturalists would have us believe, free will turns out to exist even at the particle level, and many scientists now believe that the universe may fundamentally be one of mind rather than matter. As the distinguished British astronomer Sir James Jeans put it: "The stream of knowledge is heading toward a nonmechanical reality; the universe begins to look more like a great thought than like a great machine."[35]

Further, it has become apparent that this "great thought" is not subject to the natural laws that regulate the activity of matter within the physical world. It is quite literally "supernatural."

For example, physicist John Stewart Bell demonstrated that when two particles interact and then separate, they continue to influence each other instantaneously—which is to say, faster than the speed of light. Since it is known that nothing in our three-dimensional universe *can* exceed the speed of light, Bell concluded that there must be some "deeper" level of our universe where quantum particles are instantaneously connected—*an invisible, causal dimension which exists outside the natural world and is not subject to the constraints of space and time.*[31] This is, of course, what mystics have been saying for thousands of years.

Some physicists in this century have concluded that mystics were correct all along in suggesting that matter is only a perceptual illusion generated within the mind. And if the universe truly is a "great thought," surely it is not unreasonable to wonder about the Thinker. What is the unimaginable intelligence that stands outside of nature—the formless architect of all physical form? As we shall see, although contemporary physicists have given it many names, it is apparent from their descriptions that they are referring to the same entity mystics call God.

According to physicist Werner Heisenberg, this "deeper" level of the universe is a dimension of information that creates form out of formlessness by orchestrating the behavior of energy.[31] It quite literally places energy "in formation," causing it to exhibit the properties of matter. This means that the palpable, three-dimensional world of our everyday experience arises out of, and depends for its existence upon, a formless, unmanifest dimension of ideas. Heisenberg proposes that there is an infinite sea of knowledge in which some scientists are beginning to recognize the causal, supernatural realm that mystics call the mind of God.

A Scientific Perspective on Miracles

Let us pause for just a moment to note the significance of all this. If nature represents the orderly and predictable progression of events in space and time, then miracles are instances where space and time are "interfered with"—brought into a new configuration—by an intelligence that stands beyond them. Indeed, *A Course in Miracles* refers to miracles as "out-of-pattern time intervals"—interludes during which space and time are readjusted to suit our needs.[21]

Remember that deliverance seems often to be associated with detachment from ordinary reality and a dreamy sense of timelessness. For example, an automobile accident that is actually occurring with blinding speed appears to be unfolding in slow motion. It is as if individuals who experience miracles of deliverance temporarily shift their focus into a timeless dimension of thought where they find themselves in a position to *decide* what will happen next. Now some physicists are telling us that there really is a timeless, causal dimension out of which our minds create our experience of physical reality. Let us take a closer look at what they are saying about it.

The "Deeper" Level of the Universe

Physicist David Bohm proposed that the physical world comes into existence when minds interact with what he called hierarchies of "implicate informational structures."[36] Within this conceptual "implicate order," Bohm hypothesized that all possible futures are "enfolded" as potential. These possible futures exist only as ideas, but Bohm said that when a particular idea becomes the focus of someone's attention, it is conceptually "unfolded" from the implicate order and brought into physical form as a set of circumstances that symbolically embodies that idea. This is to say that a thought has been "made manifest" through the interest of an observing consciousness in having the corresponding experience. Science writer Norman Friedman elaborates on this crucial point as follows:

> One of the basic postulates of quantum theory states that an initial system can potentially develop into a number of states, each with given probability of occurrence. We know, though, that only one probability can actually take place. According to the accepted interpretation of quantum theory, the actual or "real" state of these probabilities is specified by an observation; that is, the "real" state is brought into reality by an observer. *The observer thus becomes a creator and gives the system its form.* [The emphasis is mine.] Without the observer, the system is in a state of potential, waiting to come into existence.[31]

Creating the Physical World

Spiritual masters have long maintained that a thought in the mind of God is "made manifest" in the physical world through the concentrated attention and belief of those who experience it. Through prayer and positive affirmations, for example, a person focuses consciously upon creating the outcome she or he desires. Yet, if these physicists are correct, whether or not we intentionally do these things, our thoughts are always busily creating whatever possibilities we believe to be real.

I have been suggesting in this book that miracles become possible whenever someone makes a sudden mental shift from fear or anger into a peaceful altered state of consciousness. Nineteenth-century physics had no room for such a view—if mind was not real, then there was no way that changing the mind could affect the physical world. However, we now know that mind *is* real. Not only does it "influence" physical things, it quite literally brings the physical world into being.

If our thoughts *create* the physical world, then it should be obvious that changing our thoughts can *change* the world. Is it possible that in studying the way the physical world is brought into existence by the activity of the mind, scientists have been quietly elucidating the mechanism of miracles without realizing what they have been doing?

Changing Your Reality by Changing Your Mind

Let us make this idea that we are all creators a bit more concrete by applying it to the familiar deliverance situation. If physicists are correct in saying that, at the quantum level, we are each creating whatever "reality" we experience, what might that mean in terms of ordinary behavior? In what sense are we choosing what will happen to us next?

All of the people I am calling "miracle workers" faced danger with what initially appeared to be an irrational conviction that everything was going to work out fine. They seemed to feel that their ultimate well-being was assured, no matter what happened to their physical bodies. I am suggesting that this "faith" in their continued well-being may have played a vital role in creating the positive outcomes they experienced. Could it be that one's mental attitude is the key to selecting which one of a number of possible futures will be actualized? Let us see how this might work.

Heidi

Heidi is a San Diego teenager who broke her back in an automobile accident. She was cut out of the wreckage paralyzed from the waist down, and it was greatly feared that she would remain

179

that way for the rest of her life. Many people, including her doctors, believe that Heidi's recovery from this serious spinal chord displacement was miraculous.

Heidi's neurosurgeon described her injury as the worst he'd ever seen of its kind. On a scale of 0 to 5, her doctors estimated her chances of ever being able to walk again as "O to 1." Although they did not want to be discouraging, they admitted when pressed that they had never seen anyone come back from such a severe spinal chord displacement. As one of her physicians privately confided to her rehabilitation nurse, "That's one kid who will never walk again!"

Heidi reports that her constant prayer throughout her ordeal was, "Lord, just get me through this. You can let me die, or you can let me walk away, or you can help me accept what will happen. But just get me through this somehow."

Notice that, like many others who received miracles, Heidi asked for divine help but did not presume to tell God specifically what the oucome should be. If it was God's will that she die or that she survive as a paraplegic, she was prepared to accept her situation and try to make the best of it. It seemed to her that with God's support, she could somehow be all right no matter what happened to her. Her focus was upon maintaining a sense of inner peace and well-being, whatever occurred.

Nevertheless, Heidi believed in miracles, and she never let go of the hope that she would walk again. Whenever her doctors and nurses commented on her poor prognosis, Heidi's response was always, "Never tell me that!" She knew her chances were slim, but she was determined to do everything in her power to make a complete recovery. Like others who experienced deliverance, Heidi denied the *inevitability* of a negative outcome, although she did not deny its *possibility*.

Heidi said that as her days in the hospital wore on with no evidence of improvement, it was increasingly difficult to keep her hopes alive. Finally, in desperation, she prayed, "Lord, just give me *something*—some small sign of progress that I can work to improve on." The next day, she discovered that she was able to wiggle a toe ever so slightly. As far as Heidi was concerned, it was the sign from God for which she had been praying. She set to work with all her concentration, focusing upon this little movement and working to expand it. By concentrating totally on the one encouraging sign she had been given, I believe that Heidi focused the power of her mind to actualize a very improbable, but nonetheless possible, future. Against everyone's predictions, Heidi walked out of the hospital one month after her accident. When I met her, she was walking almost normally—a slight limp all that remained of her former paraplegia. She is convinced that her recovery was a gift from God, but I want to emphasize that it was also one she had a hand in co-creating. By relentlessly maintaining the necessary mental focus, she found a way to bring something that was only a distant possibility into physical manifestation as her "reality." This is how miracles are created.

Here we see yet another instance of a person who insisted on believing that everything was somehow going to be all right, despite all the information she was receiving that it would not. This provides a good example of the way an individual can create the "reality" of his or her choice through mental attitude. How might this work?

I suspect that when Heidi responded to the threat of lifelong disability calmly, she was investing her belief in the comforting thought "God is with me, everything is going to be all right." In so doing, she was automatically selecting an experience of "all rightness" from among the infinite possibilities available within the implicate order. This is to say that her positive, optimistic mental state accessed its experiential counterpart from the causal dimension.

Notice also that the idea of full recovery would have been rejected as "unrealistic" by a person who lacked Heidi's faith in God. She understood very well that it would take a miracle to heal her, but that did not mean to Heidi that she could not hope to be healed. "Yes! A miracle *could* happen," she thought. God *could* cure me, and I'm going to do everything I can to make it happen!"

The deliverance stories we have considered all support the spiritual view that our decision about how to interpret our experience causes an outcome to manifest that corresponds to, and justifies, that interpretation. Because Heidi responded to her bleak prospects with faith and hope, she felt peaceful in the midst of adversity. Her optimism then created a result that made faith and hope appear justified. In the same way, when we respond with fear, we access frightening possibilities, and when we believe that anger is justified, the universe cooperates by supplying an infuriating turn of events.

[Fear] not only injures us psychologically and aggravates world tensions, but through such negative concentration we tend to attract the things which we fear. If we fear nothing and radiate love, we can expect good things to come.

—Peace Pilgrim

Some physicists now seem to be agreeing with mystics that the world is only a perceptual illusion that looks different to each person. According to this view, *your* world will appear any way *you* have decided to believe it is. Such a thing once seemed scientifically impossible, but science is now explaining how our thoughts could determine our physical experience.

This means that our conclusion about what emotional reaction is "called for" by a situation influences the direction things will take in the next moment. When Elizabeth decided to believe that her knife-wielding assailant was really a decent guy who would behave with integrity if reminded of his responsibilities, this was the possible future she went on to actualize. When Karen and Mike sailed off a cliff in the dark, but decided to believe that this was not a cause for concern—that everything was going to turn out just fine anyway—that was the possible future they brought into manifestation. When Brian treated rioting prisoners like buddies who would appreciate a good joke, that is what they became in his world. I suspect that whenever anyone says—and truly believes—"there is nothing to get upset about," it turns out to be true!

Indeed, even if the "worst" happens and someone dies, that does not necessarily mean that their peaceful altered state failed to exert a positive influence upon their future. Many cosmologies teach that the state of mind of a dying person determines the experiences that follow death. Individuals who die in "a state of grace" may achieve immediate entry into a heavenly realm where their faith and love earn them a well-deserved reward. In any case, inner peace is its own reward.

Changing Collective Reality

Both physicists and metaphysicians seem to be converging upon the realization that we each create our own experience. The only difference between miracle workers and others is that miracle workers are aware that their thoughts can influence the way things turn out. Anyone who understood this would instantly recognize the folly of expecting the worst. Remember Kathleen steadfastly refusing to believe that the man who raped her would also kill her? She knew better than to put any mental energy into actualizing the possibility of her own murder.

> *The mind is very powerful, and never loses its creative force. It never sleeps. Every instant it is creating. It is hard to recognize that thought and belief combine into a power surge that can literally move mountains.*
> —*A Course in Miracles*

Enlightened self-interest would compel anyone who understood the power of the mind to abandon negative, judgmental thoughts in favor of peaceful, loving ones. This is the reason so many spiritual paths emphasize positive thinking and faith in God's grace. For example, in the following quote from his book *Mastering Your Hidden Self: A Guide to the Huna Way*, Kahuna Serge King explains that the mind's power to create our physical experience is at the basis of Hawaiian mysticism.

> The most fundamental idea in Huna philosophy is that we each create our own personal experience of reality, by our beliefs, interpretations, actions and reactions, thoughts and feelings. It is not that our reality is created for us as a result of these personal expressions, but that we are creators, co-creators with the Universe itself. Huna is all about learning to do that consciously. This idea, however, is not unique to Huna. It is shared, though often only in the esoteric teachings, by virtually every religion known to man. Sadly, it is seldom widely taught or practiced.[38]

Choosing Your Future

The generic supernatural theory we are considering predicts that by investing mentally in the possibility that X will occur, we make it much more likely that X will happen. If only one person is concerned with X, then it is entirely up to that individual whether or not to imagine X into existence.

For example, because Heidi's disability directly affected only herself, she was probably in complete control of the outcome. The prayers and positive thoughts of her loved ones undoubtedly helped to encourage and support her in trying for a miracle, but, ultimately, it was up to her what outcome to actualize. But what if a situation involves the fates of many people? For example, what if X represents "world peace"?

According to mystics, changing collective illusions requires collective action. By expecting, and working for world peace, an individual increases the likelihood that it will occur. However, everyone else contributes a vote as well. As long as the majority of people on earth think they have something to gain through aggression, wars will continue.

Nevertheless, every time we persuade someone else to seek solutions that are fair to everyone involved, peace on earth comes closer. According to this view, the great world events that affect all of us are decided upon by a democratic process in which everyone has a say. What actually occurs represents the sum of everyone's thoughts about it. When enough of us decide to act only from love, peace will prevail.

> One day a lady said to me, "Peace, I'm praying with you for peace, but of course I don't believe it's possible." I said, "Don't you believe peace is God's will?" "Oh, yes," she said, "I know it is." I said, "How can you tell me that which is God's will is impossible? It's not only possible, it's inevitable, but how soon is up to us."
> —Peace Pilgrim

Cooperating with the Universe

Now I realize that it is a considerable leap from the findings of quantum physics to the dynamics of the deliverance phenomenon, but I believe that they will ultimately turn out to be connected. What else does it mean to say that our mental choices determine what will happen in the physical world? We are literally *thinking* our world into existence and if we change our minds, the world must change, too. This is how miracle workers throughout history have explained their ability to influence reality. Some physicists now say that this is the way things *must* work, and the reports of the people who experienced deliverance indicate that this is the way they *do* work.

It would seem that, despite the differences in their approach, modern scientists and ancient mystics have been groping the same "elephant" after all. Miracles may come down to the mind's abil-

185

ity to drop an unsatisfying implicate strand being manifested in the physical world and actualize another instead. People who create miracles seem adept at refocusing their attention in order to imagine their world differently. Gino, for example, imagined that his liver was healing. Many of the individuals who shared their astonishing reversals of fortune seemed guided from within to simply imagine that—appearances to the contrary—they were not really in any danger. As the Bible puts it, "As you believe, so is it done unto you."

Now that we have some idea how a supernatural phenomenon such as miracles might be scientifically valid, let us see what mystics have had to say about the nature of God and the universe.

13

What Is God?

Theist and Atheist: The fight between them is as to whether God shall be called God or shall have some other name.

— Samuel Butler

We saw in the last chapter that some modern physicists appear to be stumbling upon a causal, supernatural dimension of reality that bears a striking resemblance to the descriptions mystics offer of God. But does God really exist?

If this question means, "Is there evidence of an all-powerful and all-knowing but somewhat temperamental old gentleman who sits in judgment of mortals?" I suspect that the answer is no. However, while this concept of God is fairly common in religions throughout the world, it is an obvious attempt to simplify and anthropomorphize a much more complex and sophisticated concept of God intuitively apprehended by the mystics of diverse faiths.

In this chapter, I am going to attempt to articulate what might be called a "generic" mystical view of the universe, which we can compare to the current scientific one. It is stitched together using metaphors from different spiritual traditions and traces a common core of belief that underlies many of them.

In the past, it has often appeared that science contradicted religion and that different religions contradicted one another. Yet I believe that if we focus upon the broad outlines of what the most enlightened members of different faiths believe to be true, we will find a surprising amount of common ground. Although they use different metaphors to describe what they see, the great thinkers of the world—ancient and modern, sacred and secular—actually agree more than they disagree with respect to the nature of the cosmic "elephant."

I believe in the fundamental Truth of all the great religions of the world. I believe that they are all God-given.
—Mohandas Gandhi

The Nature of the Universe

The generic spiritual view asserts that there is an external, infinitely loving and intelligent higher power that created everything that exists out of itself. Many mystical traditions describe God as the very ground of being. As the original source of consciousness that gave "birth" to all of the individual minds manifesting in this physical dimension, God is often compared to a "heavenly father" or a "great mother." However, those who wish to avoid such anthropomorphism describe God as a formless higher power, love, the fertile void, the creative principle of the universe, divine law, the prime mover, or the Great Way of Things.

Terms such as these bear a striking resemblance to the descriptions physicists give of the invisible realm of ideas that gives rise to the natural world. We have seen that some scientists now view the universe as a living being, every particle of which appears to think, communicate, and make choices. A few even agree with metaphysicians that we are not bodies but minds, and that we exist within a vast universal mind of unimaginable intelligence and complexity—a supernatural dimension of thought that sustains our existence and grants our desires by giving form to whatever ideas our minds entertain.

Creation—the Scientific View

Like mystics, modern scientists speak of a "time" before the illusion of separation in time and space when there was only oneness. According to physicists and astronomers, all of the stuff of the cosmos was once compressed into a nearly dimensionless point. At some moment in eternity, the energy within the point exploded outward in all directions. Scientists do not claim to understand what triggered this "big bang" in which the three-dimensional universe was born.

The naturalistic view holds that as the compressed energy rushed forth, it created the dimensions of space and time and took on the aspect of physical matter. According to this view, on at least one of the chunks of matter generated by this cosmic explosion—the planet Earth—life accidentally developed and began to evolve.

However, as we have seen, many physicists now believe that matter can only be brought into existence by the activity of an observing consciousness. This would seem to imply that the physical universe could not manifest before some preexisting universal Mind thought it into being. Like the commonly held spiritual view of creation, this places Mind at the *beginning* of the causal sequence, rather than at the end.

The current scientific perspective holds that the physical universe will continue to expand until the momentum of the "big bang" is no longer able to overcome the gravitational attraction of the parts for one another. Then it will reverse its direction and begin to contract, eventually collapsing back into a dimensionless point once again. Time, space, and matter will all cease to exist as if they had never been. There will again be only eternal oneness.

Creation—the Mystical View

Time is nothing but the measurement of the duration of corporal bodies and that which is not a body is beyond time and measurement of duration.
—Saadya Gaon, Emunath V'deoth 2:5

189

The world's great spiritual traditions put it somewhat differently. They hold that the big bang theory represents a spatiotemporal metaphor for events that are really taking place in consciousness.

According to many spiritual traditions, God initiated the process of creation by extending itself into one, original child of God—in Judaism, Christianity, and Islam, the biblical Adam. God is said to have created this first being out of a desire to have an object for its love.

Like the Creative Force itself, the first child of God also longed for greater joy through the creation of other beings with whom to share love. With the One Mind's complete approbation, that first creation extended the mind of God farther, bringing other children of God into being. All of these new "brothers" and "sisters" were creators as well. In this fashion, mystics say that a universe of constantly multiplying—individual but interconnected—minds (spirits) came into existence.

The mystical perspective holds that only mind (spirit) is ultimately real, since that is all that God is, and therefore all that it created out of itself. If this view is correct, then it is our minds and not our bodies that are created "in the image and likeness of God." Thousands of years before scientists began to suspect that mind was real and matter, illusory, meditators were being shown the same thing through intuition.

The Separation

It is also widely believed that once the One Mind had extended itself into other beings, some of us decided to become independent of our Creator. While we could not do this in reality, we were able to *imagine* that we had, using the same process of psychological dissociation (motivated forgetting) we continue to employ to this day.

According to this view, we elected to forget about our eternal equality with all other children of God because we wanted to find out what it would feel like to be "special" and better than others. Thus, the excursion into a separated state was intended to allow us to seem different, so that we could compete with one another and prove ourselves worthy of *special love*—that is, love that is given to some and denied to others.

In order to keep score, we became extremely attentive to differences among ourselves and assigned values to all of them. This led to an obsession with judgment. "I am prettier (and therefore better) than you!" "Yes, but I am richer (and therefore better) than you!" "But I am kinder (and therefore better) than either one of you!" Each characteristic we assumed within the physical illusion was intended to distinguish us from others, and entitle us to special love (or, failing that, to special hate). The important thing was to be special—separate and different.

Mystics predict that the illusion of separation will end when the attraction of *unconditional* love overcomes each individual's desire for *special* love. The moment we children of God lose all desire to judge ourselves or others *unworthy of love,* we will joyfully reunite with one another. At that point, separation in space and time will no longer serve any purpose. The children of God will once again peacefully rest in the awareness of eternal equality and oneness.

Although scientists arrived at the big bang theory in the twentieth century, it is apparent that spiritual thinkers have been discussing something very much like it for thousands of years. Instead of a mechanical explosion, they speak of a decision to separate. Instead of the force of gravity, they speak of the attraction of Love. Where naturalistic metaphors characterize the universe as random and meaningless, mystics have long thought of it as a great mind in which things occur for intelligible reasons.

The Role of Judgment in Maintaining Separation

Mystical traditions throughout the world agree that the desire to judge caused, and maintains, our sense of being separate from God and one another. The Book of Genesis, for example, says that

Adam and Eve ate the fruit of the Tree of Knowledge and this made them aware of good and evil, a distinction that had never before existed in their minds. This is to say that they forgot about unconditional love and began to conceptually divide God's universe into things that were "good," and therefore "worthy of special love," and those that were "evil," and therefore "unworthy of love."

Many spiritual traditions regard love that has been contaminated by judgment and rendered conditional as a pale reflection of the Unconditional Love that can be experienced in the absence of judgment. This means that we children of God who decided to analyze our experiences into good and evil—loving only the parts of reality that met our expectations and rejecting all others—necessarily forfeited the joys of unconditional love. Since God *is* unconditional love, we also forfeited the awareness of our ongoing relationship to the ground of our being. Through our decision to entertain judgment, we effectively "cast" ourselves "out of Paradise."

The Physical Illusion

Spiritual systems throughout the world agree that in adopting judgment we created the illusions of space and time. We began to imagine ourselves within an illusory material universe where everything was separated from everything else. Hindus call this dualistic physical illusion *maya*. In his *Autobiography of a Yogi*, Swami Paramahansa Yogananda summarized the ancient Vedic perspective of the physical universe as follows.

Physical science, then, cannot formulate laws outside of maya: the very fabric and structure of creation. Nature herself is maya; natural science must perforce deal with her ineluctable quiddity. Science thus remains in a perpetual flux, unable to reach finality; fit indeed to discover the laws of an already existing and functioning cosmos but powerless to detect the Law Framer and Sole Operator. To surmount maya was the task assigned to the human race by the millennial prophets. To rise above the duality of creation and perceive the unity of the Creator was conceived of as man's highest goal.[37]

The enlightened thinkers of many faiths have compared this illusory physical universe to a dream being dreamed by God's children. For example, the Bible says that Adam fell asleep in Paradise, and it makes no reference to his ever having awakened. There is widespread agreement that the only true "awakening" is achieved through spiritual enlightenment (salvation)—a process in which we reverse our dissociation and remember who and what we really are. This awakened state, in which we penetrate all illusions to remember our relationship to God, is variously called Christ consciousness, Krishna consciousness, realizing one's inner Buddha nature, living in harmony with the eternal Tao, dancing one's dream awake, merging with the Godhead, and so forth.

The Roots of Suffering

Since judgment leads to separation, religions throughout the world designate it as the source of all suffering. For example, the Buddha characterized the roots of human misery as clinging and aversion—the tendency to judge everything and then cling to some experiences while attempting to separate ourselves from others. Being rich is an experience to which many people would like to cling, while poverty is widely regarded with aversion. According to the Buddha, an "enlightened" individual is "even minded," declining to place any value judgments upon the things that seem to occur within the physical dream.

I believe that the attitudes of the people who experienced deliverance provide a glimpse of this dispassionate consciousness. For example, Heidi, whose recovery from a devastating spinal chord displacement we discussed in the last chapter, did not cling to the idea that she could only be happy if she could walk, or terrify herself with frightening images of the miserable life she might have if she were not healed. Certainly she preferred to walk again and did everything in her power to actualize that possibility. But if necessary, Heidi was prepared to be satisfied with whatever life brought. In all of the deliverance stories, we see miracle workers contemplating the prospect of injury or death with a remarkably even-minded willingness to accept reality on its own terms.

The Buddha also taught that when we surrender judgment once and for all, we will be restored to awareness of our "inner Buddha nature" and discover that the physical dimension was really nothing more than an illusion. Why pass judgment upon a dream you yourself have chosen to entertain? If you don't like what you are dreaming, the sensible thing to do is to dream it differently or, better yet, to wake up.

This attitude toward judgment is virtually universal within mystical thought. Consider, for example, these comments by a Taoist master.

*The Great Way is not difficult for those who have no preferences.
When love and hate are both absent, everything is clear and
    undisguised.
Make the smallest distinction, however, and heaven and earth are
    set infinitely apart.*

—Third Chinese Patriarch

Jesus expressed the same idea through his emphasis upon forgiveness. Forgiveness reverses a prior decision to judge against someone or something. Jesus recognized that all of his brothers and sisters were entitled to unconditional love, no matter what role they played within the physical illusion.

Heaven and Hell

With their emphasis upon mind rather than matter, mystics regard the once and future unity of being as a state of oneness with God, or "heaven." In this view, the separation from God through judgment is regarded as an act of will that must be consciously reversed—not because it is morally reprehensible, but simply because it is unsatisfying. A separated state inevitably leads to conflict and alienation.

For one thing, having forgotten that we are eternally connected to, and sustained by, the Mind of God, we experience a terrifying sense of isolation and vulnerability. Within the physical illusion, we appear to be bodies, and bodies can suffer and die.

Further, since the meaning of our lives is not comprehensible without reference to our relationship to the universe, people who lack a belief in God generally conclude either that their lives have no meaning or that it is up to them as individuals to create their own meaning. If you think about it, this amounts to the same thing.

The attendant sense of alienation, meaninglessness, and despair, which existentialists regard as the human condition, is what mystics call "hell." Jean-Paul Sartre once said, "Hell is other people," and, indeed, the perception of hell results from the idea that there *are* other people—that we are separate individuals with interests that conflict.

If space and time are illusory, then hell cannot be a "place" where the dead are tormented after death, but only a painful and frightening state of mind of the eternally living. Nor is hell inflicted by God as a punishment for sin. Hell is the natural consequence of imagining that you are separate from God, and what would the omnipresent Being of which everything is composed know about separation? We may imagine ourselves separate from God, but God is not similarly deluded.

Heaven and hell are states of being. Heaven is being in harmony with God's will; hell is being out of harmony with God's will. You can be in either state on either side of life. There is no permanent hell.

—Peace Pilgrim

Judgment Leads to Fear

Many spiritual philosophies identify the ego as the deluded aspect of our minds that we specialized to entertain the concepts of separation and judgment. When we judge others—concluding that they are unworthy of love and deserve to suffer for what they have done—we inevitably project our own faultfinding tendencies onto the universe. This leads us to imagine that God wants to punish us for our shortcomings, just as we want to punish others for theirs. To the ego-identified, God is a terrifying figure—the ultimate punitive parent from whom no sin is hidden.

This means that everyone who identifies with the ego is chronically fearful and guilty. Spiritual teachers say that this is true whether or not we consciously believe in God. The more we judge, the more we dread divine judgment. Atheism may be a last-ditch effort to avoid this fear and guilt without actually removing its cause.

The ego attempts to cope with the negative effects of judgment by projecting them outside the mind, onto the physical illusion. There, guilt and fear take on the form of external punishing circumstances such as sickness, attack, loss, and rejection. Some spiritual teachers propose that by making ourselves suffer in these ways, we unconsciously hope to lessen the punishment we anticipate from God for our defection. Unfortunately, this strategy does not actually relieve our distress, but merely obscures its cause. Now the problem appears to be medical, economic, or social, instead of originating in our own judgmental thoughts.

Abdication of Judgment Produces Miracles

Individuals who use meditative techniques to extricate their minds from identification with their egos discover that judgment no longer makes any sense to them. Spiritual enlightenment manifests, in part, as an attitude of general acceptance and reverence for all beings. The complete disavowal of judgment allows enlightened individuals to love even their former enemies without reservation.

Notice that this is precisely the consciousness we see in people who experience deliverance. They lay judgment aside and reflect nothing but unconditional love, even to those who are about to take their lives.

Releasing judgment makes one "miracle minded" because it represents a shift away from identification with the ego's chronically frightened and resentful perspective. According to mystics, the dramatic shifts in the physical illusion that we call "miracles" are produced by corresponding mental shifts into unconditional love.

Because the world is only an illusion projected by our minds, a peaceful mind projects a peaceful world. Thus, a person who is willing to grant the "all rightness" of everyone, looks out upon a physical illusion that is suddenly all right again. Once it is forgiven, the "betrayal" of a friend turns out to be only a foolish misunderstanding. A peaceful mind quickly brings a skidding automobile back under control, and those who are not invested in the importance of a dreadful diagnosis often find that it turns out to have been unduly pessimistic. In this way, unconditional love truly does redeem the world from pain and darkness.

If fear is the inevitable result of entertaining judgment, then the moment someone embraces unconditional love, his or her fear should instantly evaporate. The Bible, for example, says, "Perfect love casteth out fear." Again, this is precisely what we see among people who report deliverance. Their "enlightened" state may last only a few moments, but in those moments they become utterly unafraid. Then their conviction that the universe is ultimately safe and loving is projected into their physical experience as a miraculous turn of events, converting a nightmare into a happy dream.

The Last Judgment

Although we imagine that God cherishes judgment as much as we do, enlightened spiritual teachers throughout the world maintain that this is not the case. The belief that judgment is sometimes appropriate is precisely what *separates* us from God. Indeed, according to *A Course in Miracles*,[21] the much-feared "Last Judgment" mentioned in the New Testament will not be an act of God at all. Instead, it will be nothing more than each individual's eventual decision to lay judgment aside. When you personally have made *your* "last judgment," you will finally be free to unite with others in the heaven of unconditional love.

We ultimately escape from hell and return to heaven by recognizing that we have neither the right nor the ability to judge anyone. Judgment is always a justification for withholding love. Salvation lies in the recognition that there *can be no* justification for withholding love. If we are all created out of Love, then love is what we *are*. To imagine that we can limit love, or express anything else, is to live within an illusion.

In this chapter and the last, we have seen that there are important voices within both physics and metaphysics that agree that consciousness creates the physical world and that our choices about what to think, feel, and believe determine what will happen to us. I believe that by applying this principle intelligently, all of us can hope to become miracle workers. Now that we have some theoretical grounding, let us look more closely at the practical application of this principle.

14

The Lord Will Provide

If you realized how powerful your thoughts are, you would never think a defeatist or negative thought. Since we create through thought, we need to concentrate very strongly on positive thoughts. If you think you can't do something, you can't. But if you think you can, you may be surprised to discover that you can. It is important that our thoughts be constantly for the best that could happen in a situation—for the good things we would like to see happen.

—Peace Pilgrim

If our beliefs and expectations determine what is possible in our world, it means that those who meet danger with an optimistic sense that nothing can interfere with them should be able to overcome all obstacles. This includes the obstacles presented by natural laws. If miracles are real, then nothing is truly "impossible."

Mystics have long maintained that the "immutable laws of the universe" are better thought of as the rules of a game the children of God are playing on the board of three-dimensional space/time. They are collective agreements—the constraints within which we ordinarily agree to work. Yet, throughout history, there have been miracle workers who have discovered that they were free to violate physical laws.

Miraculous abilities that defy natural laws are called *siddhis* by yogis. While some spiritual adepts deliberately seek personal power through the cultivation of these mystical "powers," the practitioners of many paths are advised to simply ignore them as distractions from the ultimate goal of spiritual liberation. Fascination with *siddhis* could hold a person back by tempting him or her to feel special, and to seek gratification within the world of illusion, instead of going beyond it to union with God.

Nevertheless, many people discover that miraculous abilities arise spontaneously when they center their minds in unconditional love. For example, there are accounts of levitation during meditation by individuals as diverse as Saint Teresa of Avila and Swami Nagendra Nath Bhaduri. A Hindu woman named Giri Bala as well as a Bavarian Catholic named Theresa Neumann are said to have developed the ability to live on universal energies without ingesting food for decades. The Muslim fakir Afzal Khan reportedly materialized objects out of thin air just as the modern Hindu avatar, Sai Baba, is said to do, and there are tales of Hindu and Sufi saints who walked upon water just as Jesus is reputed to have done.

Whether or not one has intentionally cultivated miraculous powers, miracles seem to occur naturally whenever someone enters a peaceful, nonjudgmental, "enlightened" state of consciousness. The evidence from the deliverance stories we have considered indicates that God can and does protect those who rest in unconditional love. The people who shared their narrow escapes with me had not developed mystical abilities through long practice. Their deliverances were not so much the result of "personal power" as of "divine grace."

The Role of Free Will in Miracles

Many religions teach that allegiance to Love can create a safe place for us wherever we happen to be. Unfortunately, few people know how to withdraw into unconditional love when destructive experiences are being foisted upon them by others. We all have inviolable free will, but as the mystic Gurdjieff pointed out, few of us use it.[39] Like Dorothy in Oz, most of us walk around in our "ruby slippers" without understanding the extraordinary power they confer.

The exercise of free will is very much the exception rather than the rule. The vast majority of people simply assume that when you are faced with death, you *have to* become frightened. When people threaten to harm you, you *have to* hate them. These defensive reactions are conditioned into our egos from early childhood, but they are grounded in our biology as well. It doesn't seriously occur to most people to *try* to love their "enemies." When we use our free will to center our minds in peace and offer unconditional love to everyone, we become invulnerable, but few people realize that this is so.

A Son of God can recognize his power in one instant and change the world in the next. That is because, by changing his mind, he has changed the most powerful device that was ever given him for change.
—*A Course in Miracles*

The Key to Miraculous Invulnerability

If free will guarantees everyone's right to decline to become involved in harmful interactions, how exactly does this work? Let us consider the case of Dona—the woman who was stalked to an isolated laundry room by a rapist.

You will recall that Dona mentally conveyed to her would-be assailant that the rape he had envisioned was not "for her"—that he had "the wrong person." Without judging him, or his desire to rape *someone*, she made it clear that *she* was not prepared to undertake the role of victim in the exploitative interaction he proposed. According to mystics, when someone exercises free will to release judgment and opt out of a harmful situation as Dona did, their word is law. It leaves a would-be assailant to either give up on the assault or to recruit someone else to play the complementary victim role.

Free will means that a victimizer cannot proceed without some minimal mental cooperation from the intended victim. First of all, the person being attacked must consent to regard their mutual interaction *as* an attack. If the intended victim decides to treat belligerent behavior as a call for love—as Phil did when the drunk threatened to punch him—no business will result.

Further, the intended victim must also agree to play by some mutually acceptable rules with respect to what is possible. People like Jeanne, who maintain that it is not possible to rape them, or like Dona, who insist upon turning into towering giants, are making up rules of their own as they go along. What is a rapist supposed to do with a victim who can't be raped, or one twice his size? It just isn't fair!

Invulnerability

When we drop judgment and reinstate our minds in unconditional love, we are safe, just as we would be if we touched "base" in a children's game. As long as we remain in contact with the base, our opponents cannot touch us. In the same way, God ensures our safety as long as we abide in love.

This means that a person resting in unconditional love is quite literally invulnerable. Spiritual traditions throughout the world regard fearlessness, compassion, and unshakable inner peace as the identifying characteristics of enlightened individuals, and these qualities are everywhere believed to confer miraculous protection.

Shamanic Training

One African group traditionally takes young boys suspected of having potential as shamans out into a jungle clearing. The heavily armed elders make noises to attract the attention of a lion and then hide in the trees leaving the child to his fate. If the lion kills the boy, they conclude that he must not have been a shaman.

As an adult, one individual who survived this initiation recalled

202

his encounter with the lion. He had been about three years old at the time and had had no conscious understanding of what was going on. He remembers sitting in some tall grass enjoying the sunshine. When the great beast sauntered up, he was overwhelmed by a sense of its beauty and majesty. Delighted with this magnificent new friend, he gazed into the lion's yellow eyes with wonder and adoration. For what seemed like a long time, the two simply drank each other in. Then the lion turned and went away, and the boy was taken off to be trained as a shaman.

While this method of vocational guidance is a bit heavy-handed for my taste, it is nonetheless clear that these people understand that spiritually aware individuals respond to threats by becoming utterly peaceful, loving, and fearless. Instead of attempting to defend themselves, they take refuge in a meditative state. As *A Course in Miracles* succinctly puts it, "love without attack" is the necessary and sufficient condition for miracles.[21]

If people are safe whenever they decide against attacking others through judgment, it also means that no one can truly be victimized against his or her will. Yet it certainly seems as though people *can be* hurt against their will. What is going on?

Willing Versus Wishing

It may be useful here to make a distinction between *willing* and *wishing*. *Wishing* is a weak and erratic activity engaged in by the ego—the part of our mind that believes in the physical illusion. Because the ego is split into many parts, the wishes of one ego state frequently conflict with those of others. For example, "I wish they would make me president of the company" may coexist with "I wish I had more time for my family," and "I wish I didn't have so many responsibilities."

Willing, on the other hand, is the expression of a unified purpose. Mystics say that we create whatever we wholly desire—whatever we will without conflict or reservation. Were the people who experienced deliverance "willing" their escapes, or merely "wishing" for them? Let us take a closer look at Dona's case.

In the moment in which she locked eyes with her antagonist, Dona recognized that she *used to* think there could be some psychological gain in casting herself as the victim of a brutal man. Perhaps this anticipated benefit involved sympathy from others, or self-pity, or the possibility of later manipulating the victimizer through guilt. We really do not know.

But whatever the motivation had been, in the time that had passed since she had been mistreated by her stepfather, Dona had grown to realize that being a victim no longer offered anything she wanted. She was through being exploited, and nothing this man could do was going to change that.

This is unified purpose. This is the exercise of free will. Dona understood that she had a *choice* about how to respond to her would-be assailant, and she also realized that nothing on earth was going to make her respond to him as a victim from a position of fear or anger. As far as Dona was concerned, this man might have the power to injure her body, but he could not dominate her mind unless she let him. And she was not about to let him.

Notice that had Dona become frightened or angry, she would have been interpreting her position in the same way as her attacker. This would mean unwittingly cooperating with him in selecting a possible future in which he had the power to hurt her. Instead, she created a personal reality where her would-be assailant was no match for her. And because the focused power of Dona's peacefully united will was so much stronger than the weak and confused wishes of the rapist, she succeeded in turning the tables and dominating *his* mind. A hulking thug was induced to scramble out of the way before this petite young woman walked right over him!

Elizabeth's interaction with the veteran who abducted her at knifepoint illustrates the same point. After going into a state of inner peace, Elizabeth was able to calmly reduce this highly trained killer to a sweating, baffled, emotional wreck. She simply refused to entertain the idea that he could possibly hurt her, and he was unable to actualize that possible future without her mental co-operation.

The fact that these women were not as *physically* powerful as the men who intended to hurt them was irrelevant. Mind is the creative force. Faced with a total lack of mental agreement about what could, and would, happen between them, these men could not proceed

The bottom line is that if you are coming from the level of your ego, you may *wish* for deliverance, and even *pray* for deliverance, but you cannot *will* deliverance. Willing presupposes a mind that has released judgment and is united in inner peace. No one who is fearful or angry is in a position to will anything.

Further, since our higher power refuses to interfere with our freedom of choice, it can only help us by guiding us in the correct use of our will. God will not remove dangerous judgmental thoughts we prefer to entertain. This means that even prayer may not work for people who cling to their ego's point of view.

The thoughts of people identified with their egos are riddled with judgment. As a result, they often mistakenly pray for vengeance, or ascendency over others, rather than for peace. God, however, cannot side with one person over another, or grant an unloving prayer. All things are possible when a happy outcome all around is our only goal, but miracles cannot be accessed by those who prefer to see themselves as the embattled victims of "wicked" people who "deserve" punishment. The self-righteous and vindictive are on their own. They have not properly invited divine intervention.

Choosing a Better Future

If our thoughts structure our perception of reality, then our present interpretation of a situation is a choice point, branching off into many possible futures. The paths we choose in the confidence that peace and love are justified lead on to good fortune.

The ones we select out of fear, resentment, sadness, indignation, and guilt take us downward into conflict and loss. It is as if there are two worlds—one heavenly and the other hellish. Through our thoughts, we choose which one to live in. In the following selection, psychotherapist Jacquelyn Small explains the way fear and anger create the illusion of an unrewarding world.[40]

> My consciousness, for this moment in time, is residing in a world that I created, where all negativity about this particular subject hangs out! Until I choose to shift out of this "place," this negativity builds upon itself, attracting more just like it, and I can become overwhelmed. If I opt for a positive experience, I *ascend* into another universe that immediately cooperates, and instantly, forces begin moving to manifest a positive result. And as the positive gains momentum, I find myself feeling wonderful, delighted by the beautiful world about me.[40]

Every moment offers an opportunity to choose again. Let us take a closer look at this process of choice through which our personal reality is created.

Manifesting Physical Reality

The dynamic African-American preacher Reverend Ike makes an illuminating analogy between attention and money. He points out that every person has an equal capacity for "paying" attention, and that from this point of view, we all have equal power to actualize our will. What makes the difference in our fortunes is *what* we elect to pay attention *to*.

In Reverend Ike's amusing monetary metaphor, we actually "purchase" experiences for ourselves by "paying" attention to them. We quite literally "buy into" different illusions. The attention that purchases an experience of danger or rejection is no different from the attention that purchases an experience of peace or love. The content of the illusion is different, but the method by which our minds bring it into physical manifestation is the same.

Reverend Ike points out that successful individuals usually display a resourceful, "can-do" attitude that makes short work of obstacles. Whether they attribute their good luck to their own abilities or to the power of God acting through them, they nevertheless invest attention and belief in the idea that there is a power within that can overcome every difficulty. They believe that they deserve to succeed and confidently work toward a possible future in which they get what they try for. As a result, a happy outcome soon manifests in their lives.

Using precisely the same creative process to produce a different result, we may decide to indulge the idea that we are someone's victim, temporarily enjoying the feeling of righteous indignation we get in complaining about injustices. However, unbeknownst to us, our thoughts are relentlessly calling up their likeness from the implicate order.

Without realizing it, each of us is continually placing a demand on the universe to prove that our chosen point of view is justified by the facts. When I say, "I can handle this," or "I am sick and tired," or "There is no justice in the world," the universe automatically arranges my physical circumstances in such a way as to make my beliefs true in my experience. By paying attention to only those aspects of a situation that support my preconceived ideas, I create for myself a private illusion in which things happen according to my convictions. Then, sure enough, in *my* world you *can't* beat City Hall, and men *do* only want "one thing."

This means that we are all living in different worlds, where different kinds of things occur. What is realistic in one person's universe is out of the question in another's. For example, I will never forget a woman named Nancy, with whom I used to work. She expressed wistful envy over my account of an enjoyable trip to a distant city.

"You have some vacation time coming," I reminded her. "Why don't you go there yourself?"

"Oh!" Nancy replied in a shocked tone. "I couldn't do that! If I left town, everyone would think I had gone away to have an abortion!"

The idea that *anyone* would make such a bizarre association would simply never have crossed my mind, but this woman was living in a private reality where "everyone" would leap at an opportunity to condemn her. This was one scary little universe she had going, and I was glad that I was not obliged to live there myself.

The idea that our thoughts determine what happens to us accounts for both the continuity we ordinarily experience as well as the "miraculous" discontinuity that is possible. Most of us allow our beliefs to be molded by external influences, such as family, culture, religion, and education. By always thinking and reacting as we have been conditioned to do, we continually access the same sorts of outcomes from the infinite possibilities available within the implicate order. In this manner, we produce for ourselves the experience of a stable, predictable world, although not necessarily a rewarding one.

If the spiritual view is correct, then there is a supernatural power within our minds that can perform miracles to support and protect us when our minds are at peace. Some teachers have compared this power to a genie that supplies our every need. All that is necessary to access this miraculous help is that we peacefully rely upon the promptings of love, rejecting the idea that judgment— and its attendant fear and anger—is ever justified. The following excerpts from Swami Paramahansa Yogananda's *Autobiography of a Yogi* provides some delightful examples of the way our higher power can take care of us when we rely upon it in all things.

The Lord Will Provide

Swami Yogananda, at the time an adolescent called by his boyhood name "Mukunda," was determined to quit school to go and study with his guru. His family was equally determined that he must go to college and become a businessman. Here, Mukunda's brother Ananta seeks to prove to him the folly of pursuing a spiritual life.

"So you feel quite independent of Father's wealth." Ananta's gaze was innocent as he resumed the barbs of yesterday's conversation.

"I am conscious of my dependence on God."

"Words are cheap! Life has shielded you thus far. What a plight if you were forced to look to the Invisible Hand for your food and shelter! You would soon be begging in the streets."

"Never! I would not put faith in passers-by rather than in God! He can devise for His devotee a thousand resources besides the begging bowl."

"More rhetoric! Suppose I suggest that your vaunted philosophy be put to a test in this tangible world?"

Ananta challenges Mukunda, and his fellow disciple Jitendra, to go to the city of Brindaban without a single rupee for food or for their return train fare, and with the restrictions that they must not beg for food or money, nor reveal their predicament to anyone. Ananta, confident that his naive little brother is about to learn a valuable lesson, says that if they do not miss any meals and are able to return before midnight, he will allow Mukunda to initiate him as his disciple. The boys accept the challenge.

Jitendra maintained a lugubrious silence as the train covered the miles. Finally he bestirred himself; leaning over, he pinched me painfully on a tender spot.

"I see no sign that God is going to supply our next meal!"

"Be quiet, doubting Thomas; the Lord is working with us."

"Can you also arrange that He hurry? Already I am famished merely at the prospect before us. I left Banaras to view the Taj mausoleum, not to enter my own!"

"Cheer up, Jitendra! Are we not to have our first glimpse

of the sacred wonders of Brindaban! I am in deep joy at the thought of treading the ground hallowed by the feet of Lord Krishna."

The door of our compartment opened; two men seated themselves. The next train stop would be the last.

"Young lads, do you have friends in Brindaban?" The stranger opposite me was taking a surprising interest.

"None of your business!" Rudely I averted my gaze.

"You are probably flying away from your families under the enchantment of the Stealer of Hearts.* I am of devotional temperament myself. I will make it my positive duty to see that you receive food, and shelter from this overpowering heat."

"No, sir, let us alone. You are very kind; but you are mistaken in judging us to be truants from home."

No further conversation ensued; the train came to a halt. As Jitendra and I descended to the platform, our chance companions linked arms with us and summoned a horse cab.

We alit before a stately hermitage, set amidst the evergreen trees of well-kept grounds. Our benefactors were evidently known here; a smiling lad led us without comment to a parlor. We were soon joined by an elderly woman of dignified bearing.

"Gauri Ma, the princes could not come." One of the men addressed the ashram hostess. "At the last moment their plans went awry; they send deep regrets. But we have brought two other guests. As soon as we met on the train, I felt drawn to them as devotees of Lord Krishna."

"Good-by, young friends." Our two acquaintances walked to the door. "We shall meet again, if God be willing."

"You are welcome here." Gauri Ma smiled in motherly fashion. "You could not have come on a better day. I was expecting two royal patrons of this hermitage. What a shame if my cooking had found none to appreciate it!"

*Hari; an endearing name by which Sri Krishna is known to his devotees.

The pleasant words had a surprising effect on Jitendra: he burst into tears. The "prospect" he had feared in Brindaban was turning out as royal entertainment; his sudden mental adjustment proved too much for him. Our hostess looked at him with curiosity, but without remark; perhaps she was familiar with adolescent quirks.

Lunch was announced; Gauri Ma led the way to a dining patio, spicy with savory odors. She vanished into an adjoining kitchen.

I had been premeditating this moment. Selecting the appropriate spot on Jitendra's body, I gave him a pinch as painful as the one he had given me on the train.

"Doubting Thomas, the Lord works—in a hurry, too!"

A sumptuous meal consumed, Jitendra returns to doubt. The dinner was just a lucky fluke. How will they see Brindaban or return to Ananta's without money?

"You forget God quickly, now that your stomach is filled." My words, not bitter, were accusatory. How short is human memory for divine favors! No man lives who has not seen some of his prayers granted.

"I am not likely to forget my folly in venturing out with a madcap like you!"

"Be quiet, Jitendra! The same Lord who fed us will show us Brindaban, and return us to Agra."

A slight young man of pleasing countenance approached at rapid pace. Halting under our tree, he bowed before me.

"Dear friend, you and your companion must be strangers here. Permit me to be your host and guide."

It is scarcely possible for an Indian to pale, but Jitendra's face was suddenly sickly. I politely declined the offer.

"You are surely not banishing me?" The stranger's alarm would have been comic in any other circumstances.

"Why not?"

CREATING MIRACULOUS SOLUTIONS

"You are my guru." His eyes sought mine trustfully. "During my midday devotions, the blessed Lord Krishna appeared
in a vision. He showed me two forsaken figures under this
very tree. One face was yours, my master! Often have I seen
it in meditation. What joy if you accept my humble services!"

Their benefactor takes the boys on a tour of various shrines
and prevails upon them to accept his gift of sweetmeats and a bun-
dle of rupee notes. Mukunda repays him by initiating him in Kriya
Yoga. The two "Cinderellas" return before midnight to shower
Ananta's table with rupees.

"Jitendra, the truth!" Ananta's tone was jocular. "Has not
this youngster been staging a hold-up?"
But as the tale was unfolded, my brother turned sober,
then solemn.
"The law of demand and supply reaches into subtler
realms than I had supposed." Ananta spoke with a spiritual
enthusiasm never before noticeable. "I understand for the first
time your indifference to the vaults and vulgar accumulations
of the world."
Late as it was, my brother insisted that he receive diksha
[instruction] into Kriya Yoga. The "guru" Mukunda had to
shoulder, in one night, the responsibility for two unsought
"disciples."[37]

Notice that even as an adolescent, Yogananda had learned to
rely upon God in all things. He received miracles constantly because he remained peaceful and loving at all times and because
he confidently *expected* them. Yogananda trusted that he—and indeed everyone—was being watched over by a loving and generous higher power. Extensive experience had convinced him that
there was an invisible hand that lovingly arranged to fulfill his
every need.

212

15

Your Miraculous Invulnerability

Though a thousand fall at your side,
ten thousand at your right hand,
you yourself will remain unscathed.
                                    —Psalm 91:**7**

If a relentlessly loving person is literally invulnerable, then unconditional love is the ultimate form of self-defense. This has led to the study of martial arts as a spiritual discipline in the East. In martial arts such as kung fu, aikido, and karate, physical combat provides a laboratory for learning the fearless, peacefully alert, intuitively attuned state of mind involved in advanced spiritual awareness. It is understood that, in any contest, whichever individual has the greater ability to remain calm and loving in the face of danger will prevail. Brute strength and physical skills are of decidedly secondary importance.

The consummate martial artist uses his or her skills only in the defense of self or others—never to attack or dominate. Focused in one-pointed awareness, "peaceful warriors" tune in to intuition and seem to know what their opponents are going to do before they know themselves. Somehow, the spiritual adept is always poised to respond with minimal effort and maximal result.

The concept of a *peaceful warrior* may initially seem like a contradiction in terms to some Westerners, but it will be familiar to

213

many through an inspiring book called *Way of the Peaceful Warrior* by Dan Millman.[41] As Millman explains, personal power is appropriately cultivated and expressed through self-mastery rather than by dominating others. It involves the use of strength to protect, rather than to terrorize or exploit. The peaceful warrior endeavors not to fight at all, but when combat is necessary he or she is fearless and utterly efficient.

Consider the example of the American soldier Alvin York. Many readers will remember the popular movie called *Sergeant York*, in which Gary Cooper portrayed this simple man who became the most decorated hero of World War I.

Sergeant York

Alvin York was a "hillbilly" who had been much addicted to drinking and brawling before a spiritual experience turned his life around. Transformed by his new sense of personal connection to God, he humbly sought the forgiveness of people he had offended and began to pursue a life of sobriety, rigorous honesty, and total nonviolence. When World War I broke out and his neighbors were enlisting, York applied for Conscientious Objector status.

However, because his religious sect was a small one, without an established tradition of nonviolence, he was denied a deferment. Drafted into the army, York had to decide whether or not to serve. He meditated intensively upon his conflicting responsibilities to God and his country, and he ultimately concluded that it would not necessarily be immoral to kill in a situation where killing a few people was the only way to save many lives.

When York's unit was pinned down in the open by German forces, this nonviolent man faced the very situation he had decided might justify violence. Turning within for guidance, he was moved to take matters into his own hands. The slaughter must be stopped. York directed his men to remain under cover as much as possible, while he crept off to work his way behind enemy lines.

This uneducated mountain man now pitted his hunting skills

against the vastly superior resources of the German army. Years spent stalking game for food had taught him to move silently and remain invisible to his prey. The extraordinary marksmanship that had won him prizes in turkey shoots at home now enabled him to pick off German snipers, and systematically destroy their seemingly impregnable pillboxes.

The Germans had no defense against this silent and deadly opponent behind their own lines. They became frightened and confused. As one soldier after another fell to the invisible assassin, they concluded that they were being attacked from all sides. When York called out to them that they were surrounded and demanded their surrender, they were quite prepared to believe that it was so. By the time the dust cleared, Alvin York had single-handedly won the battle and personally captured nearly a thousand enemy soldiers!

Sergeant York's feat was hailed as a miracle by many. He was awarded the Congressional Medal of Honor in this country, as well as the highest honors of England and France. With characteristic modesty, York maintained that he had only done what anyone else would have done in the same circumstances.

This phenomenal warrior always regretted the fact that he had had to kill so many Germans. Despite the fact that he was a poor man, he refused to profit from his hero status after the war by accepting money for commercial endorsements. To his way of thinking, killing people might sometimes be necessary, but it was not something to brag about.

Sergeant York provides a wonderful example of a peaceful warrior. He did not hate or fear the Germans; he simply wanted to prevent them from slaughtering his exposed comrades. Single-handedly, this conscientious man did what scores of well-armed soldiers had not been able to do. And while York did kill a number of people in the process, it is clear that he saved many more lives—both allied and German—by quickly ending the battle and taking hundreds of prisoners. Both sides rationalized their glorious war with the idea that God was on their side, but God—as always—was guiding the hand of the man who loved his enemies and only wanted to stop the violence.

Resolving Conflict Peacefully

People who follow the path of the peaceful warrior find that most conflicts can be resolved without bloodshed. Actual combat is the exception rather than the rule. The following account written by Terry Dobson and reprinted in the book *How Can I Help*, by Ram Dass and Paul Gorman, provides another extraordinary insight into the peaceful, compassionate, consciousness that is considered the "secret" of success in martial arts.[42] Notice how closely this account corresponds to the deliverance experiences we have been discussing. Here, as there, the "enemy" is not bested in physical combat, but rather quietly transformed into a friend.

Aikido in Action

Here Terry Dobson describes a moving experience from his travels in Japan.

The train clanked and rattled through the suburbs of Tokyo on a drowsy spring afternoon. Our car was comparatively empty—a few housewives with their kids in tow, some old folks going shopping. I gazed absently at the drab houses and dusty hedgerows.

At one station the doors opened, and suddenly the afternoon quiet was shattered by a man bellowing violent, incomprehensible curses. The man staggered into our car. He wore laborer's clothing, and he was big, drunk, and dirty. Screaming, he swung at a woman holding a baby. The blow sent her spinning into the laps of an elderly couple. It was a miracle that the baby was unharmed.

216

Terrified, the couple jumped up and scrambled toward the other end of the car. The laborer aimed a kick at the retreating back of the old woman but missed as she scuttled to safety. This so enraged the drunk that he grabbed the metal pole in the center of the car and tried to wrench it out of its stanchion. I could see that one of his hands was cut and bleeding. The train lurched ahead, the passengers frozen with fear. I stood up.

I was young then, some twenty years ago, and in pretty good shape. I'd been putting in a solid eight hours of Aikido training nearly every day for the past three years. I liked to throw and grapple. I thought I was tough. The trouble was, my martial skill was untested in actual combat. As students of Aikido, we were not allowed to fight.

"Aikido," my teacher had said again and again, "is the art of reconciliation. Whoever has the mind to fight has broken his connection with the universe. If you try to dominate people, you are already defeated. We study how to resolve conflict, not how to start it."

I listened to his words. I tried hard. I even went so far as to cross the street to avoid the Chimpira, the pinball punks who lounged around the train stations. My forbearance exalted me. I felt both tough and holy. In my heart, however, I wanted an absolutely legitimate opportunity whereby I might save the innocent by destroying the guilty.

"This is it!" I said to myself as I got to my feet. "People are in danger. If I don't do something fast, somebody will probably get hurt."

Seeing me stand up, the drunk recognized a chance to focus his rage. "Aha!" he roared. "A foreigner! You need a lesson in Japanese manners!"

I held on lightly to the commuter strap overhead and gave him a slow look of disgust and dismissal. I planned to take this turkey apart, but he had to make the first move. I wanted him mad, so I pursed my lips and blew him an insolent kiss.

217

"All right!" he hollered. "You're gonna get a lesson." He gathered himself for a rush at me.

A fraction of a second before he could move, someone shouted, "Hey!" It was earsplitting. I remember the strangely joyous, lilting quality of it—as though you and a friend had been searching diligently for something, and he had suddenly stumbled upon it. "Hey!"

I wheeled to my left; the drunk spun to his right. We both stared down at a little, old Japanese man. He must have been well into his seventies, this tiny gentleman, sitting there immaculate in his kimono. He took no notice of me, but beamed delightedly at the laborer, as though he had a most important, most welcome secret to share.

"C'mere," the old man said in an easy vernacular, beckoning to the drunk. "C'mere and talk with me." He waved his hand lightly.

The big man followed, as if on a string. He planted his feet belligerently in front of the old gentleman, and roared above the clacking wheels, "Why the hell should I talk to you?" The drunk now had his back to me. If his elbow moved so much as a millimeter, I'd drop him in his socks.

The old man continued to beam at the laborer. "What'cha been drinkin'?" he asked, his eyes sparkling with interest. "I been drinkin' sake," the laborer bellowed back, "and it's none of your business!" Flecks of spittle spattered the old man.

"Oh, that's wonderful," the old man said, "absolutely wonderful! You see, I love sake too. Every night, me and my wife (she's seventy-six, you know), we warm up a little bottle of sake and take it out into the garden, and we sit on an old wooden bench. We watch the sun go down, and we look to see how our persimmon tree is doing. My great-grandfather planted that tree, and we worry about whether it will recover from those ice storms we had last winter. Our tree has done better than I expected, though, especially when you consider the poor quality of the soil. It is gratifying to watch when we take our sake and go out to enjoy the evening—even when it rains!" He looked up at the laborer, eyes twinkling.

As he struggled to follow the old man's conversation, the drunk's face began to soften. His fists slowly unclenched. "Yeah," he said. "I love persimmons, too . . . " His voice trailed off.

"Yes," said the old man, smiling, "and I'm sure you have a wonderful wife."

"No," replied the laborer. "My wife died." Very gently, swaying with the motion of the train, the big man began to sob. "I don't got no wife, I don't got no home, I don't got no job. I'm so ashamed of myself." Tears rolled down his cheeks; a spasm of despair rippled through his body.

Now it was my turn. Standing there in my well-scrubbed youthful innocence, my make-this-world-safe-for-democracy righteousness, I suddenly felt dirtier than he was.

Then the train arrived at my stop. As the doors opened, I heard the old man cluck sympathetically "My, my," he said, "that is a difficult predicament, indeed. Sit down here and tell me about it."

I turned my head for one last look. The laborer was sprawled on the seat, his head in the old man's lap. The old man was softly stroking the filthy, matted hair.

As the train pulled away, I sat down on a bench. What I had wanted to do with muscle had been accomplished with kind words. I had just seen Aikido tried in combat, and the essence of it was love. I would have to practice the art with an entirely different spirit. It would be a long time before I could speak about the resolution of conflict.[42]

The narrator of this story recognizes the essence of aikido in the old man's actions, although this elderly Japanese may very well have known little or nothing about martial arts per se. The miraculous power of unconditional love appears to be a "secret" that has been discovered throughout the world by educated and un-

219

educated people alike. When we use it, dangerous "enemies" can be miraculously disarmed by small children, ballerinas, and frail old men. Nevertheless, the courage, awareness, and self-mastery that the peaceful altered state reflects remain the crowning achievements of a human lifetime.

Ahimsa [infinite love, nonviolence] is a weapon of matchless potency. It is the summum bonum of life. It is an attribute of the brave; in fact it is their all. It does not come within the reach of the coward. It is no wooden or lifeless dogma but a living and lifegiving force. It is the special attribute of the soul.
— Mohandas Gandhi

Unconditional Love in Tiananmen Square

He does not contend, and for that very reason no one under heaven can contend with him.
—Tao Te Ching

Wang Wei Lin

My chapter on miraculous invulnerability would not feel complete without some mention of the Chinese youth Wang Wei Lin, who faced down a tank in Tiananmen Square during the 1989 student revolt in Beijing. Many of us who watched the spectacle unfold on videotape will never forget this young man's courage. The soldiers had orders to run down any demonstrators who got in their way, and had been doing so. But this particular student seemed utterly oblivious to danger as he stepped in front of a tank and ordered it to halt.

Blocked by the shouting, gesticulating student, the driver of the tank hesitated, and then stopped. He tried repeatedly to steer around the young man, but whichever way the tank moved, the demonstrator simply stepped in front of it again. The youth seemed almost to be *dancing* with the tank—man and machine moving together in a bizarre and deadly tango. Finally Wang Wei Lin climbed up onto the tank itself. He pounded on the steel plating and seemed determined to gain entry. I expected to see the young man shot, or run down at any moment, but eventually other demonstrators broke the stalemate. They ran out of the crowd, seized the student, and carried him away to safety.

Witnesses at the scene later reported that Wang Wei Lin had not been yelling accusations or threats, but rather calling to the tank driver to come out and talk with him. Like my deliverance subjects, he had met aggression with love, and treated an "enemy" like a misguided brother. I am personally convinced that he was acting under the direction of his higher power and that he was protected by a miracle.

Like other Chinese youths, Wang Wei Lin had almost certainly been raised to be an atheist. Nevertheless, his lack of religious convictions did not make the slightest difference to his ability to access a miracle. What clearer evidence could we have that true spirituality is not a matter of saying religious-sounding things, or being a dues-paying member of the "right" church? It begins and ends with the willingness to express nothing but unconditional love. Since unconditional love can be as real to atheists and agnostics as it is to religious people, miracles occur in modern China as easily as in ancient Jerusalem, the mountains of Tibet, or the streets of Los Angeles.

If inner peace can make us invulnerable to attack by others, might it not also protect us against attack from within our own bodies? In the next chapter, we will consider some of the ways people have used miracle mindedness to heal themselves physically.

16

Miracles of Healing

'Tis as dangerous to be sentenced by a Physician as a Judge.

— Sir Thomas Browne

The miraculous safety that unconditional love provides does not mean that the body of a truly spiritual person will never die. Souls live forever, but bodies do not. We are all going to lay down our physical forms sometime, and miracles of deliverance cannot be used to prolong physical existence indefinitely.

The evidence from numerous deliverance stories suggests that if you achieve the peaceful, compassionate, detached, state of consciousness that constitutes "miracle mindedness," your higher power *will* help you. However, the nature of that help is not necessarily predictable.

If it is not your time to leave the physical plane, divine help may take the form of a narrow escape, as it did for those who shared their stories of deliverance. If it *is* your time to go, God's help may come in the form of an easy transition out of the body and a smooth translation to a joyful afterdeath experience. Even when divine intervention does not prolong our existence, it may nevertheless improve the quality of our life by showing us how to heal our relationships and find a sense of meaning in our suffering.

For example, the Frenchwoman Elizabeth Paige spoke with on the Greek island of Páros died of cancer not long after their conversation.[5] Yet, from her deathbed she reached out to express her gratitude to Ms. Paige for helping to restore her ability to love and forgive. This woman seemed to feel that peace of mind was a treasure in and of itself, even if it did not prevent her death. Inviting divine intervention insures the best outcome, but the "best outcome" is not always that life continue in its present form.

Indeed, even if perfect miracle mindedness *did* render us completely invulnerable to accidents, assaults, and illnesses, that would just mean that death would eventually have to come to us in some other form. The passing of Swami Paramahansa Yogananda in 1952 can serve as an illustration.[37]

Yogananda's Death

When Paramahansa Yogananda realized that his work on earth was done, he held a banquet for his followers at the Biltmore Hotel in Los Angeles. After completing his after-dinner speech, and inviting his guests to take some final photographs, Yogananda went into meditation for the last time and left his body, never to return. Among yogis, this final, conscious exit from the body is called "taking mahasamadhi." Physical death does not necessarily have to be violent or painful for those who have given up all investment in suffering.

The Healing Effects of Inner Peace

If it is true that our mind creates our body, then when our thoughts no longer sustain a disease process, the illness should disappear. However, while this is "simple," it is not necessarily "easy." It is one thing to rapidly shift gears in an emergency to derail an accident or an assault, but quite another to sustain the ongoing sense of inner peace needed to reverse a serious illness.

Holding onto inner peace may be especially difficult in the case of disease, because the danger usually does not pass away quickly. Sick people may find it all too easy to become discouraged when their constructive efforts are not rewarded by immediate and permanent relief. Besides, pain and disability can be depressing in and of themselves. Negative thoughts undoubtedly contribute to illness, but it is equally true that illness is conducive to negative thoughts.

If our health is being influenced by our thoughts on a moment-to-moment basis, conflicted thinking can be expected to produce variable results. This means that the sporadic episodes of peaceful, miracle mindedness that prevent an accident or an assault may not be sufficient to produce permanent and complete healing. Each time we lapse back into negative mental patterns we may create the same problem for ourselves all over again.

The difference between temporary change and permanent healing is clearly illustrated by the following account.

Lou

Some years ago I was experiencing recurring concern about a friend who had AIDS. Lou had been a psychology student at the graduate school where I taught but had had to drop out as his illness worsened. I had not seen him in some months and had only spoken with him a few times on the phone.

Thoughts of Lou kept coming up for me one evening on the way to my meditation group, and I felt directed to lead the others in a visualization in which we mentally gathered together people who were having health problems and poured energy into them. I visualized Lou in the center of the circle and then added a few other people I was aware of who were in need of healing. About a week later I received a call from Lou.

"Carolyn, did you do a healing on me last Tuesday at nine in the evening?" he began.

I had to think about it. Tuesday. That was my meditation night. And nine was about the time we had started the actual meditation. What had we been focusing on last Tuesday, I wondered.

Oh, yes. We had offered healing energy to a number of people, and Lou had been one of my candidates.

"Yes, I guess I did," I replied. "How did you know?"

Lou said that last Tuesday night he had felt so ill that he had gone to bed very early, although he knew that he would not be able to sleep.

"Around nine I felt you come into my room and do a healing on me," Lou went on. "I knew it was you because I meditated with you that one time, and I know what your energy feels like. You did a healing on me, and then I fell into a deep sleep—I actually slept through the night for the first time in months. When I woke up in the morning, all my spots were gone! [He had Kaposi's sarcoma, which mottles the skin.] I felt wonderful—better than I've felt in the last half year. My appetite came back, too, and I've put on fifteen pounds in the past week. I just had to call to thank you!"

Lou was no more surprised by this dramatic result than I was. Many spiritual authorities maintain that our higher power will intuitively prompt us to offer miracles to people who are currently in a position to accept them, just as Jim was impelled to offer healing to Sam on the very day that he decided to leave his fate in God's hands. Clearly, my higher power directed me to send healing to Lou at a moment when he was in a state of miracle readiness.

However, I must also report that Lou's symptoms did eventually return and that he died of AIDS about a year after this incident. It can, of course, be argued that it was merely a coincidence that Lou had a temporary remission that he attributed to the spiritual energy I utilized, at the precise time when I was praying for his healing. However, the possibility also exists that Lou really did receive some miraculous benefit from prayer, but that it was not permanent. Why might even miraculous healing be transitory? And might there be cases where permanent healing is not even desirable? If we want to comprehend why people die in a particular manner, at a particular time, we must first understand why they live in the first place.

Living and Dying

Even entertaining questions about the purpose of life and death will undoubtedly strike some readers as a dramatic departure from a "scientific attitude." Naturalistic science contends that life is an accident, and that to ask "why" is to make the error of attributing a purpose to a purely mechanical process. However, as we have seen, there are spiritually inclined scientists as well as mystics and philosophers who hold that life does have a purpose—that our illusory physical world is actually a school that spiritual beings attend in order to overcome fear and learn to love.

As with any other school, we are ready to leave when we have completed our studies. If we have fully utilized our opportunities and gained all there is for us to gain from the experience, we are ready to move on. Although it may be sad for those who are left behind, such a graduation is timely at any age.

I suspect that this accounts for the extraordinary complacency with which the people who told me of their narrow escapes contemplated the possibility of their own deaths. Looking out on events from the perspective of higher consciousness, they did not feel *ready* to die, but they were *willing* to go, if it was the decision of their higher power that they had completed their learning. Having momentarily broken free of identification with their egos, the prospect of physical death did not appear horrifying but merely somewhat disappointing. Perhaps those who are genuinely ready to leave do not even experience disappointment.

Thus, the spiritual perspective implies that physical death may sometimes be timely, appropriate, and even welcome. For example, many people who have had near-death experiences report that they returned to this life out of a sense of duty and that they eagerly look forward to the time when their work here will be done, so that they can be reunited with loved ones in a nonphysical dimension. Death does not appear to hold any terror for those who have seen it "up close and personal."

Choosing One's Death

Many mystics say that we all actually choose the time and manner of our deaths, although—unlike Yogananda—most of us do not do this consciously.

Edgar Cayce

Many years ago, the great American psychic Edgar Cayce was about to step onto an elevator, when he noticed that there was something peculiar about the people already on board. Looking more closely, Cayce realized that not one of them had an aura. (The *aura* is an emanation of colored light that, according to psychics, permeates and surrounds living bodies.) Cayce had never before seen people walking around without auras, so he stepped back and let the elevator leave without him. A moment later, the cable broke, the car plunged to the bottom of the shaft, and all of the occupants were killed.

The fact that no one on the elevator had an aura suggests that these souls had already left their bodies. Mystics say that when we are ready to end our incarnations, we unconsciously arrange accidents, assaults, and illnesses to dispose of our physical vehicles. A situation such as Cayce experienced, where people preparing to die are unconsciously guided to leave their bodies on an elevator that is about to crash, may be the counterpart of the stories we have discussed where someone who was not ready to die was psychically warned to avoid a potentially fatal situation. It suggests that apparently accidental deaths may actually be planned well in advance at some other level of consciousness. It also suggests that the souls that once inhabited those bodies may have made a safe and painless transition, leaving only unoccupied bodies to go through the process of physical death.

Death Is Not Tragic

Remember, where specific lessons are at issue, a long, easy life is not necessarily more valuable or fulfilling than a very brief or difficult one. Some individuals may enter the physical illusion in order to accomplish learning that is complete within minutes or hours and may die soon after birth, having succeeded in everything they came here to do. Others may die at a ripe old age, having failed to accomplish anything at all.

According to this view, it is possible that Lou's goals in this life included the lessons to be learned in dying of AIDS. Religions the world over say that we choose to face trials and tribulations in order to learn qualities such as courage, patience, forgiveness, and faith. And although it may be difficult to understand, I have heard many AIDS and cancer patients declare that their years of battling their illness were the most rewarding, and meaningful, of their entire lives. Faced with a potential death sentence, some people quickly sort out the important from the trivial and begin experiencing life very intensely. A serious illness can provide the stimulus to heal relationships, grow spiritually, and experience love at levels the individual never imagined possible.

A death that seems tragic from our perspective within the physical illusion may represent a resounding triumph over fear and disability when seen from another level of consciousness. Perhaps people suffering through terminal illnesses might be compared to marathon runners undergoing an agonizing, but self-chosen, test of strength, endurance, and commitment. However difficult it may be to watch a loved one go through such a painful ordeal, free will means that no one has the right to decide for another which challenges to undertake.

Our Thoughts Create Our Reality

If the spiritual perspective is correct, every painful physical condition is being held in place by the conscious and unconscious thoughts we invest with belief. Some illnesses may reflect our unconscious intention to challenge ourselves, but there are also cases where the illness serves no truly useful purpose, and is merely the result of bad mental habits. Our hostile, guilty, and fearful thoughts may manifest as a sickness or a handicap that only seems to justify further resentment and depression. In such cases, healing would depend upon our ability to identify the thoughts that are causing the problem and change our minds about them completely.

Miss America

In the early 1980s, I remember seeing the then-Miss America interviewed on the *Merv Griffin Show*. This guest, who had recently been selected as one of America's most beautiful and accomplished young women, said that this title had been her goal ever since she was old enough to remember. She had always believed that she would someday grow up to be Miss America.

As a young girl, she had suffered through two major automobile accidents, each of which had put her into the hospital for months. Among many other serious injuries, she had had much of the flesh ripped off her face when she was thrown through a windshield and several inches of bone surgically removed after one of her legs was crushed.

Merv marveled at the quality of cosmetic surgery she must have received to restore her face to its current beauty, but the young woman replied that she had never had any plastic surgery at all. The doctors had simply stitched her face together as best they could after the accident. She showed him that, underneath her makeup, her complexion was actually seamed with a network of faint scars.

She recovered beautifully from the accidents except that one leg was now several inches shorter than the other. This caused her to limp and necessitated her wearing a prosthetic shoe. Despite her awareness that people do not become Miss America if they limp through the bathing suit competition in a prosthetic shoe,

229

this young woman never lost her conviction that she would some-day win that title.

After years of living with her problem, Merv's guest said that her spiritual adviser had finally convinced her that God had no reason to want her to suffer with a short leg. When she realized that this must be true, her short leg instantly grew out to the same length as the other one. Despite the surgical, radiological, and photographic evidence that the bone had been removed, and that her injured leg had been significantly shorter, it was now obviously the same length as the other. If I am remembering correctly, she went on to win Miss Congeniality in her first Miss America Pageant, and her Miss America title on her second attempt.

This story beautifully illustrates the miraculous power of a shift in consciousness to literally undo all physical effects of past beliefs. Once she became conscious of her underlying belief that God wanted her to suffer for her sins, this young woman was able to consider it rationally. How could it be that divine love could want one of its creations to suffer? How could she be exempt from forgiveness? She realized that her suffering could not be God's will.

Further, if reality is God's will, how could her disability be part of reality? If God did not will her to have a short leg, and she did not will herself to have a short leg, how could she have a short leg? She couldn't. She didn't.

Have faith in only this one thing, and it will be sufficient; God wills you be in Heaven, and nothing can keep you from it, or it from you.
—A Course in Miracles

A miracle of this sort, where physical "reality" is dramatically changed in an instant, is hard for most people to credit. Yet if the physical world is really only our dream, it is no more difficult to change it totally than it is to change it slightly. When we truly uncover and discard the beliefs that were causing the problem, we yank the very foundations out from under an unwanted physical condition. Lacking any present cause to support its continued existence, such a condition should rapidly disappear.

Permanent Healing Depends Upon Permanent Mental Change

The spiritual view suggests that there are actually two distinct types of healing. The first is temporary, and is based upon trading one illusion for another. People who imagine themselves ill now imagine that a powerful doctor, healer, or drug provides a cure. Or those who have been sick may simply lose interest in the illusion of illness, and occupy their minds with something else instead.

In such cases, people tentatively set aside the mental conflict that has been causing illness, without recognizing the significance of what they have done. They relax, cheer up, and hope for the best. They take a renewed interest in life. This shift to a more engaged and optimistic outlook manifests as relief from physical symptoms.

Many readers will be familiar with instances where people recovered quickly from chronic, or supposedly terminal, conditions after life handed them an interesting new assignment. For example, the grandmother of my friend Samantha was bedridden with rheumatoid arthritis. She felt very much a helpless victim of this disease until her daughter skipped out, leaving three young grandchildren in her care. This elderly woman, who had never expected to walk again, was up and doing in no time. She lived a long and productive life, and the arthritis, which had once virtually immobilized her, was relegated to the role of "darned nuisance."

However, this trading of one illusion for another leaves a person open to relapse. If we are healed when we change our dreams, our illness may be recreated if our thoughts return to the original pattern. For example, it may be that Lou was open to the possibility of miraculous healing for a time, but the remission was maintained only as long as he continued to hold his mind aloof from whatever form of discouragement, resentment, or self-rejection was manifesting physically as a viral attack upon his body. Miracles proceed from a peaceful state of consciousness, and if judgmental thoughts are permitted to intrude, we may eventually recreate the problem and wind up back where we started.

The guiltless mind cannot suffer. Being sane, the mind heals the body because it has been healed. The sane mind cannot conceive of illness because it cannot conceive of attacking anyone or anything.

—A Course in Miracles

The Will to Live

For deliverance to occur, the spiritual view implies that the individual must have some important goal in continuing to live. If there are no further obligations to be performed, or lessons to be learned, the person's own higher consciousness would welcome an opportunity to withdraw. None of us would wish to repeat a difficult course of study we had already mastered. In truth, although our egos are desperately afraid of death, *most of us are not really having such a wonderful time here.*

Friedrich Nietzsche said, "He who has a 'why' for living will always find a 'how.'" For example, I have heard of many cases where people in peril decide that they quite simply *cannot* die, because of the effect their death might have on a loved one. It is almost as though such individuals dispassionately review their commitments and discover important unfinished business. Death is not regarded as terrifying—just absolutely out of the question.

Christine

In August 1989, Christine was diagnosed with breast cancer. She underwent a radical mastectomy in September, followed by three rounds of aggressive chemotherapy, but by December she was worse. Just before Christmas, she was rushed to the hospital with pneumonia, and it was discovered that the cancer had metasta-sized to her lungs.

At that point, Christine's cancer specialist, Dr. Jeffrey Scott, was compelled to admit that her prospects were grim. "It's the worst prognosis if someone is getting the best therapy and the cancer comes back. And the lungs are a very bad place for it to come back to. Then it really predicts for doing poorly." He estimated that this patient had less than six months to live.

At Dr. Scott's suggestion, Christine sought a second opinion. However, the new doctor told her she was likely to be dead within three or four months. It was time for Christine to put her affairs in order and make some arrangements for her eight-year-old daugh-ter Rachel.

Throughout the dismal process of diagnosis and treatment, this dying woman had been tormented by worry about her child. Christine knew all too well what it felt like to lose one's family. Except for her daughter, she was alone in the world herself, and she could not bear the thought of leaving Rachel in that position. So great was her distress over this that Dr. Scott began to suspect that her emotional turmoil might be interfering with her response to treatment.

"Christine and I got very close," Dr. Scott reports. "I knew her mother had just died, and that she didn't have any family members that she could feel comfortable leaving Rachel with." One night Dr. Scott discussed his patient's painful dilemma with his wife. The next day this generous man assured Christine that when she died, he and his wife would adopt Rachel and raise her as their own.

"I want to emphasize that we were talking about 'when' she died—not 'if.'" Scott adds. "I thought aggressive chemotherapy might prolong Christine's life, but there was really no question of her getting well again. I never tell anyone that they are going to die unless there is no alternative, but we had to be frank because she had Rachel, and she had to know the score."

Christine's mind was more at ease, now that her physician had promised to provide a loving home for Rachel, but she still could not bear the thought of what her daughter would go through in losing her only parent. Casting about for anything she might try as a last resort, Christine remembered a passage from the Bible that says that if people are ill, the elders of the church should be assembled to pray for them. Since medicine could offer her no hope of a cure, Christine asked the minister of her church if he and some of the other parishioners would assemble and pray for a miracle.

"I grew up Pentecostal," Christine explained, "but I'm a Southern Baptist now, and they don't usually do that. But my minister is a good man, and he said yes. He got some of the deacons together, and some of my friends were there, too. One week before they prayed for me, tests showed that I was covered with cancer."

Dr. Scott supported Christine in her decision to seek miraculous healing, although he insisted that she continue her medical treatment as well. "I know that miracles occur," he told her, "but they don't happen every time. It's important that we use every tool we have."

Christine was in complete agreement. "I knew that God could heal me but that I had to use my head, too. God gives you a brain to work with, and he also guides Dr. Scott's hand."

The members of her congregation had never done anything quite like this before, but under their minister's guidance they willingly gathered to ask God to heal their friend. However, despite their best efforts, Christine had to admit that she did not feel any dramatic change in her condition as a result of the prayer meeting.

A few days later, Christine celebrated a birthday everyone assumed would be her last. The friends who gathered to share this bittersweet occasion presented her with a beautiful cake ablaze with thirty-eight lighted candles. It was time to make a wish and blow them out.

"All I could think about was Rachel," Christine says. "I closed my eyes and made a wish that I would be free of cancer, so that

I could be there for her as she grew up." Then this woman who was recovering from pneumonia, and supposedly dying of lung cancer, drew in a mighty breath and effortlessly blew out every one of the thirty-eight candles!

"I knew that it was a sign from God," Christine laughs. "I must have been healed, or I couldn't have done it. I arranged for a lung scan, and sure enough, my cancer was completely gone!"

Asked what his reaction had been to the discovery that the lung cancer had disappeared, Dr. Scott exclaimed, "Shock! I thought we must have made a mistake. Maybe the breast cancer hadn't really metastasized to the lungs, and somehow it had just been the pneumonia we had been seeing. But we looked back at the biopsy, and it hadn't been a mistake. There's no question that Christine really had advanced, metastatic lung cancer, and there's no doubt that it had completely disappeared a week after she was prayed for.

"I can't explain why she is still here and well four and a half years later," he went on. "If it's a miracle, I don't care, because I'm thrilled. I believe in God, and as a physician I know that things happen that we can't explain."

Christine followed through on her medical treatment, despite the fact that there was no longer any trace of the cancer. Three years later, Dr. Scott had the pleasure of walking his former patient down the aisle, as he gave her away to a new husband. As of this writing in the spring of 1994, Christine continues in good health. She attributes her healing to a miracle, jointly performed by the members of her church and her beloved friend and cancer specialist, Dr. Jeffrey Scott.

Notice all of the features that this story has in common with the other deliverance stories we have discussed. Christine faced the prospect of her own death realistically, but she did not stop trying to find a cure. She was not *afraid* to die, but the prospect of dying was unacceptable because of its implications for her daughter.

Getting Rid of Fear and Anger

We have seen that the will to live is critical to miracles of deliverance. However, the spiritual view also implies that an individual who desires a permanent cure would need to uncover and reject all of the conscious and unconscious attitudes, ideas, and motives that express themselves in the form of disability or disease. These ideas would all be different versions of the belief that fear and anger—and all their variants, such as guilt, resentment, condemnation, shame, remorse, indignation, and so forth—are sometimes justified and appropriate.

Thus, someone might be unambivalent about their desire to survive but continue to harbor a worldview that must inevitably lead to their early demise. It is not that they *want* to die. It is just that they mistakenly choose to continue investing in destructive beliefs and attitudes.

All of these dangerous ideas represent some form of mental attack—either upon ourselves or someone else. Each is grounded in the idea that people can be bad and deserve to suffer for what they have done. But miracles occur when we love *without* attack, if only for a moment. As long as we continue to believe that anyone deserves punishment, miracles will not manifest.

Remember Elizabeth's impulsive desire to give her assailant her phone number? Remember Debra's compassion for the suffering of the terrorists who were about to murder her and her husband? Whatever their feelings about the assault afterward, none of my subjects was focused upon retribution at the moment of deliverance. Each redeemed a bad situation by overlooking the transgressions of a seeming enemy and treating him like someone who still deserved respect and kindness.

According to the spiritual view, the same forgiveness that heals a relationship, when extended to another, heals our own body when it rests upon ourselves. General amnesty is the key to miracles. When we decide to forgive, our peaceful mental state projects instantaneous healing into any situation to which it is applied.

This means that people who remained in this miracle-minded state throughout the day would see miracles sprouting all around them to smooth their path through every situation. Yogananda's experiences in Brindaban provide an excellent example of the way our higher power can tenderly watch over us when we rely upon it in simple faith. However, even folks like those who shared their stories of deliverance—people whose mastery of higher consciousness is not yet total and who utilize unconditional love only at critical moments—will nevertheless see love transform that one situation. If the spiritual view holds true, miracles are the generic solution to all of our problems. However, until we fully grasp this fact, we may reach for them only as a last resort.

The Healing Effects of Inner Peace

Writer Norman Cousins's book *Anatomy of an Illness* traces his cure from a dangerous disease of the connective tissue, partly through the use of humor.[43] During a long hospitalization, Cousins discovered that time spent roaring with laughter over funny films and TV shows paid off in hours of pain-free sleep, increased mobility, and improved blood-test results.

Notice that if it is true that illness results from inner conflict, Cousins's shift into a humorous, carefree state of consciousness should have been expected to produce an improvement in his disease. By watching one amusing show after another, he was nourishing his mind with happy thoughts, and stimulating himself to meditate upon them.

Cousins's account also indicates that when he stopped focusing on funny material, his mind would wander back to its usual concerns, and his pain and disability would gradually return. Clearly, this is an example of the temporary form of healing discussed above—the trading of one illusion for another, more congenial one. Cousins very sensibly decided to spend a great deal of his time in the hospital laughing instead of worrying about his condition, and he attributed his recovery at least partly to this decision. While there is no evidence that he uncovered the unconscious roots of his disease, doesn't it sound as if Cousins intentionally cultivated a peaceful altered state of the sort that saved the people I interviewed?

From the spiritual point of view, unifying the mind in peace gives sick bodies a badly needed rest from the self-torture to which they are being subjected the rest of the time by conscious and unconscious conflictual thoughts. For the moment at least, negativity is not being projected into their bodies and environment. But when people's minds return to their habitual preoccupations, the vacation is over. The disease, which symbolizes their fear, guilt, and resentment, may take up where it left off.

The brief, or even momentary, shift in consciousness achieved by the people I interviewed is probably child's play compared to the extensive and permanent mental revision necessary to heal a "terminal" disease, such as AIDS or some cancers. Nevertheless, the spiritual view maintains that our higher power is always available to direct us through the process, and that healing is within the reach of anyone who truly wants to live and is willing to question and revise every basic assumption. After all, *whose mind is it* that is creating your problems? It is *your* mind, and with considerable hard work you can learn to focus it more productively.

The Relationship Between Miracles and Inner Peace

It should be apparent by now that there is a direct relationship between inner peace and miracles of healing and deliverance. However, it is critically important that we understand the direction of causality in this relationship. Many people who believe in miracles seem to think that they cause inner peace: "If God would only heal me, then I could be happy again." But this is putting the cart before the horse, a bit like saying, "If only my hunger could be satisfied, then I could eat."

The peaceful altered state permits miracles to happen. *Inner*

peace leads to miracles, but miracles may, or may not, lead to inner peace.
As we have seen, some people receive them with neither recognition nor gratitude. Thus, the decision to shift into a loving, peaceful, mental state is the *necessary precondition* for miracles, not their inevitable result.

Similarly, miracles do not produce faith; faith produces miracles. We must trust and follow inner guidance before we will be able to see the positive results. People who say, "Let my higher power prove its existence with a few miracles, and then I will believe in God" have it backward.

All of this means that you can create miracles of healing in your own life by refusing to believe that accidents or diseases can have any power over you. If you are dreaming your body, why not dream it hale and hearty?

But isn't this just neurotic denial, you may be wondering? When we forget about real danger and opt to believe instead that everything is going to turn out all right, aren't we really just "zoning out" and failing to cope? And won't denial lead to somatization, psychopathology, and other serious negative consequences? In the next chapter, we'll explore this important issue in greater detail.

17

To Hope or Not to Hope?

*Hope is the only God common to all men; those who
have nothing more, possess hope still.*

—Thales of Miletus

Readers well versed in psychology will perhaps have noticed certain points of similarity between the behavior of people who experience deliverance and that of neurotic individuals who hide from unpleasant realities through defensive denial. For example, in both cases the person reports a sense of well-being that does not appear to be justified by the facts. Is it really sensible and adaptive to feel calm and self-assured when you are looking down the barrel of a gun?

Further, in the cases of both neurotics and people who report deliverance, measures of autonomic nervous system arousal might tell a very different story about the amount of emotional turmoil the individual was actually experiencing at the physical level. Remember Elizabeth, who felt completely self-possessed while dealing with a knife-wielding assailant, but went into shock afterward? And I developed a phobia after my narrow escape from skidding over the edge of a cliff. Many people who told me of their extraordinary peace and love in the face of danger also said that they had quickly fallen back into fear and anger afterward. Is it possible that what appeared to be inner peace was really just some sort of temporary emotional paralysis induced by extreme terror?

I am suggesting that a peaceful altered state of consciousness

240

protected the people who told me of their narrow escapes. But defensive denial is commonly associated with maladaptive reactions to emergencies that place the individual in even greater danger. Is it possible that these people were simply out of touch with their feelings? Are they best understood as models of miraculous consciousness, or were they just neurotics who got lucky? In order to decide this question, we need to have a better idea of what neurotic denial entails.

Defensive Denial

The term *denial* can be used in more than one sense. In ordinary usage, we deny assertions if we believe them to be objectively false (or if we wish others to think we do). However, it is the psychological usage with which we will be concerned here. Clinically, *denial* refers to a defense mechanism used by neurotics—an unconscious strategy intended to shield them from harsh realities when they feel in danger of being overwhelmed by negative experiences.

Persons resorting to defensive denial unconsciously choose to distort their perception of reality so as to make themselves more comfortable. As a result of this distortion, disturbing emotions are pushed out of awareness. Having consigned the aspect of their minds that knows how upset they really are to oblivion, they feel better. Now they can "truthfully" assert that they are not at all bothered by what is happening. Defensive deniers hide their true feelings *not only from other people, but also from themselves.*

The medical and psychological literatures are filled with well-documented accounts of the problems that people create for themselves when they resort to denial.[44] At the interpersonal level, it is very difficult to work out conflicts with other people when we cannot acknowledge our true feelings. The first step in resolving a problem is to admit that you have one, and this the defensive denier refuses to do.

Further, use of this defense mechanism takes a serious toll on one's health. It has been shown that when emotional turmoil is pushed out of awareness, it will be projected into the body, producing a stressful state of chronic arousal. Thus, defensive denial retards healing from disease and is associated with a high incidence of stress-related illnesses.

Not only does the use of this defense mechanism cause illness, there is also evidence that reversing defensive denial promotes healing. For example, Type A (hard-driving, aggressive) heart attack survivors who learned to acknowledge and express their negative feelings in psychotherapy were *50 percent less likely to experience a second heart attack* than were comparable controls who received only normal medical care. When women with breast cancer shared their feelings with others in group therapy, they lived significantly longer than did patients who lacked this emotional outlet.

Psychotherapy has been shown to facilitate healing from many physical complaints, and one reason for this may be that talking honestly about one's feelings counteracts denial. When we allow ourselves to consciously recognize and voice our emotional distress, it dissipates. As painful thoughts and feelings are aired, arousal within the autonomic nervous system decreases, immune functioning improves, and health-care visits are reduced.

Giving Up

I suspect that one reason denial has so many negative consequences is that people resort to it only when they have already given up. Denial originates in our cognitive appraisal of the situation. If we interpret it as one with which we may be able to cope, we set about taking constructive action. However, if the problem seems overwhelming, we may conclude that there is nothing we can do. Conceding defeat and withdrawing emotionally in order to minimize the pain of an inevitable tragedy, the defensive denier waits passively for the proverbial axe to fall. Unfortunately, this tends to foreclose any possibility of discovering creative solutions.

Giving up can be deadly when it comes to coping with a crisis or fighting off a disease. In his book *Love, Medicine and Miracles,* cancer surgeon Bernie Siegel cites numerous examples of patients dying quickly once their doctors tell them that they have only a few months to live.[6] Individuals with comparable problems survive much longer and sometimes even recover if their doctor does not state that the disease *must* be fatal. It seems that once people accept the idea that there is no hope for them, they yield to the "inevitable." Yet without their acquiescence, an immediate death might not *be* inevitable.

The research cited earlier on spontaneous remission supports this point as well.[7, 8, 9] Those who recover after a terminal diagnosis are often the ones who reject their physician's gloomy predictions and seek out alternative healing methods. Instead of politely withdrawing into defensive denial, they express their negative emotions openly and then mobilize their resources to search for a cure.

Not only does a sense of hope motivate people to seek out valuable new therapies, but the "placebo effect" shows that hope is sometimes curative in and of itself. Patients occasionally make astonishing recoveries from life-threatening illnesses when told that they are receiving a "miracle drug," even though it is only a saline injection or a sugar pill. There is also evidence that people recover more quickly from surgery when the anesthetized patients overhear their doctors and nurses speaking of their satisfaction with the operation and their positive expectations for rapid and complete recovery. It is clear that patients readily accept their doctors' suggestions, and that they frequently act to fulfill their expectations. We sometimes literally live or die because we believe that that is what we are *supposed* to do!

Hope Is Always Appropriate

Individuals who are permitted to hope often find a way out of a desperate situation. Indeed, as the spontaneous remission data indicate, even people who are *not permitted* to hope sometimes hope anyway, and then go on to find a solution where none appeared to exist.

Individuals facing some sort of danger are confronted by a choice: They can continue hoping—and, therefore, trying—or they can decide that hope is no longer appropriate and give up. Which they choose will depend upon their assessment of (1) the situation, (2) their own abilities, and (3) other available resources.

Once we opt to accept the idea that we are helpless, we have a further choice between panic and defensive denial. People who panic express their negative emotions in an uncontrolled, disorganized manner, while those who resort to defensive denial numb out and wait for the end passively. In neither case does the individual search vigorously for solutions. When hope dies, we suspend our efforts to improve our position.

Thus, *defensive denial may be regarded as the silent and chronic form of panic.* Biologically, it is probably the human equivalent of the freezing response seen in some animals. Inaction may be an excellent strategy for a rabbit hiding from a fox, but it is not much use to humans psychologically "hiding" from their cancer.

The alternative to giving up is continuing to hope. But what can one hope for in a situation that is obviously "hopeless"? What but a miracle? When the chips are down and it is apparent that your chances are nil, miracles hold out the possibility that there is still something that might save you. Miracle workers remind themselves that something out of pattern can suddenly occur to reshuffle the deck. Their assailant could have a change of heart. They might find an unconventional cure for their disease. A beaver pond may be waiting for them in the darkness at the bottom of the cliff.

I said earlier that our decision to hope or not depends upon our assessment of the situation, our abilities, and other available resources. God comes under the heading of "other available resources." Miracle workers look the situation over and see no glimmer of light. They survey their own abilities and find no reason for optimism there either. So as a last resort they entertain the possibility that some power greater than themselves might wish them well and intervene on their behalf. Acting on this hope, they disregard fear, suspend their ordinary thought processes, and listen inwardly for inspiration. And when it comes, they act upon it without hesitation. Consider the case of Hannah.

Hannah

The mother of my friend Larry was a Jew who escaped from six different Nazi death camps during the Second World War. Five times Hannah was recaptured, but on her sixth attempt she succeeded in walking all the way to Sweden. This woman lost her whole family to the Holocaust but went on to create a new one in the United States.

Hannah said that it was not really that difficult escaping from the various concentration camps. The guards were not particularly astute, and they weren't expecting trouble. She tried repeatedly to get others to escape with her, but most of her fellow prisoners were afraid of what the dogs and the guards would do to them if they were caught. Hannah pointed out that to stay where they were meant almost certain death, but found that most people were in denial about this. They preferred to take their chances with the evils they knew, rather than face the unknown terrors of flight across enemy territory.

I think that Hannah's story very clearly illustrates the difference between defensive denial and miracle mindedness. When push comes to shove, people who pull off miraculous escapes do not become paralyzed with fear or comfort themselves that everything will turn out all right if they just go along with the program. Nor do they react with hysteria.

Instead, they watch for their opportunities and are ready to take them. Miracle workers regard their illnesses and enemies more as wily opponents to be outwitted than as cruel victimizers to be impotently hated and feared. Rejecting the inevitability of a tragic outcome, people relying upon their higher power figuratively say to the world, a disease, or an enemy, "So, you think you can beat me? Well, go ahead and try. But don't think I'm going to make it easy for you. You may win in the end, but I'm going to give you a run for your money!"

In his book *Head First,* Norman Cousins points out that dangerously ill people who experience unexpected healings and remissions are usually those who regard their illness as a major challenge that will require their full attention.[45] They deny the *inevitability* of a negative outcome, but not its *possibility.* They realistically acknowledge the correctness of the diagnosis and then do everything in their power to improve their chances of survival, knowing all the while that they may not succeed. Yet their very efforts at healing indicate some degree of hope that a new approach can still change things.

Cousins also reports that people who simply deny their diagnosis and try to go on with "business as usual" do not fare well. They do not initiate the medical, psychological, and lifestyle changes that might otherwise make the difference.

Hoping for a Miracle Denies Illusion, Not Reality

It should be clear by now that the value of denial depends upon what you are denying. Miracle workers deny that disaster is inevitable—not that it is possible. They deny that the way things have happened up to this point means that they must continue on the same trajectory.

Hope is always justified. If we are co-creators, this means that a dangerous situation taking shape before us is sustained by our own present thoughts and attitudes. It would be *foolish* to deny that our thoughts have placed us in real danger, but *sensible* to deny that disaster is inevitable. Right up until the moment of death, we are always in a position to opt for inner peace and follow guidance to a miraculous solution. Unfortunately, this may be difficult to do when others are urging us to be "realistic" about our problem. If we do not understand that it *is* realistic to try for a miracle, we will not do so.

The spiritual view holds that no outcome is ever inevitable. This is because the past does not *directly* influence the present or future. Even though our mental actions up to this point have produced very undesirable results, the present is being created *right now*. A person who is truly finished with old and unrewarding ways of thinking is free to start over.

A number of years ago I heard Dr. Gerald Jampolsky tell a story about a patient he had treated whose case seems to illustrate this well.

Gerald Jampolsky

Dr. Jampolsky's patient was a college student who had been blind since birth. A premature baby, her life had been saved by placing her in an environment with high oxygen content, but, sadly, the same treatment had destroyed her retinas.

When she first went to see Dr. Jampolsky, this young woman asked him if he thought she would ever be able to see. He replied that he believed in miracles and that anything was possible, but said he did not feel that that should be the goal of their work together. The focus of their sessions became forgiveness.

It turned out that this young woman was unconsciously carrying a deep sense of grievance against the doctors who had made her blind, against her parents for permitting it to happen, and against all sighted persons for having a gift that had been denied her. Under Jampolsky's guidance, she began to rethink these resentments and to forgive.

As she relinquished one source of grievance after another, her sight began to return. Although there was no physical basis for such a thing to occur, the healing progressed swiftly. This patient was soon able to give up reliance upon her guide dog, and eventually she married and moved away to begin a new life. Just prior to the lecture at which I heard Jampolsky speak, his former patient had called and invited him to lunch. When she picked him up at his office, she was driving her own car. This formerly blind woman now gleefully flaunted a driver's license for uncorrected vision!

Here we see another dramatic example of the way changing our thoughts changes our reality. By giving up her cherished resentments, this young woman surrendered her claim to any emotional payoffs to which her blindness might otherwise have entitled her. In effect, she decided to stop regarding herself as a victim, no longer blaming others for her difficulties, or insisting that those who were "more fortunate" owed her something in compensation for her disability. This decision brought about a miracle. As we shall see in the next chapter, miracles become possible whenever we decide to give up the victim role.

Co-Creating Miracles

Miracles are the result of a collaboration between our own creative ability and divine guidance. When we turn within and attend to our intuition, God offers us a more loving interpretation of our situation—one where terrifying assaults, accidents, and illnesses turn out to be harmless. If we embrace this new interpretation—having faith that it is true and acting in accord with it—it becomes true for us. Ugly scenes dissipate the way nightmares vanish when we awaken.

Defensive deniers regard themselves as helpless victims, and this, in itself, is evidence that they are not accepting their higher power's interpretation of reality. God knows each one of us to be an equally powerful co-creator, with sovereign will. This is the way we were created, and it is the way we remain.

This means that no child of God can ever be weak or helpless. We can certainly imagine for ourselves an illusion in which we are weak and helpless if it pleases us to do so, but even then, our apparent weakness is only further evidence of the sovereign power of our minds to dictate our own physical experience. There are mystics throughout the world who agree that nothing can happen to anyone that they have not imagined for themselves, in the confident belief that it is what they deserve.

This means that to avert a disaster that *we ourselves are imagining into existence*, we must squarely face the fact that it is our own belief that our anger, guilt, fear, resentment, and so forth are justified that lies at the root of the problem. Dr. Jampolsky's blind patient, for example, found herself healed when she took a critical look at her own resentments and withdrew belief from them. If things are going wrong in our lives, it should alert us to search our minds for the unloving thoughts that are causing the trouble.

However, acknowledging negative thoughts is precisely what defensive deniers refuse to do. Instead, they push them out of awareness, where they are unconsciously projected into their physical illusion. This leads to the perception of being attacked from without by rejections, accidents, assaults, and illnesses.

Defensive deniers are misusing their God-given creative power in order to imagine a personal illusion which is punishing. Since they have faith in the illusion they have created, they accept the idea that they are doomed to suffer, withdraw emotionally, and stop trying for a solution. This passive acceptance of an unkind "fate" is a little like locking your plane's controls on autopilot, despite the fact that you do not like the destination for which you are headed.

Detaching From the Ego's Negativity

How can we be sure that the people who reported experiencing a peaceful, altered state of consciousness just before they escaped from danger were not just in denial? *By the very fact that they escaped.* The proof that they had truly divested all negative thoughts

249

of belief lies in the fact that violent possibilities disappeared from their physical illusions. Had negative thoughts still seemed to them to be justified, the projection of those thoughts into the environment would have been automatic, and things would have turned out badly.

However, this does not mean that negativity was absent from the *egos* of our miracle workers, only that at the critical moment, *their minds were not identified with their egos.* According to spiritual thought, the ego *always* believes in the reality of the physical illusion it creates. It *cannot help* believing that fear and anger are justified when it is confronted by the prospect of the death of the body with which it identifies. However, if we are not confusing our *selves* with our egos, *we* will not be unduly disturbed by the prospect of physical death. Spiritual mastery is not about perfecting our egos—which are inherently deluded—but rather about transcending them, to embrace our higher power's view instead.

For example, it is clear from my later phobic response that my ego had been terrified by my near-fatal accident on the Angeles Crest Highway. But while it was occurring, I was fearless because my mind was not identified with the body that was about to plunge over a cliff.

On the later trip to Sedona, I had slipped back into identification with my ego and was tormented by its exaggerated fear of skidding over cliffs on icy, mountain roads. But because I reached for God's help, the message from my higher power on the radio succeeded in reminding me of what was really going on. I was not a weak, frightened creature at the mercy of an unkind fate, but a beloved child of God, protected by miracles. I was once again able to joyfully detach from my ego. Instead of allowing it to project an accident to "prove" how dangerous winter driving can be at the higher elevations, I successfully invited and accepted an experience of divine protection.

Whenever we are distressed by the physical illusion our ego is creating, we have two choices. We can mentally step away from the ego and solicit God's guidance in finding a more benign interpretation of our experience. Or we can continue to identify with the ego's perspective, and then project the fear and anger it provokes back into our physical illusion, causing the situation to go from bad to worse. One strategy leads to miracles and the other, to disaster.

Miracles and the Process of Dying

In the 1960s, Elisabeth Kübler-Ross formulated the following stages that people facing death by disease tend to go through: denial, anger, bargaining, depression, and eventually, acceptance.[46] Later researchers have argued that there is not an invariant progression through these stages—that people may go back and forth among them. Nevertheless, there is general agreement that these are experiences a terminally ill person can expect to have.

I find it interesting that all of these reactions imply a sense of powerlessness. Each one reflects identification with the ego and the fate of the body. These may very well be the stages that people dying of disease typically go through, but notice that they do not appear to characterize "terminally" ill individuals who surprise us by *not* dying.

First of all, like others who experience deliverance, people who achieve spontaneous remissions tend to accept their situations realistically, without denial. It is as though they never seriously imagined that they were going to live forever, in any case. The realization that death may be imminent shocks them, but upon reflection they are quite prepared to believe that such a thing could indeed happen. Again and again, miracle workers reported that their first reaction to danger was, "Oh, I guess maybe I'm going to die now. How about that?"

Nor do miracle workers linger in anger. They typically hold everyone harmless, including the doctors who cannot help them, the loved ones who will survive them, and even, surprisingly, the disease that is about to kill them. I have heard many terminally ill individuals express gratitude for their illness and the things it

251

has taught them. As we saw earlier in our discussion of spontaneous remission, sick people fighting for a miracle may sometimes become annoyed with physicians who behave like prophets of doom, but these momentary flashes of anger do not constitute a "stage."

Further, miracle workers do not attempt to bargain with fate on the theory that if they are extra "good" God, or their disease, may decide to spare them. Indeed, the attitude of people who achieve spontaneous remissions seems to be, "To hell with being good! If I'm going to die anyway, I might as well spend what is left of my life doing what I want to do."

Promising to be extra good implies guilt and an attempt to placate God. But miracle workers seem to be comfortable with their relationship to their higher power and to regard death as simply a fact of life that in no way reflects upon them personally. As far as they are concerned, we are all going to die sometime. If your days are numbered, you might as well live boldly and authentically for whatever time remains. After all, what have you got to lose?

Depression does not characterize miracle workers either. Self-healers tend to maintain an "unreasonably" optimistic attitude and are too busy searching out, and working for, a cure to indulge in extended periods of despondency.

And while they do display some sort of "acceptance" or "surrender," it should not be confused with the kind Kübler-Ross discusses, which causes people to give up and submit to their fate. Miracle workers "accept" their situation in the same sense that one "accepts" a challenge. Now the problem has their full attention. For them, acceptance of a death sentence represents the *beginning* of their struggle for survival, not its end. This attitude is reflected in the maxim, "When the going gets tough, the tough get going."

Miracles Do Not Involve Defensive Denial

Despite a few superficial similarities, the behavior of people who experienced miracles of deliverance does not really resemble that of neurotics. Where neurotics become rigid or disorganized under stress, miracle workers demonstrate extraordinary poise, creativity, and mental flexibility. The folks who told me their stories pushed fear aside not to comfort themselves in their despair but in order to concentrate on finding a way out. Instead of falling apart, or passively acquiescing in their own destruction, they hung in there and kept trying.

This probably accounts for the popular impression that "God helps those who help themselves." People like Hannah, who escaped from the Nazis, display a unique combination of persistence, audacity, and creativity that snatches victory from the jaws of defeat. There is nothing numb, neurotic, or unrealistic about them.

Hoping and *trying*, then, would appear to be activities that clearly distinguish miracle workers from defensive deniers. The bottom line is this: Miracles cannot coexist with a sense of helplessness, hopelessness, and victimization. The spiritual view says that physical life is a dream. Either you are dreaming with your ego that you are being overwhelmed by circumstances beyond your control or you are dreaming along with God that you have resources that may yet turn the trick. These versions of personal reality are mutually exclusive and lead to very different outcomes.

In the next chapter, we will explore the reasons so many of us opt to see ourselves as victims instead of becoming miracle workers. If we want to truly understand why miracles are not more common, we must fully appreciate the subtle attraction that a sense of helpless victimization holds for us.

18

Choosing Miracles
Over Victimhood

*Although others may feel sorry for you, never feel sorry
for yourself: it has a deadly effect on spiritual well-being.
Recognize all problems, no matter how difficult, as
opportunities for spiritual growth, and make the most of
these opportunities.*

—Peace Pilgrim

We have touched upon a number of reasons miracles might
be rare. The most fundamental is that when faced with an overwhelming threat, most of us automatically take refuge behind the
assertion that we are victims. Because of the projective nature of the
physical illusion, this decision can have catastrophic consequences.

Psychological theories designate the *ego* as the aspect of the
mind that is adapted to living in the physical world. Freud said
that the ego begins to develop out of the unconscious mind during infancy. Throughout childhood, our ego uses our personal
experience of the world to learn how things work so that it can
get our needs met most effectively. In one family, the children's
egos might learn to ask politely for the things they need. In another,
operating according to different norms, the children's developing
egos may learn to take what they want when others aren't looking.

By the time we are adults, our egos are the repositories of
a lifetime's accumulated "wisdom" about manipulating the environment to our advantage. And since we were all once helpless and

dependent, most adult egos share a fundamental belief that being helpless has important compensations. As children, we all experienced the easy payoffs dependence upon others can bring. In growing up, some of us discover better sources of satisfaction in our own abilities, while others continue to fall back upon a portrayal of littleness.

The Uses of Victimhood

What are the payoffs for portraying ourselves as victims? First of all, the ego associates "victim" with "innocent" and concludes that to be a victim is to be morally superior. After all, if I am a victim, it is others who are aggressive and bad, not I. What better evidence could there be of my innocence than the fact that I am cruelly abused by wicked people?

Further, "innocent victims" are entitled to be angry about what has been done to them, so they alone are allowed to aggress against others with impunity. Isn't the rationale of every child, "But they started it!"? What would be "viciousness" in anyone else must be excused as "righteous wrath" and a wholesome desire for "justice" in an "innocent victim." Whenever individuals, groups, or nations assert that they are someone's victim, be assured that naked aggression will not be long in coming.

However, the attraction to victimhood goes beyond the ego's desire to enlist support, regard itself as innocent, and aggress against others with impunity. The ego actually anticipates profit from maintaining resentments. Its reasoning goes something like this: "If you have hurt me, then you owe me a moral debt. If I can make you acknowledge this obligation, I may be able to control you to my advantage. Further, if you owe me something, you cannot in good conscience leave me until our accounts are settled." To the ego, *grievances entitle one to compensation and hold relationships together.* They are like money in the bank.

As adults, we find it hard to get over the idea that a convincing portrayal of the victim role will entitle us to sympathetic attention and rich rewards. Making ourselves small has the added advantage of avoiding conflict and competition with others. There is a trade-off—others get to feel larger and more powerful, but at the cost of having to take some responsibility for our well-being.

The ego proposes that we present ourselves as victims whenever it thinks that we are more likely to succeed by manipulating others through guilt than by exercising our own abilities. In a seemingly "hopeless" situation, our ego anticipates only failure through its own efforts and therefore automatically regresses to the strategy that worked for it earlier in life—loudly protesting that it is all terribly unfair. Unfortunately, an accident, illness, or assailant is not nearly as concerned with being fair to us as our parents once were. Trying to elicit pity is seldom the most adaptive posture for an adult.

There Are No Victims

The spiritual perspective says that we are never really anyone else's victim, and in proof of this, it offers the miracle. After all, *if you can change what happens to you instantly, just by changing your mind, then the problem must have been in your mind all along.* And if the problem was really in your own mind, then no one else is guilty of having "made" you suffer, and no one deserves punishment. To recognize this is to "forgive the world" by acknowledging that we alone are responsible for our pain.

Most of us consider that we have some degree of responsibility for the things that happen to us. In fact, many psychotherapists would agree that a good rough index of mental health is the amount of personal responsibility a person accepts. The psychologically immature and maladjusted generally imagine that the deck is stacked against them. They blame others for their difficulties and feel helpless. Such people often portray themselves as mentally or emotionally *disabled*, and they do not experience themselves as responsible in the sense of being *able to respond* adaptively.

At the other extreme of the mental health continuum, Abraham

Maslow's self-actualizing subjects felt very much in control of their lives and well able to accomplish their goals.[23] Healthy, effective individuals do not waste time blaming their problems on others. Nor do they feel entitled to easy victories. They expect to work hard for success, and when they fail, they reevaluate their strategy and try again.

Still, even exceptionally responsible people may find it difficult to believe that their responsibility is total. Yet *the whole explanation of miracles rests on this idea that our own consciousness is creating the world we experience.* You can change your "reality" in a moment precisely because your world is nothing more than a projection of your present conscious and unconscious thoughts about it. What you say goes. If you say you are the victim of a cruel world, you will be a victim. If you say your problems can be solved, you will find a way out of difficulty.

You may believe that you are responsible for what you do, but not for what you think. The truth is that you are responsible for what you think because it is only at this level that you can exercise choice. What you do comes from what you think.

—A Course in Miracles

The Ego's Limited Point of View

Most people make no distinction between themselves and their egos. They think the ego—the personality they have developed in the course of their lifetime—is who they really are. Further, because the God within us speaks only when spoken to, most of us are completely unaware of its presence. We do not realize that we could appeal to it for help, and instead rely exclusively upon our ego's limited resources.

And the ego's resources *are* limited. Because it is only aware of the skills it has personally developed through experience in the physical world, it has no more idea of how miracles occur than

257

your dog has of why the light always comes on when you walk into a darkened room. The ego can be awed by the miraculous things that happen when we turn to our higher power, but it is clueless when it comes to *making* them happen.

My ego knows how fast I can run, how persuasively I can talk, how skillfully I can drive, and so forth. Faced with an emergency, it takes a rapid and relatively realistic survey of the situation, its own abilities, and other resources that are available within the physical illusion. If these resources are clearly insufficient to solve the problem, it concludes that the problem is insoluble and gives up. Its only remaining trick is to characterize itself as a victim and hope that someone—and as a last resort, God—will take pity on it.

However, our deliverance stories indicate that no situation is ever truly hopeless. Each one can be reinterpreted by our higher power in such a way as to become benign. But in order for that reinterpretation to occur, there must be a moment in which the self withdraws investment from the ego's depressing perspective and turns within in silent anticipation of help. Then our higher power can intuitively guide our thoughts and those of others who might help us. It specializes in dreaming up happy endings for our "cliff-hangers."

It doesn't matter that life has suddenly turned into *The Perils of Pauline.* The last episode may have ended with our heroine tied to the railroad track while the 4:15 bears relentlessly down on her. Nevertheless, the moment our higher power is invited to take over the production, it becomes a new episode. We can be sure that the plot will now go through whatever contortions are required to pull poor Pauline off the tracks a split second before that train roars through.

Perhaps a team of ground squirrels will conveniently gnaw through the ropes to get at the acorns Pauline just happens to have hidden in her pockets. Perhaps the villain will find religion and repent of his evil deed before it is too late. Perhaps the next episode will begin with Pauline awakening in her bed and realizing that it was all just a horrible dream. The essential point is that however seemingly impossible the situation, if we hand the pen to our higher power, we are going to wind up with a happy ending. As in the case of Karen and Mike's beaver pond, that ending may be so shamelessly contrived that no self-respecting editor would permit it in a work of fiction. But, by golly, it will be happy!

Perhaps the ancient Greek playwrights had the right idea with their deus ex machina endings. Dramatists could feel free to paint themselves into corners, creating a plot so convoluted that it was incapable of resolution. At the end of the play, they would simply write in a god who would descend into the middle of the action and miraculously put everything right. Our higher power is available to serve this function upon request.

The Ego's Resistance to Responsibility

Once we accept responsibility for having helped to dream things the way they are, we are free to dream them differently. However, the ego can be counted upon to resist our higher power's liberating message of personal responsibility with all of the resources at its disposal. This means that to the degree that people identify with the ego, they will experience themselves at the mercy of circumstances beyond their control. In recognizing the world as a self-created illusion, one approaches spiritual liberation, and it is the ego's mission to delay this final enlightenment as long as possible.

After all, the ego is the aspect of our mind to which we have assigned the task of "creating" the physical illusion by believing in it. As the master of illusion, it has no intention of allowing us to wander off into heavenly realms where it cannot follow, connecting up with a spiritual reality it cannot perceive. Thus, the ego is always ready with "good" reasons why we should continue to view the world through its distorting lens. Its continual distraction and interference with our spiritual growth is so utterly predictable that virtually all religions agree upon the necessity for some sort of "ego death" or "ego transcendence."

One of the ego's most ingenious ploys for maintaining the illusion of victimhood is to suggest that our higher power is actually our enemy and that by urging us to understand our responsibility for what happens to us it is being cruelly abusive. This unique form of "persecution through personal empowerment" it calls "blaming the victim." This is a logical trap that capitalizes on the widespread confusion between *responsibility* and *blame*. If we fall for this trap, we will misinterpret our higher power's efforts to liberate us from all suffering as attack and reject these efforts accordingly.

The confusion of *blame* and *responsibility* begins early in life. Parents and teachers of young children are constantly trying to sort out which child was responsible (that is, "to blame") for misbehavior. They know very well that the kitten didn't get into the refrigerator by itself, and their concern is to identify the culprit and apply consequences that will discourage any repetition. As a result, the child's developing ego concludes that being "responsible" is the same as being "to blame."

In the ego's view, to accept responsibility for having made a mistake is tantamount to admitting that one is bad and deserving of punishment. This is something it is understandably reluctant to do. The spiritual perspective, on the other hand, maintains that while we are all responsible, no one is to blame and everyone is unconditionally entitled to love and support. We may very well make mistakes, but *mistakes call for correction, not punishment*.

For example, loving parents would not be content to blame and punish a child for putting a kitten in the refrigerator—instead, they would want to help the child understand the suffering this behavior could cause. In the long run, gently educating a child to feel empathy for others will be a much more effective strategy than punishment. The spiritual perspective suggests that we are all doing our best given our limited understanding, but that we all have much to learn.

Once blame and punishment are laid aside, it is easier to see the value of responsibility. The fact that we are responsible for our pain can then be recognized as good news, since it means we have the power to change things. In this view, to see someone as a helpless victim is actually to do them a real disservice. Our only hope for a better life lies in recognizing the power of our destructive thoughts so that we can correct them.

When we suggest that people are the victims of circumstances beyond their control, we disempower them, diverting attention from the level at which they have the ability to change things. This would be like telling a heart patient, "Don't bother exercising, reducing stress, and following that low-cholesterol diet— your heart condition isn't your fault, so you don't have to do anything about it." Of course it isn't anyone's "fault," but that doesn't mean that our behavior has not contributed to our problem and that a change in that behavior might not help.

To accuse others for one's own misfortunes is a sign of want of education; to accuse oneself shows that one's education has begun; to accuse neither oneself nor others shows that one's education is complete.
                                                                    — Epictetus

Victimhood Is Attack

According to the generic spiritual view we have been discussing, in any conflict there is never really a "victimizer" and a "victim"—just two frightened people, each of whom believes it is necessary to defend himself or herself from the other. Whichever one resorts to a defensive act first will be regarded as the attacker by others, but he or she will not share this appraisal. The so-called "aggressor" will view himself or herself as simply responding to intolerable threat and provocation. For example, people who regard themselves as the "victims of society" can be among the most dangerous on earth. Self-righteously convinced that they are entitled to revenge against those who have oppressed them, such people make up the ranks of ruthless criminals and terrorists.

Miracles occur when we put our faith in love rather than fear. When we forget about being a potential victim, we find ourselves in a position to reinvest our faith in the alternative possibility—that the situation actually calls for love. This involves entertaining the idea that our antagonists are basically decent people like ourselves who would rather get their needs met in a civilized manner if that seemed possible. They *look* hostile, but perhaps they are just frightened and confused. Maybe if we reach out to them in friendship, they will calm down and behave more reasonably.

By acting upon the assumption that the other person is a brother or a sister who deserves kindness and respect instead of counterattack, a loving person mentally restructures the whole situation. Now it is a misunderstanding among friends that can easily be resolved. The happy ending that results from moving our faith from fear to love will look like, and indeed be, a miracle.

What it comes down to is this: You can elect to defend yourself against someone you see as bad, or you can elect to love without attack and have a miracle heal the situation, but you cannot simultaneously do both. Consider John's experience.

John

While visiting San Francisco on business, John found time in his schedule for dinner at a neighborhood bar and grill with a woman friend he hadn't seen in years. However, as the two chums settled in to catch up on old times, their conversation was violently disrupted. A wild-eyed man lunged through the door and began laying about him with a metal pipe. Slashing at everyone and everything within reach like an avenging fury, the madman knocked several patrons to the floor before anyone had time to react.

John was then a powerfully built man in his forties who had done a stint as an M.P. in the army and had worked briefly as a prison guard in his youth. In his later careers as a photojournalist and then a private investigator, he had often carried a gun and was by no means a stranger to violence. Yet his response in this emergency was atypical for a man of his background and training.

John reports that the minute he saw what was happening, he knew what he had to do. With a profound sense of inner guidance, he walked up to the man brandishing the pipe. Ignoring his threatening gestures, John stood there peacefully with his hands at his sides, making no attempt to defend himself from the hovering blow.

John gazed steadily into the madman's eyes and said with great compassion, "You must be in terrible pain to do a thing like this." As his words and tone registered, he saw uncertainty replace the maniacal fury on the other's face.

John now held out both hands, palms upward, silently urging the deranged man to surrender the pipe to him. After a few moment's hesitation, the rage in the attacker's face dissipated. He placed the pipe in John's hands and began to weep. John handed the weapon to a bystander and took the man in his arms, comforting him as he sobbed out the tale of his rage and frustration.

"It works every time!" John laughed as he concluded his story. "It's like they say—if you defend yourself, you get attacked. My life has been a whole lot safer since I stopped trying to protect myself!

"You know," he went on, "it's a funny thing. For years I carried a gun for protection and it seemed like people just couldn't help shooting at me. I stopped carrying in 1986, and not a blessed soul has taken a shot at me since!"

An eventful career spent uncovering secrets that others would kill to keep hidden has led John to the conclusion that loving is the only way to ensure his safety. He has come to believe that all of his efforts at self-defense only made danger real in his experience. These days he places his reliance not upon weapons but upon his human connection with others. He sleeps the more soundly for having done so.

It is hard to believe a defense that cannot attack is the best defense. This is what is meant by "the meek shall inherit the earth." They will literally take it over because of their strength.

—A Course in Miracles

The Healing Power of Defenselessness

The extraordinary healing power of defenselessness is also to be seen in this beautiful story from Peace Pilgrim's book. Peace Pilgrim was an elderly woman who spent many years walking around North America talking about the importance of peace to anyone who would listen.

Peace Pilgrim

Here is the story in Peace Pilgrim's words.

Once I was hit by a disturbed teenage boy whom I had taken for a walk. He wanted to go hiking but was afraid he might break a leg and be left lying there. Everyone was afraid to go with him. He was a great big fellow and looked like a football player, and he was known to be violent at times. He had once beaten his mother so badly that she had to spend several weeks in the hospital. Everybody was afraid of him, so I offered to go with him.

As we got up to the first hilltop everything was going fine. Then a thunderstorm came along. He was very terrified because the thundershower was very close. Suddenly he went off the beam and came for me, hitting at me. I didn't run away although I guess I could have—he had a heavy pack on his back. But even while he was hitting me I could only feel the deepest compassion toward him. How terrible to be so psychologically sick that you would be able to hit a defenseless old woman! I bathed his hatred with love even while he hit me. As a result the hitting stopped.

He said, "You didn't hit back! Mother always hits back." The delayed reaction, because of his disturbance, had reached the good in him. Oh, it's there—no matter how deeply it is buried—and he experienced remorse and complete self-condemnation.

What are a few bruises on my body in comparison with the transformation of a human life? To make a long story short he was never violent again. He is a useful person in this world today.[47]

Victimhood as an Excuse

All of this talk about defenselessness and forbearance is not to say that criminals should not be incarcerated. It is undoubtedly necessary to protect society from certain misguided people. The spiritual view holds that no matter what the provocation, we are all responsible for our actions. If you do the crime, you do the time.

However, it is currently popular to believe that victims are *not* responsible, either for what was done to them or for the things they do in retaliation. What began as a compassionate appreciation of the reasons why people do shocking things, has ended as universal permission to behave badly. Since victimhood is so widely regarded as the ultimate excuse, it is small wonder that it is now being tried as a legal defense.

The Menendez brothers' trials, for example, raised the question of whether people may be excused if they murder the parents who allegedly mistreated them. Elsewhere in Los Angeles a jury grappled with the issue of whether an individual who attempted murder was himself a "victim" of the "mob psychology" that "made" him do something he says he would not otherwise have considered. In New York, jurors were asked by counsel for the defense to excuse the Jamaican gunman who massacred Long Island Railroad commuters, on the grounds that he was himself the victim of our racist society.

This way lies madness. If "victims" cannot be held responsible for their actions, what is to stop anyone from claiming to be a victim? All of us have suffered. All of us think that we have "good" reasons for the cruel things we do. If angry or frightened people must be excused for reacting with aggression, who can be held responsible for anything?

It is well known, for example, that most violent people got that way at least partly through childhood abuse. However, if we are to be consistent we must also sympathize with the individual's abusive parents, since they were probably the "victims" of their own abusive families. It is a chicken-and-egg situation. No matter where we try to lay the blame, it can always be shifted one step back.

However, if we adopt the spiritual view that no one is to blame, yet everyone is responsible, we can get criminals off the streets without either hating or fearing them. In an ideal world, incarceration would be used constructively to help convicted persons understand their mistakes so that they could eventually be welcomed back into society. This suggests that prisons should become "penitentiaries"—literally places where people go to contemplate their mistakes, become penitent, and change their ways.

If we can release the goal of punishment—the desire to make people suffer for the way they have made others suffer—then rehabilitation might become a realistic goal, at least for some. As psychoanalyst Alice Miller points out, people who wantonly hurt others are usually those who have had to endure extreme cruelty themselves as children.[48] If personal suffering leads to hostile and aggressive behavior, it is ridiculous to expect that further pain and rejection will correct it.

It would be interesting, for example, to see what would happen if first-time offenders convicted of lesser crimes were sentenced to six months under house arrest in a happy, loving home in some distant part of the country. Prisoners would be taken out of their accustomed environment and temporarily reduced to the legal status of minors—required to obey their new "parents" and contribute to the household as they directed. "Condemned" to work side by side with kind, moral people who want to help them get their lives together, I suspect that many fewer criminals would go on to commit a second offense.

19

The Miraculous Power of Love Without Attack

To understand all is to forgive all.
—Buddha

When we pass up an opportunity to portray ourselves as someone's indignant victim and come from love instead, miracles enter to transform the situation. The miraculous power of love was recently illustrated by a rabbi who felt moved to reach out to a neo-Nazi radio broadcaster who had been using his show as a forum for racial hatred. I happened to see these men interviewed on television last year, and I will never forget their amazing story.

The Rabbi and the Nazi

Listening to the Nazi's radio show one day, the rabbi felt moved to call the station—not to complain about the dangerous racist and anti-Semitic content of the broadcast, but to speak with the broadcaster. When he got the young skinhead on the line, he gently asked, "I'd just like to know—how can you hate me so much when you don't even know me?"

The rabbi's simple question provoked a flood of abuse, and the Nazi broadcaster quickly hung up on him. But the rabbi would not give up. He called again and again, day in and day out, always gently coming back to the same point. "Look, if you get to know me and then hate me, I'll understand. But how can you hate me when you don't know me? It doesn't make any sense."

267

In a situation where most people would agree that he had a right to be outraged, the rabbi declined to take offense. He did not regard himself as anyone's victim, but rather as an older and wiser person who was sincerely intent upon trying to understand what could have made the broadcaster so violently racist. He never criticized the Nazi or responded to his denigrating remarks with counteraccusations. Despite being continually insulted and hung up on, he persisted in his good-humored calls, continually holding out the hand of friendship and playfully asking, "Why not get to know me? Then you can *really* hate me."

Somehow, despite the Nazi's virulent hostility, a dialogue began to emerge. The skinhead was a lonely young man who had known little kindness in his life. As the calls went on, he gradually began to open up. At first he would only expound his racist theories, but as time went on, he began to reveal glimpses of his personal life.

The rabbi found himself experiencing great compassion for this emotionally wounded young person. The older man was a good listener, and little by little the Nazi began to secretly look forward to his calls. It wasn't so bad, having some sympathetic attention, even if it did come from a Jew. The insults began to diminish as the rabbi checked in frequently to discuss the day's broadcast and see how his young antagonist was doing.

One day when the rabbi called, he happened to catch the broadcaster in a moment of personal crisis. In a fit of despair, this unhappy young skinhead could not resist the impulse to pour out his heart about the many problems in his life. The rabbi lent a sympathetic ear.

Deeply concerned, the rabbi insisted that they get together to talk further. At the older man's urging, the broadcaster reluctantly agreed to accept an invitation to the rabbi's home for dinner. There, despite his fears, he was welcomed by a loving family, which was grateful to him for being willing to come and meet them. He and the rabbi talked far into the night.

Gradually, this lonely, hostile young man became a regular

visitor to the rabbi's home. His previous offensive behavior was completely forgiven, and he met with only kindness and understanding. In time, it became impossible to continue affirming his racist convictions, and he gave them up.

Not long after that, he converted to Judaism. He said that the choice had been entirely his—the rabbi had never encouraged him to take that step. However, in the course of his interaction with this family, and through them, with other Jews, he had developed enormous respect for Jewish values and traditions. He said that he simply wanted to be part of a community that had shown him so much more kindness and love than he had ever encountered elsewhere.

Is this awakening of a soul to love any less miraculous than the saving of a life? There are many kinds of torment in this world and the charitable attitude that forgives an "enemy" is the key that releases us from all of them.

Love Without Attack

We have seen previously that love without attack is the necessary and sufficient condition for miracles, and I think that the preceding story beautifully illustrates this truth. To see yourself as someone's victim is to attack him or her. When you elect to forgo the victim role and take no offense, you love without attack and miracles ensue.

I think it is obvious that the people who shared their stories of deliverance from assault did elect to love without attack, and there is no need to belabor this point. But where accidents were concerned and the danger was not even *ostensibly* caused by another person, who could possibly have been the object of the miracle workers' "love without attack"? In these cases, I think the recipients of forgiveness were vaguely defined others, the individuals themselves, and God.

Remember that just because there is realistically "no one to blame" for what is happening does not necessarily mean that we do not blame someone all the same. Often we experience a general sense of grievance directed at the one who is supposed to make things safe—that is, the people who maintain the roads, repair our cars, or police our streets. Danger (or even mere inconvenience for that matter) often triggers a resentful sense that there must have been culpable mismanagement somewhere along the line. This very human impulse to find someone to blame for our troubles constitutes an attack thought that places us beyond the reach of miracles.

Attack thoughts can be directed at ourselves as well as at others. We may think we deserve punishment for having been "stupid" enough to get ourselves into such an awful predicament. For instance, Carmela recognized that she had been foolish to climb down the bluff, but she dismissed the idea that she was therefore guilty and must expect to pay for her error with her life. She continued to love herself without attack despite the realization that she had made a mistake. This is to say that she forgave herself and blamed no one for her predicament, maintaining a miracle-minded attitude throughout.

And finally, the background to all of our grievances against ourselves and others is often an ongoing sense of grievance against God or fate. If we believe that there is some higher power controlling our destinies, we will necessarily wonder why it "makes" or "allows" us to suffer so. Regardless of whether we experience ourselves as the victim of our own stupidity, the system, another person, the workings of fate, or God, our sense of victimization continues to project threat into our physical illusion.

Thought Creates "Reality"

A sense of victimhood is dangerous because our unconscious mind is subtly programming the things that seem to "just happen" to us in such a way that our expectations are always fulfilled. Each of us "finds" in our world whatever our thoughts proclaim is there. If we declare that we are victims, the situation will conform to our expectations, and we will discover that we are indeed suffering through the carelessness or cruelty of other people. Let's explore some examples in order to see exactly how such attack thoughts endanger the people who hold them.

Lauren

Lauren was driving on the freeway in light traffic when a speeding motorcycle unexpectedly swooped in front of her. Startled, she had to brake hard to avoid an accident. Her rush of fear quickly turned to anger as she got a better look at the person she'd almost hit.

"The rider was a longhaired, tattooed guy in his late thirties. He wore biker colors and he was lying forward on his stomach with his feet stretched out behind him, swooping in and out of traffic like a kid showing off on a bicycle. And he kept cutting it really close, pulling in only a few feet in front of the drivers."

When she realized that the biker had cut her off intentionally, Lauren was outraged. "That guy is going to kill himself," she thought, "and he nearly killed me too! How dare he jeopardize my life with his irresponsible behavior!"

However, this train of thought set off an alarm in her consciousness. Through her spiritual studies, Lauren had learned to mistrust her own motives when she found herself feeling righteously indignant about someone else's behavior. She said that she suddenly realized that her sense of outrage could be the prelude to a real accident if she did not change her mind immediately.

"I quickly reminded myself that only my own thoughts determine what happens to me. I chose to be all right whatever the motorcyclist did. My immediate need was to forgive him before my ego whipped up an accident to prove his guilt."

The next moment, a few cars ahead of Lauren the biker swerved in front of another vehicle. This time the startled driver overreacted and crashed into the truck on his right, setting off a chain reaction of cars smashing into one another in front of her.

"It looked bad, but I reminded myself that I had chosen not to regard myself as the biker's victim, so I could not suffer through him. I concentrated on remaining calm and hoping that everyone would be okay.

"I had to swerve all over the road to avoid hitting the crashing cars in front of me, and I was forced off onto the left shoulder, but I came to a safe stop without hitting or being hit by anyone. Then I got out and ran to see if anyone needed first aid. Although there were injuries and several people were taken off in ambulances, no one appeared badly hurt."

Lauren said that eleven vehicles were damaged to some degree or other while the motorcyclist sailed off untouched, seemingly unaware of the wake of devastation he'd left behind him. She is convinced that if she had not made that quick decision to release her resentment against the biker, she would have cracked up, too.

Like John's experience, this one provides a rare glimpse of someone consciously employing the method of miracle working we have discussed. Lauren caught herself flirting with a sense of victimization and stopped in time to avoid the unpleasant consequences of her attack thoughts. As is the case with most of the deliverance stories, this *could have been* just a coincidence, but it is interesting to note that when someone made a point of applying the method recommended for achieving miracles, she did avoid an accident of which she might easily have been part.

Lauren's attack thoughts were directed at the biker, but self-directed ones can be equally destructive, as Richard's case illustrates. In the grip of hopelessness induced by his own self-judgment, Richard foresaw no happiness in life and unconsciously concluded that it would probably be best for everyone if he just quietly folded a losing hand.

Richard

Richard was in his early twenties when his life started coming apart at the seams. A popular college student with a bright future, he was engaged to a wonderful young woman. Her family adored him and was in many ways more loving and supportive to him than his own. Richard and Angela were to marry shortly, and then Richard would graduate and join her father in their lucrative family business. The problem was that he could no longer avoid the realization that he was gay.

It had taken a long time for Richard to allow his homosexuality into consciousness, but now that it was there, it could not be denied. He loved Angela very much, and his position seemed hopeless. If he concealed his homosexuality and went ahead and married her, it would be unconscionable. But this was in the 1960s when *homosexual* was very much a dirty word. If he "came out of the closet," it would shatter Angela's regard for him, and everyone would have to know why the wedding was off. He would be a disgrace to his family and would certainly be rejected by nearly everyone else. The wonderful life he had planned for himself was cruelly denied him. Why did he have to be different?

Richard was walking home one snowy winter night from a late class, still perched on the horns of this dilemma. "I've got to come clean about this. Angela is entitled to my honesty. But how can I face life as a known homosexual?" His route home took him through a local park. As he approached the frozen lake in the center, he decided to take the shortcut across the ice rather than walk around.

"That was something that never would have occurred to me under ordinary circumstances. It was still early in the season, and there were warning signs posted all around about not going out on the lake because the ice was not solid. But somehow that night it seemed like a good idea, and I didn't give any thought at all to the reason why I shouldn't cross the lake. I just walked on out there.

"And then it gets even weirder. Because in retrospect I now realize that I was out of my body. It was as if I was somewhere above and behind myself, floating in the air watching Richard walk out onto the ice. Now you'd think something like that would be unusual enough to get your attention, right? But I thought nothing of it. I know now that I was trying to 'accidentally' end my life. I guess it just somehow seemed easier to die than to have everyone know that I was gay.

"When I was way out in the middle, the ice broke, and I fell through. I felt the freezing water close over my head, and as my clothes became saturated and I sunk to the bottom, I didn't even struggle. I was at peace with the whole thing.

"But then, it was as if I suddenly changed my mind! I just knew that I wanted to live. And there I was on the bottom of a frozen lake! It sounds ridiculous, but it felt to me like my soul suddenly shot back into my body through my head. Just VOOM! I felt a shock go through me like lightning, and suddenly I was back. And I was determined to live.

"I began to swim like a maniac. I coudn't even tell you exactly how I did it, but I somehow got my head above water and then dragged myself back up onto that fragile ice and slid on my belly back to the shore. Then I ran like hell to get home before I froze to death.

"You know, that experience was like some kind of weird baptism. I fell into that lake a kid miserable about his sexuality, and I came out of it a proud gay man. Because ever since the moment my soul came back into my body, there has never been a doubt about the direction I would have to take in life.

"I came out to everyone. And it did cause a lot of pain and rejection, but a lot of the important people in my life, including Angela, decided to go on loving me anyway. And since then, I've never looked back. I am gay and proud. This is who I am, and it's just fine!"

Richard had been attacking himself with the belief that as a homosexual, he was sinful and did not deserve love. However, a few moments spent in that peaceful altered state just before death showed him that this was not true. He returned to his body with an unconditional appreciation of his own worthiness, which has stood him in good stead ever since.

From Richard's case, we can see that what appeared to be an accident was actually an unconscious suicide attempt. Although no one else knew it, he had given up on his life. This was probably also the case in the drug-related death of Becky, the cousin of a friend of mine. While many things will never be known for sure, the facts Pam unearthed are suggestive.

Becky

Pam's cousin Becky was a registered nurse who had been divorced for about five years and had recently become engaged to be married to a wonderful man. Becky spoke of him in glowing terms, and everyone who knew her rejoiced in her good fortune. However, a month before the wedding, Becky died of an accidental cocaine overdose. It seemed cruelly ironic that a nurse of all people would so badly miscalculate her own tolerance for a drug.

At her funeral, everyone commented on how especially sad it all was considering Becky's upcoming wedding and her high hopes for the future. How tragic that she should die just when she had "everything to live for."

Becky's ex-husband attended the funeral also, and Pam gathered from one of his comments that he had spoken with Becky several days before her death. Unable to put it out of her mind, Pam called him up the next day. "It's none of my business, but if you wouldn't mind my asking, what did you and Becky talk about that last time?"

Becky's ex-husband said that actually he was relieved to be able to tell someone. Becky had called and pleaded with him to get back together. He had explained as kindly as he could that he did not see any possibility of ever reuniting with her. He made it clear that his life was moving in new directions and that she would have to make her plans without him.

When she heard that, Pam realized that things had not been the way they had appeared. Becky had convinced everyone that she was happy with her new love, but in reality she was unwilling to face the prospect of life without her ex-husband.

Like Richard, Becky appeared to be attacking herself with the idea that happiness was no longer possible for her in this life. As a result of this thinking, she consciously or unconsciously created an accident to end her problems.

I think that cases like these also underscore the fact that we are seldom in a position to know what is really going on in someone else's life. If Richard had died at the bottom of that frozen lake, no one would ever have suspected the painful dilemma that had made him feel so hopeless. And it was only a fluke that Pam discovered Becky's hidden despair.

Even the people to whom such things occur are usually not aware of their reasons for creating accidents, assaults, and illnesses. Richard realized in retrospect that he had unconsciously decided to kill himself, but he did not suspect this at the time. Lauren didn't consciously want to be involved in a traffic accident, yet if she had continued to indulge her hostile thoughts at the biker's expense it might have happened. According to the spiritual perspective, nothing occurs to anyone that they have not created at some level, but that level is not necessarily a conscious one.

Once again, it isn't that we *want* to suffer. It is just that we want to continue indulging the attitudes, beliefs, and emotional reactions that *lead to* suffering. We feel entitled to see ourselves as victims and resent any suggestion that this might be destructive, just as a young child resents a parent for taking away a dangerous, but attractively shiny pair of scissors. Nevertheless, attack thoughts create their likeness in the physical world as surely as loving ones create miracles. We will never be truly safe until we discipline our minds to avoid them.

Forgiveness Ends Suffering and Loss

What all of this means at a practical level is that if you want miracles, you must forgive the people who seem to be hurting you and resist the temptation to see yourself as anyone's innocent victim. Only then will you be truly harmless to others. Only then can you achieve the sense of peaceful inner attunement that makes divine intervention possible.

The desire to regard yourself as a victim sounds like a small thing, but do not underestimate its destructive power. *If you are willing to be a victim, you will be a victim.* Once you have chosen to play the role of "sufferer" of your own free will, not even God can release you from it. God will never contradict *you.*

The only hope for those of us who have endangered ourselves by foolishly opting for victimhood is to quickly change our minds. We have unfairly judged against ourselves or another, and the only way to restore peace now is by deciding to withdraw the judgment.

Forgiveness means resolutely overlooking someone's apparent guilt and working to bring their eternal innocence into focus instead. If we saw all attack as coming from a beloved brother or sister who was simply frightened and confused, this would be easier. A handy, all-purpose formula for forgiving is the one Jesus used: "Forgive them, Father, for they know not what they do."

Remember John saying, "You must be in terrible pain to do a thing like this," or Peace Pilgrim thinking, "How terrible to be so psychologically sick that you would be able to hit a defenseless old woman!," or the rabbi's generous concern for the Nazi broadcaster who hated Jews? Each overlooked guilt and sought to comfort the suffering person who was behaving badly. Through forgiveness, miracle workers release themselves and their antagonists from a hell both unwittingly had a hand in creating.

That is how miracles of deliverance work. Within the physical illusion, we are condemned to do battle with the projections of our own minds until we decide to forgive. We hate and fear others not because of what they have done but for the guilt we have unfairly imputed to them. In the absence of our need to see them as bad and undeserving, they are just people making correctable mistakes.

Those upon whom we project guilt look to us like dangerous adversaries, because that is how we have chosen to see them. But the moment we truly forgive, we recognize them as beloved brothers and sisters who are simply making a sad mistake. Think of Debra's compassionate response to the Arab terrorists.

The mind that serves spirit is invulnerable.
—A Course in Miracles

Mystics say that the mind that rests in complete forgiveness is invulnerable. When we recognize the perfect innocence of ourselves and others, Divine Love creates an invisible demilitarized zone around us—a safe place where others are welcome to join us in peace. With each such decision, the world becomes a safer place. It is partially redeemed each time someone recognizes a former enemy as a friend. Miracle workers do not fight evil; they dismiss the illusion of evil and refuse any longer to project it onto others or the world.

We have seen how divine grace protects the forgiving, but what about people who offer miracles to others? What is it like to create miracles intentionally? In the next chapter, we will hear from some women who have learned to do just that.

20

How the "Pros" Work Miracles

The humble, meek, merciful, just, pious and devout souls everywhere are of one religion, and when death has taken off the mask, they will know one another, though the diverse liveries they wore here make them strangers.

—William Penn

We have talked a good deal about how miracles work and emphasized that they are available to everyone, all the time. If the supernatural view is correct, our higher power wills our security and happiness at every moment. The limiting condition is not God's willingness to help us, but our own willingness to accept the help that is offered.

But if this is true, what is the role of miracle workers who purport to perform healings for others? For example, many miracles occur in the context of religious ceremonies where an individual who appears to have unusual powers heals members of the public. Such people are often regarded as having a special gift from God that is to be used in the service of humanity.

In order to understand this "gift," let us explore the experiences of some contemporary miracle workers. These women were selected simply because their work is known to me and because I believe that they really have performed miracles for others. Let us see what each of them has to say about working miracles.

279

Patricia Sun's Healing Abilities

Patricia never calls herself a "healer" and does not believe that she has a God-given gift that others do not possess. She feels that she differs only in that she has developed her healing abilities and is comfortable using them. It is her contention that someday everyone will learn to utilize their own capacity for working miracles, and she regards it as her job to help them do so.

Patricia gives workshops that provide an opportunity for others to "tune in" on her way of being and get a sense of what it would be like to experience their own higher consciousness. As a part of these workshops, she leads meditations, during which she makes vocal tones which draw her listeners into expanded awareness. Many people report that these sounds boost them into an unusually deep and peaceful meditative state.

Many years ago when she was a graduate student studying to be a Marriage, Family and Child Counselor, Patricia participated in a research study on paranormal phenomena. To everyone's surprise, she got every answer right, indicating a very unusual degree of psychic ability. Curious about this, she went to see a prominent psychic for a reading and was told that she, Patricia, had been a healer in many of her past lives.

Patricia was intensely skeptical about the whole concept of psychic readings and does not believe in past lives at all, so this information left her distinctly "underwhelmed." "Oh, that's right," she thought to herself, "butter me up. I'll bet you say the same thing to everyone who walks in here!"

However, the next thing the psychic said was that Patricia's decision to have the reading that day reflected her inner wish to open up to her healing potential in her present life. At the woman's words, Patricia reports that she experienced a powerful blast of energy that radiated from her heart and filled her whole body. So strong was the energy pouring through Patricia that, despite her closed eyes, the other woman actually reeled back in astonishment, saying, "My God! You really are a healer, aren't you!"

Patricia's arms felt so thick with pulsating energy that she had to move them away from her body to allow it to flow. Tears began streaming from her eyes and a voice in her head announced, "You've come home!" Patricia says that when she heard this inner voice, she slipped into an extraordinarily peaceful and joyful altered state of consciousness where she felt bathed in bliss.

The psychic went on to say that someday Patricia would begin to make sounds as part of her healing work. Patricia remembers greeting this idea, too, with silent ridicule. "I'd like to see myself making funny noises at people!" However, although she could doubt the psychic's account of the past and predictions for the future, there was no easy way to dismiss the extraordinary energy state she had gone into during their session. There must, she thought, be something in what the woman had said.

As luck would have it, she had an opportunity to try out her healing ability later that afternoon. Returning home, she found that her little boy had hurt himself playing. Patricia allowed the energy to flow through her hands as she held them over her son's injured leg, and his pain was quickly gone. "Ooh, Mommy," he remarked with pleasure, "it feels just like a warm wind!"

From that day on, Patricia began offering to help friends who complained of physical problems. When someone would mention some minor discomfort, Patricia would say rather vaguely, "Well, I have this thing that I do that might help. Just sit there for a minute while I hold my hands over the place and see if you don't feel better." And they did. Patricia reports that these experiences helped her gain confidence in her ability. She began offering help with more serious problems and these, too, invariably yielded to treatment.

One day in her meditation, Patricia was told that she had been able to heal all of these people only because the Universe was sending her individuals who were ready to be healed. Would she be willing to work on people who were not yet ready to accept healing—ones who would not go away well?

At first Patricia was reluctant to undertake healings where her efforts might appear to fail, but she soon realized that, no matter how it looked, her help might speed the time when these people *would* open themselves to healing. She quickly acquiesced, and from that day on, her results began to be much more variable. Some people were healed completely, some partially, and others apparently not at all. Patricia learned to do her part, without worrying about how it looked to others. She is confident that those who are not healed immediately will let the healing in at some other place and time.

Patricia says that there is no really "typical" pattern that her healings take. She just does whatever she is inspired to do in the moment. She offered as an example the case of a friend she treated early on.

An Example of Healing

A fellow graduate student I'll call Linda was interning at the same mental health clinic as Patricia. During a staff meeting, Linda doubled over with pain. She explained that she always had terrible menstrual cramps, which nothing ever seemed to help, and that just now they were unbearable. Patricia suggested they retire to a more private place so that she could "do her thing."

Patricia says that she did not regard menstrual cramps as much of a challenge. Once they were alone in one of the therapy rooms, she placed her hands on either side of Linda's abdomen and began to pour in energy. As she projected energy into the affected area, she was gratified to see her friend's face begin to relax. Eventually, a surprised smile replaced the look of anguish. "Hey! The pain is gone!"

Flushed with her easy success, Patricia removed her hands. Instantly, the taut look returned to her friend's face. "Oh no! It's back."

This was very strange. When Patricia worked on a problem, it usually went away quickly and stayed away. Considerably less cocky, she repeated her treatment. Once again she got it right down to the end, only to remove her hands and have the pain return. What could be going on?

282

This time Patricia decided to investigate. It was as if she had hands made of energy that could reach right inside her friend. Patricia felt as though she could actually hold Linda's womb and feel that it was hard, contracted, and knotlike. Still "holding" the uterus, Patricia again poured in energy and again felt it relax and soften. But this time she just kept pouring in energy.

At first nothing further seemed to be happening. But suddenly she felt a shift in Linda's energy so powerful that it brought a hot rush of tears streaming down Patricia's face. At the same time, Linda began sobbing uncontrollably and babbling incoherent phrases: "Men give you brain tumors! Being a woman you get brain tumors! Sex gives you brain tumors!"

After the emotional storm had passed, Linda was calm and free of pain. She recalled with surprise that her mother had had a brain tumor when she was carrying Linda in her womb. Her mother had evidently associated her tumor with her pregnancy and somehow Linda had picked up this thought. The experience had left Linda with a lifelong fear that her own feminine nature would entail pain and disaster. Patricia's treatment appeared to have raised this troubling and deeply buried memory to consciousness where it could be released once and for all.

This story underscores the point made earlier—that physical problems have hidden psychological causes. If we are each dreaming our own physical experience, then a sick person is dreaming that there is something wrong with his or her body. The situation will only change when he or she dreams it differently.

In this case, Linda may have assimilated an irrational belief of her mother's while still in the womb, or she may have picked it up later in childhood. As a result, she formed the unconscious expectation that her femininity was dangerous, causing her to contract with fear at the first sign of menstrual cramps.

Patricia says that it was "as if" she had hands of energy that could go within Linda's body and pour energy into the affected organ. We might equally well say that she poured her loving attention into Linda's problem, gently encouraging her friend to focus her own attention upon the pain in her womb as well. It was as if the two of them meditated together on Linda's peculiar reaction to menstrual cramps. Linda's willingness to allow the memory of her mother's thoughts into consciousness dissolved the block that had been holding her frightening association between femininity and brain tumors out of awareness.

This example of a healing is especially informative because it underscores one of the reasons miracles do not always occur. Linda was healed because she was miracle ready. She was willing to allow the terrifying thought that she was doomed to burst into awareness. We can readily imagine that if Linda had not been able to find the courage to face this fear, Patricia's efforts would have provided only temporary symptomatic relief.

The fact is that no matter how strongly Patricia might desire that Linda be healed, her will could never supersede Linda's own desire to keep the cause of her problems out of awareness. After all, whose mind was it that was making the decision to contract Linda's womb? It was Linda's mind, and only she could decide to change it. A miracle worker can encourage someone to face their problems head-on, but he or she cannot take the fear away or prevent the other person from turning back too soon to get results.

So the miracle worker's role is largely that of referring the sufferer to his or her higher power. Jesus said, "Of myself I can do nothing. It is the Father within that doeth the work," and most healers, regardless of their faith, agree that one person does not heal another. The most a miracle worker can do is to lovingly encourage afflicted people to turn within, in humble willingness to be shown the mistaken thought patterns that are causing them to dream that they are suffering. Miracles result from mental correction, and it is only the individual's willingness to accept correction that makes them possible.

In some cases, the corrective thought might simply be the realization that one is forgiven and that God does not will that anyone suffer over past mistakes. Such an insight might take the form of a deep sense of inner peace—the "peace that passeth understanding." With no conscious realization of how or why the problem was created, the healed person only knows that God wills their release from suffering and that God's Will is irresistible.

I need but look upon all things that seem to hurt me,
and with perfect certainty assure myself, "God wills that
I be saved from this," and merely watch them disappear.
—A Course in Miracles

In other cases, such as Linda's, some intellectual insight is needed first in order to achieve the "perfect certainty" that there is no need to suffer. If we unconsciously think that there is some reason God does not will that we be released, we will not be perfectly certain of being healed.

For example, if the conviction that femininity condemned her to brain tumors had remained in Linda's unconscious mind, it would have reinstated the symptom at the next opportunity. Once this belief had been raised to awareness, Linda realized that however much it had frightened her mother, it was nothing but nonsense and could have no power over her. She was free to stop dreaming that there was a painful penalty attached to being a woman.

Carmela Corallo

Carmela is a spiritual teacher with a doctorate in consciousness studies who teaches about miracles and higher consciousness in Encinitas, California. She will already be familiar to the reader from her bluff-climbing exploits, which were described in the Introduction. Carmela taught me much of what I know about miracles and has a well-earned reputation for doing "the impossible."

Carmela says that she always knew that she was psychic—mystical abilities run in her Italian-American family, and no one was overly surprised when she began to manifest them. As a small child, Carmela's older brother would use her to search out the Christmas presents their parents had hidden and then get her to tell him what was inside each of the gaily wrapped packages. Her mother realized early on that there was little point in trying to hide chocolate from her.

However, Carmela soon discovered that her highly developed intuition was a decidedly mixed blessing. She was never sure what she was supposed to know about and what she wasn't. For example, her father was frequently unfaithful to her mother. Carmela has vivid memories of the frozen silence at the breakfast table one morning when she innocently inquired about his "date" with Mrs. So-and-So the night before. Somehow she was always making social gaffes and hurting people's feelings.

Over time, Carmela became a rather shy and withdrawn child, constantly afraid of saying the wrong thing. She wanted to fit in and hated having anyone know about her clairvoyance. As a teenager, in particular, it seemed terribly important to be just like everyone else.

Carmela recalls, for example, her excruciating embarrassment in high school when a math teacher caught her staring out the window, lost in a daydream. Knowing she hadn't been paying attention, he sarcastically called upon her to give the answer to a difficult problem the class had been discussing for the past five minutes.

Carmela, flustered, instantly responded with the first number that appeared in her mind, "9,473."

"Why, that's correct!" her astonished teacher exclaimed.

Carmela thought she was out of the woods until he followed up by saying, "Now explain to the class how you got that answer." Wild horses couldn't have dragged the truth out of her!

As a young wife and mother, Carmela mostly tried to ignore her intuitive abilities, although she did occasionally resort to them in emergencies. For instance, she remembers being repeatedly frustrated in her efforts to keep her dogs from chasing her ducks. A series of physical barriers failed to solve the problem, so in desperation she visualized an uncrossable boundary in her mind, silently commanding the dogs to stay on one side of it and the ducks on the other. After that, the animals kept their distance without physical restraint.

However, it was not until she was laid up with a sprained ankle when in her thirties that she began slipping into states of expanded consciousness and decided to take them seriously. Raised a devout Catholic, Carmela now studied metaphysical thinking from many spiritual traditions, exploring the connections among them. In meditation, she was shown how miracles operate, and she began to play with the power of her mind to create the conditions she desired.

During this period of her life, Carmela worked for several years doing psychic readings and developed a reputation for excellent results. But as her own spiritual growth progressed, she began to realize that her real contribution would be as a teacher of miracles and higher consciousness. What was the point of telling someone how her relationship was likely to turn out when she could be teaching her how to get things to turn out the way she wanted them to? At this point, Carmela began taking on students for enlightenment studies.

Like Patricia Sun, Carmela Corallo helps others by consulting her higher consciousness about what to say and do. Her response to each situation is unique rather than formulaic. Nevertheless, some generalizations can be made. When she sets out to perform a miracle, Carmela says that she usually visualizes the existing condition and then dissolves it in her mind and visualizes in its place the result she would prefer to have. She offers the following as an example.

An Example of a Miracle

From her perch on the roof, Carmela's student Bette watched one of her worst nightmares taking shape: A brush fire was racing toward her house. What had a short time earlier been distant smoke was now a towering sheet of flame methodically devouring everything in its path.

Bette continued grimly soaking down her roof with a hose, but when the firefighters conceded defeat and packed up their equipment, there seemed to be nothing further to do except evacuate as quickly as possible. The nearby roofs were soon deserted as her neighbors threw a few precious belongings into their cars and screeched off down the road. Bette recognized that at this point, it would take a miracle to save her home. But she had been learning about miracles from Carmela. She quickly made up her mind. "If it's going to take a miracle, then we'd better have a miracle."

She hurried to the phone to call Carmela's office. Reaching her secretary Jan, Bette quickly explained her urgent need for help and then hung up and raced back up to the roof to continue watering until the last possible moment.

Carmela was at home when her secretary called to convey Bette's request. Jan hastily explained the situation and ended, "So can you do a miracle and stop the fire?"

"I'll certainly try," Carmela replied. "Hold the line."

Carmela explained her own part in the drama as follows: "I set down the phone and went into meditation. As I tuned in on the situation in higher consciousness, I visualized brilliant orange flames sweeping through the chaparral toward some houses. The afternoon onshore breeze appeared to be driving them at a terrific rate. As I watched, it struck me that the wind was the real problem here.

"Now, I have always felt very close to the forces of nature and to the wind in particular. In this emergency, it seemed natural to call upon the elemental spirits associated with water, fire, and wind, to request their cooperation.

"In my imagination, I called up the nature spirits and pointed out the misery the fire would cause Bette and her neighbors if it consumed their houses. I asked them to help us if it were truly in the highest and best interest of everyone involved that the houses be spared. Then I waited to see what their response would be.

"At first, nothing seemed to be happening. But then as I continued to watch the scene in my imagination, the wind assumed a physical form and became two giant hands. These hands reached down and gathered in the flames the way one would gather hair into a ponytail. With the wind's "hands" gripping the fire it could no longer spread, and at that point I saw the leading edge of the blaze stop moving toward the houses. A few moments later, water formed a blue circle around the perimeter of the burning area. Picking the phone back up, I told Jan that I thought it would be all right now. I looked at my watch, and it was four o'clock."

In an unprecedented move, the afternoon onshore breeze shifted 180 degrees during the five minutes when Jan was on the phone with Carmela. It drove the fire back upon itself and held it steady. The firefighters, who had pulled out in order to form a new line of defense on the other side of the mountain, quickly seized the opportunity to get back into action and extinguish it.

From her roof, Bette felt the wind shift and watched the flames halt thirty yards from her house at precisely four o'clock. The next day, the local newspaper carried an exuberant story about the surprising turn of events, quoting the fire chief's remarks about their incredible "good luck" in having the wind reverse itself and pin down the fire right at four.

The question I hope you are asking yourself is: "Why was Carmela's help needed at all? If there are no special people, why couldn't Bette or Jan have done what Carmela did?" Carmela believes that they could have, although they didn't realize it.

While Bette believed in miracles, she may not yet have believed in herself as a miracle worker. Perhaps she could not shake off her fear in order to enter the peaceful altered state that Carmela calls "higher consciousness." Or perhaps she simply didn't believe that it would work for her.

Within the physical illusion, there did not appear to be any

289

way of stopping the fire, and we see that Bette's neighbors as well as the firefighters conceded defeat. Bette, however, remembered that there were "other resources" available and asked for a miracle. Since Bette was fully prepared to accept a miracle but unable to go into the peaceful state necessary to project one, I think that her higher power prompted her to call on Carmela. Here we see how the uncertain "miracle mindedness" of one person can be supplemented by the greater conviction of another.

> *However, as a correction, the miracle need not await the right-mindedness of the receiver. In fact, its purpose is to restore him to his right mind. It is essential, however, that the miracle worker be in his right mind, however briefly, or he will be unable to re-establish right-mindedness in someone else.*
> —A Course in Miracles

Notice that Carmela did not presume to know or to judge the purpose for which the fire had been created. She appealed to the divine will embodied in the elements to intervene and change the outcome *if, and only if, that would truly be for the highest good of everyone involved.* Carmela acknowledged that if Bette had some important lesson to learn through losing her house, the fire must be permitted to take it. But neither Bette nor Carmela was willing to acquiesce in the destruction of her house if it would serve no useful purpose, and they jointly mobilized their wills to actualize a better outcome.

It is critically important to realize that it was not Bette's remaining behind on her roof that did the trick but her realization that she could have a miracle. I am not suggesting that anyone follow Bette's example and ignore the authorities when they order an evacuation. Physical "reality" is being created in our minds, not through our physical actions.

Bette could have achieved the same miraculous result in a variety of ways. She could have called Carmela from a place of safety, or she could have gone to a safe place and visualized a better outcome herself. She could have utilized some shamanic ritual, or she could have prayed to a saint to intercede with God on her behalf, or she could have prayed directly to God, using whatever name seemed best to her. Since time and space are not real, there was no need for her to be on site at the house in order to ask for its protection. Carmela, who was safe at home many miles from the fire, had no difficulty in intuitively "seeing" the problem and its solution.

Miracles Do Not Require Sacrifice

This brings us to the popular misconception that God wants people to jeopardize their safety in order to prove their faith. For example, there are individuals who handle poisonous snakes during religious ceremonies in order to demonstrate their miraculous invulnerability. Some of them die.

Seeking out danger in order to prove that you are special to God is the sort of destructive game the ego likes to play. Since it is our own miracle mindedness that ensures our safety, a momentary lapse in our inner peace could cost us our lives if we insist upon flirting with disaster. Surely there are enough "trials and tribulations" in the world already without arbitrarily creating new ones for exercise.

Mystics emphasize that our higher power asks no sacrifice of us. God is not an abusive parent who subjects us to terrifying "tests," supposedly "for our own good." Our higher power only wants to help us escape from the problems we ourselves have unwittingly created. There may be cases where we must face adversity and times when letting go of a defense is part of the realization that our problem is not real. However, we can behave prudently and still expect to receive God's grace in the form of miracles. Like Christine, we can ask for miraculous healing and still follow our doctor's orders.

Peace Pilgrim's Life

I'd like to close this chapter with some thoughts on healing from Peace Pilgrim's book. Peace Pilgrim had spent much of her adult life lobbying for peace in the halls of Congress before being called to a slightly different spiritual mission. This mission involved walking the highways and byways of America (and occasionally Canada and Mexico), counseling anyone who wished to speak with her about the vital importance of peace at all levels.

She left behind her name, possessions, and personal history and went forth to talk about peace and God to anyone who cared to listen. Crossing deserts and mountains, striking up conversations in country truck stops, general stores, and inner-city bus stations, she made herself available to people in all levels of society. One night she might sleep in a mansion and the next under the stars with leaves or newspaper for a blanket. It was all the same to her.

This fearless woman carried no money, but neither did she beg. Like Yogananda on his visit to Brindaban, she simply relied upon God to provide everything she needed, and she was not disappointed. Despite her advanced age, Peace Pilgrim walked tirelessly until offered shelter and fasted until offered food. Along the way, she talked to anyone who approached her, curious about the sign she wore saying that she was a pilgrim walking for peace.

She also accepted every opportunity to address larger groups through the media and in churches, auditoriums, and classrooms. She was reputedly a brilliant speaker, and many who invited her onto a talk show as an amusing eccentric came away profoundly changed by her gentle integrity and comprehensive grasp of the way an individual's inner peace or the lack of it influences everything from personal success and happiness to international tensions.

Some regard this woman of no particular religion as an authentic American saint. Peace Pilgrim experienced many miracles in her life and frequently helped others to access miracles of their own. However, understanding as she did the important purpose that the problems in our lives serve, she was extremely cautious about taking over for, or interfering with, others. She understood that true healing has to do with the sufferer's own insight into the unreality of his or her condition and that this goal can be subverted if someone else removes the problem prematurely. The following excerpts from her fascinating book *Peace Pilgrim: Her Life and Works in Her Own Words* will make this clearer.

Peace Pilgrim

One must be very careful when praying for others to pray for the removal of the cause and not the removal of the symptom. A simple healing prayer is this: "Bring this life into harmony with God's Will. May you so live that all who meet you will be uplifted, that all who bless you will be blessed, that all who serve you will receive the greatest satisfaction. If any should attempt to harm you, may they contact your thought of God and be healed."

Peace Pilgrim went on to say this about healing.

Eager beaver psychic healers are those who work on the removal of symptoms and not the removal of cause. When you desire phenomena, you possess phenomena; you do not get God. Let's say I am a psychic healer living next door to you, and you have chosen to come into this life to face some kind of physical symptom until you have removed the cause. Well, when the symptom manifests, I remove it. And so the symptom manifests again, and I then remove it again, and I manage to keep that symptom removed.

When you step over to the disembodied side of life, for another reason altogether, instead of blessing me for having removed the symptom you'll say, "That meddler! I came to solve this problem but she kept removing the symptom and therefore I never solved it!"

In her book, Peace offers the following example of a miraculous healing in which she played a role.

Difficulties with material things often come to remind us that our concentration should be on spiritual things instead of material things. Let me tell you a story of a woman who had a personal problem. She lived constantly with pain. It was something in her back. I can still see her, arranging the pillows behind her back so it wouldn't hurt quite so much. She was quite bitter about this. I talked to her about the wonderful purpose of problems in our lives, and tried to inspire her to think about God instead of her problems. I must have been successful to some degree, because one night after she had gone to bed she got to thinking about God.

"God regards me, this little grain of dust, as so important that he sends me just the right problems to grow on," she began thinking. And she turned to God and said, "Oh, dear God, thank you for this pain through which I may grow closer to thee." Then the pain was gone, and it has never returned. Perhaps that's what it means when it says *"In all things be thankful."* Maybe more often we should pray the prayer of thankfulness for our problems.[47]

Treat the Mental Cause and Not Just the Physical Symptom

The miracle workers we have considered in this chapter share an understanding that problems are self-chosen challenges that stimulate the sufferer to discover and correct the mistaken beliefs that caused them in the first place. Each of these women tries to support others in recognizing that they have the inner resources necessary to overcome their problems. Their prayers are not simply for symptomatic relief but for whatever experiences Divine

Will knows to truly be in the best interest of the individual seeking healing. They also understand that a person may not yet be ready to accept help, and that this misguided exercise of free will is no reflection upon themselves or upon the grace of God. When the mind is genuinely miracle ready, the miracle always occurs.

21

Healing Your Relationships

Few find inner peace but this is not because they try
and fail, it is because they do not try.

— Peace Pilgrim

Are there any useful generalizations we can now make about accessing miracles? I think there are. We have seen that the people who actually do receive divine help in highly dangerous situations all seem to spontaneously follow the same basic procedure. There would appear to be certain mental steps a miracle worker goes through when faced with a "hopeless" problem.

In order to understand these steps more clearly, let us now take a look at their application to a less dire problem—one that involves the saving of a relationship rather than the saving of a life. How might the mental shift that delivers us from mortal threat produce a positive outcome in a typical, everyday interpersonal conflict? Consider the case of Melanie.

Melanie

A very sweet and refined young woman I used to see as a client mentioned casually one day that she had found it necessary to dump the punch bowl over her boyfriend's head at his annual office Christmas party. She dropped this little gem into a discussion of holiday preparations and quickly moved on, but I could not let it go quite so easily.

"Wait a minute. You did what?" I demanded, stunned.

"I dumped the punch bowl over Ed's head." Melanie replied matter-of-factly. "I had to."

Melanie evidently hoped that I would let her outrageous behavior pass without further comment. However, I had no intention of going along with her on this.

"You *had* to? And why exactly did you have to do that, Melanie?" I asked, affecting the cautious air of one humoring a dangerous mental patient. The more she tried to play this incident down, the more determined I was to play it up.

As I listened with growing incredulity, Melanie went on to blandly recount a series of interactions in which she felt that Ed had been trying to put her down before his associates. It was a real education hearing her calmly rationalize each step leading up to this bizarre outburst with what she obviously regarded as impeccable logic. Starting from a remark of Ed's made in a tone she did not like, Melanie built her case against him, ending her account with the statement: "So you see, Carolyn, throwing the punch over Ed was really the only thing I could have done."

"The only thing you could have done? Drenching Ed with punch in front of his coworkers was the *only* thing you could have done?!"

"Gee, do you think I did the wrong thing?" Melanie asked, feigning wide-eyed innocence.

I stared at her in amazement. "The wrong thing!" I repeated, in a distracted sort of way. Theatrically clutching my hair like someone clinging to sanity by a thread, I began to gently pound my head against a nearby table. "Yes, maybe that might have been the wrong thing, Melanie! It's *just barely possible* that that might have been the wrong thing to do!"

At this point, she dropped the innocent routine and burst out laughing. "Yeah, I really got him good! You should have been there, Carolyn. It was beautiful!"

I believe that Melanie's bizarre behavior and the events leading up to it shed light on the way the ego typically attempts to defend itself by attacking others. Despite her protestations of innocence, it is clear from her final remark that Melanie felt she had shown Ed a thing or two. It will be instructive to examine the strange chain of logic by which the ego of a polite young woman can justify even this blatantly destructive outburst. By tracing this client's inner process, we may be able to gain some insight into the dynamics of the ego and identify the point at which her higher power could have intervened to reinterpret the situation had she asked it for help.

The Turning Point

Melanie maintained that Ed had spent the entire evening "putting her down" in front of his associates and insisted that she had only responded as "anyone else would have done" in the same circumstances. And, indeed, if we accept her premise that Ed had been engaged in a diabolical plot to strip her of every shred of human dignity, her violent reaction does seem to make a certain amount of sense.

As we analyzed her thought process on the evening of this disastrous date, Melanie began to realize that she had actually felt very insecure about meeting Ed's friends for the first time. He was an architect, and she was "only" a secretary. He came from a cultured, white-collar background, while her family had been solidly working class. As we explored her reactions, Melanie realized that she had been afraid that Ed's friends would think she was not good enough for him. Reacting to her fear over the possibility that Ed's friends were going to make her feel small, Melanie got there first with a preemptive strike. She decided to find fault with him first.

Notice how quickly Melanie's ego went from unconscious guilt to the projection of that guilt onto someone else. The distressing thought "Perhaps I am not good enough for Ed" was turned into "I'll bet Ed and his friends think I am not good enough for him. How dare they!"

This is a clear example of the ego's tendency to project its own unacceptable ideas onto others. Now her doubts about her own worth were pushed out of awareness and seen as outside her own mind, coming from Ed and his friends. In a moment Melanie went from being an insecure young woman worried about meeting her boyfriend's associates to the "innocent victim" of their snobbery.

This was evidently a much more comfortable position for her to be in. Now that the guilt was seen as outside her own mind, she knew how to combat it. Melanie quickly set about punishing Ed for the sentiments her own ego had assigned him. After all, if Ed was an inconsiderate jerk, how could there be any question of *her* worthiness?

Notice how the ego skillfully manufactures the "reality" in which it has already decided to believe by behaving as if it is true. While it seems unlikely that Ed had set off to this party with the intention of showing his associates what a "loser" he was dating, I think we can safely assume that they all came away from this debacle quite convinced that Melanie was not good enough for him. And by the end of the evening Melanie had collected all the "evidence" she could possibly want that Ed and his friends were just a bunch of snobs who looked down upon her "for no reason at all."

Melanie ultimately recognized that her fear had made her vigilant for trouble from the moment Ed arrived to pick her up. Her ego was already hovering over the solution of blaming Ed for her anxiety and discomfort, but she could not proceed until he had done something she could interpret as an offense.

In each such interaction, there comes a moment when the other person first violates our expectations for appropriate behavior. In Melanie's case, this occurred on the way to the party when Ed used a questionable tone of voice in answering her inquiry about what time it was. Melanie interpreted his "sarcastic" tone as evidence that he was angry with her for making them late. This was the critical point at which the interaction branched off from friend-friend into the victim-victimizer mode.

Interpreting Ed's tone as an attack upon herself, Melanie coun-terattacked, reminding him sharply that although she had delayed their departure, it had been his idea to cut it so close in the first place. He did not respond to this remark, a fact that Melanie in-terpreted as further evidence of his contemptuous attitude toward her. From that point on, the evening was just one long downhill slide into the punch bowl.

How could a miracle-minded attitude have made this evening turn out differently? Let us take a look at the steps that miracle workers follow and see how they might have worked here.

(1) Insisting Upon a Second Opinion

The first step in calling up a miracle is to question the in-terpretation of "reality" your ego is showing you. We too often accept the ego's analysis of our situation automatically and quickly hurry on to deciding what to do about it. Yet, once we have accepted the ego's premises—that someone or something has the power to injure us against our will and is about to do so—its conclusions about what to do next are going to seem perfectly logical.

When Melanie accepted her ego's view that she was about to be the innocent victim of an unprovoked attack, she skipped right over the point where a miracle might have intervened without noticing that she had done so. This would be the point at which she decided to impute hostile motives to Ed, conceiving of him as a "bad" person who meant to hurt her.

Melanie actually projected her own fear and hostility onto the situation and mistakenly attributed these motivations to Ed. In this way, she missed her opportunity to ask her higher power if there was some other way to understand what was going on. For example, by assuming that Ed was angry with her in the car, Melanie lost her opportunity to find out that he was really only nervous or preoccupied.

(2) Peacefully Turning Within for Guidance

When we respond to a confusing occurrence by leaping into a meditative state, we are tacitly affirming that we do not like the way things appear to be shaping up, and that we would like to see them differently. In this case, Melanie could have noticed the oddness of Ed's tone and turned within for help. Had she done so, she might have been directed to raise the matter in the form of a question: "Gee, Ed, you sound a little strained. Are you angry with me about something?" This would have allowed her to clarify the issue and perhaps resolve it. Instead, she consulted her ego, which saw only the impatience and contempt it expected to find in a man of Ed's obvious distinction.

(3) Clarifying Your Goal for the Outcome of the Situation at the Beginning

Selecting a positive outcome as your objective mobilizes your will and gives it direction, as well as attracting divine assistance. When we reach for a possibility that is generally beneficial, Providence arranges things to suit our needs. Bullets miss their mark, boxes of detergent break our falls, beaver ponds appear where they will do the most good.

According to the spiritual viewpoint, we adopt a role in each situation based upon our goal for it—what we (consciously or unconsciously) plan to have it prove. Melanie elected to cast herself as the plucky heroine and Ed as a supercilious creep who needed to be taught a sharp lesson. She structured the situation this way in order to prove that it was really Ed who was unworthy of love, thereby lessening the pain of his anticipated rejection, but it is clear that her own attitude actually brought that rejection about.

It is also important to remember that your objective should be the very general one of a satisfactory outcome all around. It is not appropriate to dictate to your higher power specifically how this is to be achieved.

301

For example, a woman in Melanie's position might have been tempted to set the goal of making Ed fall in love with her. However, Ed has free will too, and God is not going to try to make him do anything he doesn't want to do. Further, if Ed and Melanie are not right for each other, the happiest outcome might be for them to both realize this and go their separate ways in a spirit of mutual respect. Our egos simply do not know what will truly lead to happiness, but our higher power does.

If in invoking divine help we impose conditions and want God to help us in the way we like it, then we are still being secretly dominated by our ego.
—Haridas Chaudhuri

(4) Never Giving Up on the Possibility of a Happy Ending

We will not set the goal of a positive outcome if we allow the ego to convince us that a happy ending is no longer possible. For example, most people who had had bone surgically removed from their leg would simply concede that becoming Miss America was no longer a realistic goal. Similarly, most people spinning out of control across a crowded freeway, or lying on the bottom of a frozen lake would consider continued hope for a happy ending inappropriate. Yet, if we concede defeat, we are no longer creating the space for a miracle.

Having bought the idea that it was absurd to hope that a man like Ed might love and admire a woman like her, Melanie felt that a happy ending was not within her reach. Acting on this assumption, she settled for saving face by making the "inevitable" breakup look like her own idea.

Because miracles are always possible, there are always grounds for hope. By not giving up, we remain focused upon our goal and keep our will directed toward a happy ending. Isn't it always

302

the "fool," who doesn't understand that something can't be done, who goes ahead and does it? Do not be discouraged by the ego's bleak picture. No situation is truly hopeless until you accept it as such and act on that assumption.

(5) Willing a Happy Ending for Everyone Concerned

Miracles become possible when we unite our own will with that of our higher power. However, it is important to remember that we all share the same higher power. Just as a loving parent could not exploit one child for the benefit of another, Divine Love is incapable of helping one person succeed at the expense of someone else. When we ask for ascendancy over another person, God cannot share our goal, and so we are thrown back on the ego's meager resources. Miracles are only accessed by individuals who truly desire what is best for everyone and are willing to let their higher power decide what that will look like.

(6) Focusing on What Is Positive and Looking Past the Negative

How does our choice of a successful outcome for everyone lead to its attainment? Having chosen a happy ending, we will look for means that are consistent with it. This will lead us to focus only upon the positive aspects of the situation—those aspects that hold out the hope that our goal can be realized.

The positive aspects of a situation include our belief in our own abilities, our faith that a miracle can still turn things around, and our confidence that there is good in other people that can still come to the surface and make them reconsider their behavior. By concentrating upon our goal and looking past every factor that could interfere with its attainment, our will selects the possible future of our choice from the implicate order and then blazes a path to it.

It is not that we do not notice another person's hostile intent. We simply look past it to the good and deserving individual who has temporarily given way to fear or anger and who badly needs our forgiveness. Many people find it easy to look beyond the hostility of a loved, but momentarily cranky, child, and it is really no different when we do the same for adults.

For example, Melanie could have ignored Ed's abrupt tone and concentrated instead upon the idea that he was a beloved friend who was momentarily out of sorts and needed a little kindness. A few words of reassurance from her might have quickly pulled him out of whatever negative mental state he happened to be in. Ed would almost certainly have been grateful for her patience and understanding.

Notice that the people who experienced deliverance all steadfastly declined to focus upon their attacker's hostile intent and power to hurt them. They were aware of what the other person had in mind, but they responded with forgiveness anyway, brushing the hostility aside as if all that really mattered was the love between them.

Interactions are improvisations, and if one party to an interaction stands foursquare for the innocence of everyone involved and will not budge, it becomes very difficult for others to long resist that influence. It is extremely awkward to find oneself attacking someone who is not attacking back. Who would persist in presenting themselves as a bully if they could be someone's honored friend instead?

(7) Remembering That All Things Are Possible

We have seen many examples where a miracle-minded attitude won over a very hostile person. In Melanie's case, it is easy to see that a little kindness and maturity on her part could have made an enormous difference. But the fact is, had she opted for inner peace, she would somehow have had an enjoyable evening—even if Ed and his friends really did hold her in contempt and were absolutely determined to treat her badly. In the latter case, her enjoyment might have come through leaving the party early, or meeting someone else there, or simply appreciating the food and drink.

Let me emphasize that your well-being depends upon your own consciousness, not upon anyone else's goodwill or cooperation. *Your* mind creates *your* physical illusion, and your decision to forgive insures your safety regardless of what others choose. For example, in the movie *Schindler's List*, we see a depiction of a true incident where a Nazi officer tried to execute a man who had been working in Schindler's factory.

Scene From *Schindler's List*

Thinking he has identified a slacker in Schindler's factory, a Nazi officer seizes one of the Jewish workers and drags him outside for immediate execution. The worker, who happens to be a rabbi, tries vainly to explain that his output was unusually low today only because the machinery was down for repairs most of the morning, but the officer is not interested in his "excuses."

Flinging the worker down on the pavement, the officer whips out his pistol. Firing at point-blank range, he goes to put a bullet into the kneeling Jew's head, but nothing happens. His gun has jammed. He checks his weapon and tries again, but still without result. Each time he tries to shoot, the trigger clicks harmlessly.

A fellow officer who sees his predicament helpfully offers his own weapon, but when the Nazi tries to use this new gun, it will not work either. Then a third man tries his own gun, but this one malfunctions as well.

The Nazis stand around checking and rechecking their weapons, as all three of them try repeatedly to fire a round into the rabbi's head. All three pistols continue to click ineffectually. Eventually, the three would-be executioners become preoccupied with this strange problem and lose interest in their intended victim.

Giving the rabbi a petulant whack on the head, the Nazi officers wander off together, engrossed in their discussion of manufacturing defects. The rabbi goes on to survive his wartime experience.

I believe it is not God's will that a better man can be injured by a worse.

—Socrates

Here, the rabbi's miracle mindedness did not win over the Nazi officers, but it did make it impossible for them to take his life. He chose peace for himself, and that choice kept him safe in the presence of mortal danger.

Remember, despite their appearance of being accidental, these are miracles we are talking about here. They are not mere psychological strategies. Miracle-minded people cannot only accomplish things that are highly improbable, they can also accomplish feats that are not ordinarily regarded as being physically possible. The miracle actually readjusts time and space in order to meet your goal for the situation. This will be done unobtrusively if possible, but where necessary, your higher power will not hesitate to violate physical laws in order to fulfill your constructive intention.

(8) Never Accepting Fear as Justified

All fear is a sign of want of faith.

—Mohandas Gandhi

The presence of fear is a sure sign that you are according belief to a frightening illusion. When we put our faith in the idea that fear is justified, we are not in a position to access a miracle. If it is your decision to retain the ego as counsel, then you are not really placing your case in the hands of your higher power.

Notice that in an emergency, your ego would already have solved your problem if it had known how. Miracles are only at issue because the ego is forced to recognize that it can see no way out. When there is a gun to your head, the ego has little to offer beyond its condolences and the assurance that it is all terribly unfair.

This is because the ego has defined the problem as "insoluble." If you agree that the problem cannot be solved, then your higher power could only solve it at the cost of contradicting you, which it will not do. It can manipulate time and space effortlessly, but it regards your will as sacred and will never violate your freedom to dream your world any way you choose.

The people who reported deliverance all knew that the odds against survival were overwhelming. But remember, if we are indeed *choosing* the things that happen to us, *odds mean nothing.* If you offer me ninety-nine plates of brussels sprouts and one plate of apple pie, I am going to choose pie—not one time out of a hundred but every single time. Nor will the likelihood of my picking the pie change if you add a thousand more plates of brussels sprouts, so please don't bother! As long as I am aware of having a choice between apple pie and brussels sprouts, I am going to pick the pie. And anyone who realizes that they have a choice between a miracle and a disaster is going to pick the miracle.

Choosing a miracle, then, means choosing against a fearful interpretation of your situation. Confronted by grave danger, most of my deliverance subjects dropped their ego's terrifying perception like a hot brick and leaped into a peaceful altered state of consciousness where fear was conspicuous by its absence. However, there were a number of cases where fear continued to be present to some degree, and these are instructive.

Kathleen, who was abducted by a serial rapist and murderer, provides a striking example of the struggle to achieve miracle mindedness. She understood that believing her ego's fearful account placed her in peril, and she repeatedly brought her panicky mind back to a loving focus upon the basic decency that she knew must be present in even such a man as this.

For a miracle to occur, *it is not necessary that fear be completely absent,* only that you do not allow it to blind and deceive you.

Despite her fear, Melanie could have decided, "I'm just going to go to this party and trust that everything will be fine. Even if it looks as though Ed is being mean to me, I'll just act as if everything is all right and be nice to him." If the depressing version of reality that seemed to face her was not the one she preferred to see, the means would have been given her to see it differently.

In summary, by steadfastly holding our minds in peace and love, we cause reasons for peace and love to be woven into our physical illusion. Suddenly, people are a little friendlier, bureaucrats more accommodating, and the weather a bit more appropriate to our needs. Things that might easily have gone wrong go right. We feel lucky, and no matter what we try we can't seem to lose.

Many of us have briefly glimpsed this miraculous state of consciousness when we were falling in love. Lovers go around illuminated from within by joy, and as a result their world becomes a magical place. Even strangers on the street go out of their way to be helpful and entertaining when we are in love. If a touch of romance can so fundamentally restructure our reality, what do you imagine would happen if we all followed the spiritual prescription to love everyone all the time? The possibilities are awesome!

Indeed, if miracles are to be of any practical use, they had better not be reserved only for emergencies. It is all very well to realize that miracles can save your life, but how often do we really need our lives saved? Speaking for myself, what I need most of the time are small miracles to rescue my mornings, afternoons, and evenings from being wasted in petty aggravation and resentment. This is another, less dramatic way in which miracles can "save" our lives.

It is not necessary that you walk around in a state of saintly forbearance—*just that you be willing to be shown that you were wrong when you judged a brother or a sister unworthy of love.* The next time you are tempted to feel victimized by the government, your boss, or a loved one, why not try suspending judgment and listening inwardly for direction? Perhaps you, too, will find that reconciliation is possible. Perhaps your insurmountable problem will turn out to be surmountable after all.

HEALING YOUR RELATIONSHIPS

In this chapter we have delineated a strategy for accessing the help of your higher power. Sometimes this is all you need to do in order to receive a miracle. In other situations, our higher power's help comes in the form of intuitive guidance that must be followed if the miracle is to occur. The next chapter will clarify some of the ways in which this guidance is experienced.

22

Recognizing the Voice of God

The most important part of prayer is what we feel,
not what we say. We spend a great deal of time telling
God what we think should be done, and not enough
time waiting in the stillness for God to tell us what to do.
— Peace Pilgrim

Once you have set aside fear and opted for a peaceful outcome that works for everyone, you are miracle ready. At this point,
you need only rest in peace and wait for your higher power to
make its presence felt. Perhaps the situation will now undergo
a radical shift that appears to have nothing to do with you. Help
sometimes just seems to arrive in the nick of time.

However, in other cases miracle-minded individuals are instrumental in turning the situation around. Acting under inner
guidance, they say or do something that changes everything. Let
us consider some of the forms in which this inner guidance commonly appears.

A Voice

Spiritual guidance sometimes comes in the form of verbal instructions. You might hear a voice, as Mel did when told to "Move
to the left" while walking in the dark along that country road.
As we saw earlier, Harry Houdini had a somewhat similar experience with a voice that rescued him from almost certain death,

although the one he heard appeared to be that of his mother and seemed to be coming from a point outside his body. However, guidance is more commonly experienced as a voice within our own minds.

A Perceptual Shift

Guidance also frequently takes the form of a shift in perspective. The situation just begins to appear in a different light, and the new point of view makes some different sort of behavior seem more appropriate than the defensive reaction the ego had in mind. An "enemy" is reconceptualized as a confused person trying to get his or her needs met in an inappropriate way. Something the ego regarded as "impossible" suddenly seems worth one more try. Remember Brian entertaining the prison population with his Gary Cooper impression? It just seemed like the thing to do once he stopped considering everyone as an enemy and began to think of them as fun-loving people like himself.

Synchronous Experiences

Spiritual guidance can also take the form of a synchronous experience. We may be asking for guidance or wishing we knew what to do when some significant words on a billboard catch our eye, or we overhear a phrase that strikes us as the answer we have been seeking.

For example, a week or so after he had had cataract surgery, my husband was sitting in a restaurant gloomily wondering if his vision in the operated eye would ever be normal. The responsiveness of the pupil had not returned as quickly as expected, and Arnie couldn't help worrying about it. All at once, he noticed that his gaze was resting on the address of a business across the street: 2020 Wilshire Blvd. It occurred to him that that "2020" might be a synchronistic answer to his concern, and he felt instantly reassured. I am happy to report that his "new" eye soon tested out at 20-20.

Occasionally, the meaningful relationship between an experience and our train of thought will simply leap out at us, but some people actively seek this sort of guidance by opening a spiritual volume at random and reading the first paragraph their eye falls upon. And sometimes, as in the following case, guidance may involve a variety of modalities.

Louis

My husband Arnie, who is also a psychologist, tells of a client who was grappling with a difficult problem in therapy. At one point during their session, Louis dropped into a meditative silence, staring off into space as he considered the various ramifications of an important decision facing him. After a few moments, he startled Arnie by quietly announcing, "There's a being here with us in the room."

Asked to explain further, Louis continued, "It's like a light. It seems to want to help me with my problem."

Arnie went along with this, asking, "How will it be able to help you?"

"I don't know," Louis replied.

"Why don't you ask it and see what it says," Arnie suggested.

Louis listened inwardly while continuing to gaze at a point across the room. Then his eyes began to move. "Oh! It's trying to show me where to find the guidance I'm asking for. It moved over there by those books. It says that the answer I need is in one of them."

"Which one?" asked Arnie.

"It seems to be that fat blue one—the third book down in the middle stack. Now the light is all around it."

Arnie went over and retrieved the volume indicated from among the fifty-odd books and journals stacked haphazardly on his work table. "Do you know what book this is?" he inquired. Louis replied that he didn't—just that the light had said it contained the answer he was seeking. Then, in response to Arnie's question about where in the book they were supposed to look, Louis quickly rattled off a page, and then a paragraph number. Arnie handed him the volume and suggested that he take a look.

RECOGNIZING THE VOICE OF GOD

Turning to the indicated page and paragraph, Louis began to read aloud. Arnie said that a chill went up his spine as his client read off a passage that offered an illuminating answer to the very question they had been discussing. Louis looked up in wonder. "That's it! That's exactly what I needed to know! Hey, what book is this anyway?" Turning it over in his hands, Louis discovered what Arnie already knew—appropriately enough, it was *A Course in Miracles.*

Overshadowing

While most of the people who shared their deliverance stories with me followed inner promptings, some felt as if their higher power actually took control, speaking and acting in their place—a process that is sometimes referred to as *overshadowing*. Unlike a state of possession, the overshadowed individual's consciousness continues to be present and can intervene at any point if it wishes to do so. In overshadowing, the person voluntarily consents to being temporarily relegated to the role of spectator while his or her higher power takes over. This sounds like what happened to Debra in her conversation with the terrorists. Perhaps the following experience of mine will make this process clearer.

Laura

While directing a program for hospitalized female mental patients who had been sexually abused as children, I worked with a woman I'll call Laura, who had many serious problems. In addition to bipolar disorder, she was a low-functioning borderline and a recovering alcoholic. She had an extensive history of suicidal behavior and assaults upon others, and her children had been removed from her care as a result of the sadistic physical abuse she had inflicted upon them while in psychotic states.

One Sunday afternoon while I was at home idly flipping through channels on the TV, I received a call from Laura, who was now seeing me for psychotherapy on an outpatient basis. I picked up the phone and then snatched it away from my ear as she began screaming obscenities. As Laura continued to rave, it became clear that she had gone into a psychotic state characterized by intense paranoia. She was now threatening to kill me and then herself, having decided that, as her therapist, I was personally responsible for all of her unhappiness.

Many anxious thoughts flashed through my mind. "She's off her medication. I should have the police pick her up before she hurts herself or someone else. But how can I do that when I don't know where she is?" (I knew that Laura's home phone had been disconnected for nonpayment of the bill. She couldn't be calling from there, and in her present paranoid state she would almost certainly refuse to tell me where she was.)

I attempted to speak, but Laura simply shouted me down. How was I going to help her if I couldn't even get a word in? I searched my mind for anything I had ever learned in the course of my professional training that might help in this situation and came up empty. I simply had no idea what to do.

Since my clinical training failed to provide any useful guidelines for this situation, I turned next to my spiritual training. The first thing to do was to calm down and come back into the truth. What was the truth here? The truth, I concluded, was that I was just a limited human being who did not know what to do. However, it was also true that I could turn to my higher power for help if I chose to do so.

"God, this is your client," I said inwardly. "I think you'd better do something about this, because I sure as hell don't know what to do!"

Having said this, I guessed that I should probably try to calm down and go into a meditative state in case my higher power had any bulletins for me. If I were in a peaceful state of mind, some sense of ease might begin to penetrate Laura's terror. She would have to stop screaming to catch her breath at some point, and if she didn't hang up first I might just manage to jump into the conversation. I had no idea what I would say, but hopefully that would be clearer when the time came. As Laura continued her litany of paranoid threats and accusations, I cleared my mind to enter meditation.

The next thing I knew, I was totally absorbed in a scene from *Conan the Barbarian*! Before picking up the phone, I had evidently flipped the television to a station playing that movie. I can only guess that my eyes must have been resting on the TV set in front of me while I was on the phone, and somehow it had happened that I had become totally engrossed in the movie.

I suddenly awakened to the fact that I had been concentrating on the film as though it were the most fascinating thing I had ever seen. Although I had little sense of time, my recent memory was filled with idle thoughts about Arnold Schwartzenegger's impressive physical endowments: "Holy mackerel, look at the muscles on that guy! Can that be healthy? He must be on steroids." It was clear that my total absorption in the movie had been going on for at least five minutes, and maybe much more.

I was electrified by the realization that I was on the phone with a suicidal client and here I was watching television. "Oh my God, Carolyn!" I thought. "This might just be the worst thing you've ever done in your life!" This was rapidly succeeded by other thoughts: "Don't take time to beat yourself up now, stupid! You've got to get back to Laura and see if there's anything you can do to save the situation. Maybe she didn't notice that you weren't paying attention. Yeah, right! A paranoid client didn't notice she'd been ignored for five minutes or more. Buy a clue, Carolyn."

I jerked back to the phone call in a panic and was shocked to hear a strange voice talking in my living room. I was further astonished to realize that it wasn't a strange voice at all—it was *my* voice, speaking calmly into the phone! While I had been watching television, my mouth had been talking, and I had no idea what it had been saying. I felt that I had now truly entered the Twilight Zone.

As I started surfing on a new wave of fear, I remembered that I had asked my higher power to take over. Just maybe, it had done so. Maybe I should calm down and find out what was going on

315

before panicking further. After all, I thought reasonably, there would be plenty of time for panic later.

When I tuned in to the discussion between the voice and my client, it was a lot like overhearing the conversation at the next table in a restaurant. I initially had trouble making sense of what was being said because I was entering in the middle. However, it soon became apparent that the voice was offering an interpretation of the reason Laura had gotten so upset. I was unaware of the recent events in Laura's life to which it alluded, but as the reason was explained, I remember thinking, "Yeah! I'll bet that's right. That's just the sort of thing that would set her off."

From the other end of the line, I heard Laura say, "Yeah! I'll bet that's it, Carolyn. That must be what happened." Whatever was going on, I was amazed to see that she was now completely calm and cooperative. The psychotic intensity I had heard in Laura's voice earlier had been replaced by focused interest and enthusiasm. And, clearly, she thought I was the one talking.

Laura asked a number of questions that the voice answered insightfully and without hesitation. It ultimately reminded Laura of "our" scheduled appointment the next day and offered a few sensible suggestions for managing her anxiety until then. At the conclusion of the call, Laura thanked me profusely and apologized very sincerely for the terrible things she had said earlier. This paranoid client who always noticed and expressed suspicion about every detail of my dress, speech, and behavior was completely convinced that I had been talking to her! Then we both hung up, and I had my voice back.

Getting Out of Your Own Way

He will tell you exactly what to do to help anyone He sends to you for help, and will speak to him through you if you do not interfere.

—A Course in Miracles

Notice how well this story illustrates the proce
cessing miracles we have just been discussing. My e
self blocked at every turn and initially defined the
hopeless. Despite this, I was aware of wanting a positive outcome
for both Laura and myself. Since my ego clearly had no idea of
how to achieve this, I turned to my higher power.

So peaceful did I become after turning the matter over that
I actually forgot all about it for a while! In so doing, I am afraid
that I missed out on some really masterful psychotherapy. By the
time I got back into the game, my higher power had already
resolved all of the "impossible" aspects of the situation and was
just tidying up loose ends. The client who a few minutes earlier
had threatened my life was now my devoted friend again, her dangerous psychotic reaction gone without a trace.

Although this was the only time in my career as a psychotherapist when I actually dissociated, direction from my higher power
is an everyday occurrence. At this point, I would feel a little foolish trying to do therapy based only upon my ego's skills and
knowledge. What would be the point, when divine guidance is
available for the asking?

Although inner guidance can be as dramatic as a commanding voice, it is more often extremely subtle. Once you get
the hang of identifying the voice of your higher power, you
will realize that it has always been present in your consciousness. Not recognizing what it was, you didn't pay it any special
attention.

This is probably why people so often say, "I just knew that
this was going to happen" when things go wrong. In retrospect, we realize "something" told us what might occur, although
we didn't act on this knowledge because it conflicted with other
voices in our consciousness which we preferred to believe. All
of us seem to have many voices speaking in our mind at any
given time, so how do we know which is the voice of our higher
power?

CREATING MIRACULOUS SOLUTIONS

Characteristics of the Voice That Speaks for God

First of all, your higher power has a characteristically *charitable attitude* that the ego's many voices lack. It stands for universal innocence and is always kind to you and everyone else. Any stream of thought that promotes guilt (for you or anyone else) cannot be the voice of the higher self.

The voice of God will also seem *calm and confident.* Streams of thought that excite fear by "catastrophizing" about the danger you are in can only be generated by the ego. For example, my thoughts when I caught myself watching television instead of helping Laura clearly reflect the ego's perspective. They asserted that I had done something awful that would inevitably have disastrous consequences, called me "stupid," and laid a major guilt trip on me. This hectoring tone is typical of the ego's response in an emergency. Not knowing what to do, it casts around for someone to blame. The self is always a handy target.

While the voice of the higher self can be painfully "direct" and its messages are not always pleasant to hear, its comments are consistently *fair and constructive* rather than abusive and shaming. Remember Mel's conversation with the voice that told him to move to the left? It did not hesitate to point out Mel's stubbornness about taking advice, but even Mel recognized this as fair criticism.

The ego believes that the self has been sinful and needs to sacrifice in order to placate God. Your higher power regards you as innocent and *does not believe in sacrifice.* It might sometimes suggest that you do something difficult—for example, admitting your error to someone—but it will only do this to rectify a deteriorating situation, not to punish or humiliate you.

When the ego masquerades as our higher power, it typically becomes involved with fantasies of specialness through some sort of sacrifice or martyrdom. Always be suspicious if you are tuning in to a voice that asks you to put the interests of others *above* your own. Your higher power sees only perfect equality and will find ways for everyone to come out ahead.

Another characteristic of the voice of your higher power is that it may be *surprising*. In fact, what it has to say may at first seem to be "coming out of left field." This is because its understanding of the situation is so different from the way the ego has led you to view it. Working from an entirely different set of premises, it arrives at a different conclusion about what the problem really is.

Preventing War

For example, I recall once asking my higher power: "If, as you say, I have the power to work miracles, could I prevent war in the Persian Gulf?"

"Why would you want to?" came the prompt reply.

This seemed so bizarre that I couldn't believe I had heard right.

"Why would I want to prevent a war?" I returned with heavy irony. "Aren't you the guy they used to call the Prince of Peace? Surely this can't be that hard to follow! Am I going too fast for you here?" (As you have probably gathered, my higher power has a great deal to put up with.)

However, my inner voice went on to educate me patiently about the value of free will, pointing out that I had always "enjoyed" the freedom to screw up my life in whatever way I wished and that I had learned a great deal through my mistakes. If other people wanted an opportunity to learn through their own mistakes, why would I presume to deny their right to the same kind of education?

The voice said that if enough people wanted a war, there would be a war. If I didn't care to be involved in it, I was free to dream some other experience for myself, but it was not appropriate to interfere with others on the grounds that I knew better than they what experiences they should have. I could try to persuade others to settle their differences peacefully, but in the final analysis, the decision about what to do was theirs. I would have to be satisfied knowing that whatever happened, everyone would learn from it.

Another characteristic of the higher self is that in its view, *all people are equal.* It never exalts one group or individual at the expense of another. Your inner voice may tell you that you are Christ or Buddha, but it will also assure you that everyone else is, too. The higher self discourages the idea that any individual, culture, or religion has a monopoly on truth. It is only the ego that promotes grandiose fantasies of special virtue and entitlement.

Finally, *there is no such thing as an infallible prediction or prophecy.* If you will recall what we said earlier, it will become apparent that the most any prophet can hope to do is to make an accurate assessment of the probabilities of different outcomes given that no one bothers to exercise free will. Since it appears that few people exercise their free will on a regular basis, this can make for fairly accurate short-term forecasts.

All predictions about the future should be understood as conditional statements. Not "You will meet a tall, dark stranger," but "If everyone keeps on doing what they are doing, there is a seventy percent probability that you will meet a tall, dark stranger sometime in the next three months." Because we all have free will, however, there is always the possibility that someone will decide to change the picture.

It might be best to compare our higher power to an excellent athletic coach. The coach is eager to see us succeed if it can be done fairly, and has a fund of good information about our teammates, our opponents, and the rules of the game. A coach can realistically teach us skills, encourage us when we feel hopeless, point out our mistakes, and help us formulate our best strategy for winning. By following this advice, we will learn from our mistakes and play safely as our skills continually improve.

However, while a fine coach makes a vital contribution, there are other factors to be considered as well: our willingness and ability to follow advice, our own strength and skill and that of our teammates, the abilities of our opponents, and so on. Our higher power can show us how to maximize our efforts, but it cannot win the contest for us.

Hearing Your Higher Power

How can you learn to hear the voice of your higher power? Like most skills, this is an area where practice makes perfect. You would not expect to sit down at a piano for the first time and play a beautiful sonata, and you should not expect to confidently pick out your higher power's guidance on the first try either.

It is said that the voice of your higher power is as loud as your willingness to hear it. When you are in mortal danger, your willingness to receive guidance may instantly become all-consuming. However, we do not put much effort into willing things that seem beyond our reach. For that reason, it is a good idea to practice contacting your inner voice before emergencies arise. Your success in small things will train you to turn within for help when the stakes are higher. The ability to achieve a peaceful altered state where we contact inner guidance is greatly strengthened by regular meditation.

There are many types of meditation, but all of them involve a resolute turning away from the ego's incessant chatter in order to experience a different, more peaceful form of consciousness. Any mental or spiritual practice that stills the mind is going to make it easier to access miracles in an emergency. Nevertheless, approaches that do not emphasize that guidance is available do not actively encourage us to seek and utilize it.

For example, many people suffering from chronic pain are receiving great benefit from a process developed by Dr. Herbert Benson called the "relaxation response."[49] This highly effective technique for stilling the mind was borrowed from Eastern spiritual practices but stripped of all spiritual context in order to make it more generally acceptable. It involves focused concentration upon a single syllable.

Patients practicing the relaxation response discover that their pain diminishes when they quiet their minds and enter the peaceful altered state we have discussed. However, they are not taught that guidance is available to them in that state, and so they may not ask for it, and may even tune their higher power out if it attempts to communicate. Thus, they receive some of the benefits of meditation but not others. Whatever meditative practice you choose, remember that there is a source of divine wisdom and power within you that is eager to communicate, although it will usually not speak unless invited to do so.

Inner Guidance Meditation

Meditation is a very simple and natural activity that everyone engages in from time to time throughout the day. Have you ever spent a few minutes gazing out a window with nothing in particular going through your mind? Of course you have. That is a form of meditation.

I did not learn meditation. I just walked, receptive and silent, amid the beauty of nature—and put the wonderful insights that came to me into practice.
—Peace Pilgrim

If you do not presently have a meditation technique that you like, you might wish to try the following. Simply sit comfortably with your eyes closed after doing a few stretches and taking a couple of deep breaths. Focus upon being right here, right now, allowing yourself to be aware of your breathing, the way your body feels at this moment, and the sounds around you. As thoughts arise in your mind, simply notice them—"Oh, a thought about dinner"—and then peacefully return to being here now instead of figuratively climbing aboard your train of thought and riding it into the sunset.

At first, you will find that you go off on many such trains without noticing that you have done so. Instead of becoming frustrated or angry with yourself, simply dismount and go back to being here now. Learning to consciously control one's attention is a challenging process, and you should not expect instant success. With practice, you will learn to go into a very peaceful and detached altered state the moment you decide to do so.

However, there is no need to wait for complete success in this first stage of meditation before proceeding to the second. Your higher power is eager to communicate with you, and your limitations cannot interfere with the process unless you are prepared to let them. All you really need is a little willingness to hear what the divine wisdom within you has to say.

After trying to focus in the present for three or four minutes imagine that your higher power is sitting across from you. It is often handy to symbolize this source of guidance as a benevolent figure who represents divine wisdom to you (for example, Moses, Kwan Yin, Jesus, the Buddha, Lao-tzu, the Great Spirit, the Divine Mother). However, you can just as easily symbolize it as a light, the wind, a totemic animal, or some other physical manifestation.

Visualize this divine being across from you for a minute or two and then begin a conversation with him, her, or it. Explain the nature of your problem and ask for guidance, leaving your inquiry open-ended so that there is wide latitude for response. For example, "What can I do about my financial problems?" is a better question than "How can I make my boss give me a raise?" because it permits the higher self to put things into a larger perspective. Maybe there is no way to get your boss to give you a raise and the thing you need to do is to find a different job. Maybe your financial difficulties are the result of attitudes toward money that must be changed before any improvement will be possible.

You will be attuned to hear the answer to the question you have asked, and it may be difficult for your higher power to get through to you if your question is excessively narrow or misguided. Remember my ill-conceived question about my ability to miraculously avert a war? It was difficult for me to believe I had heard correctly when my higher power responded by asking me to reconsider my reasons for wanting to do so.

A very specific question may not give your higher power the scope it needs to provide useful guidance. But there is a further problem with "yes or no" answers—they make it all too easy for your ego to masquerade as your higher power. If you require your guide to lay out its reasoning, you can assess whether the response is intelligent, loving, and otherwise consistent with your higher power's view of the world.

For example, once my higher power had explained why an attempt to miraculously avert a war would be misguided, the answer made sense to me and reflected a respect for the sovereignty of free will that is consistent with the spiritual point of view. My ego could have supplied a yes or no, but not the enlightening train of logic I actually received.

Having asked your question, allow yourself to imagine what your guide replies. Do not worry about the fact that it may initially seem as though you are just making the whole thing up. You can always take a critical look at your results after you come out of meditation, but remember that judgment and criticisms are functions of the ego. If you attempt to employ your analytic faculties while in meditation, you will be invoking the guidance of your ego rather than that of your higher power, and this means that you are not really meditating. For a little while, just play along and dialogue with your symbol of divine wisdom in any way that occurs to you, putting judgment aside temporarily.

Sometimes people will find themselves blocked and report that their guide is not replying to their questions. If this happens to you, just say to yourself, "If my guide *could have* spoken, what would he/she/it have said?" Make up whatever occurs to you as your guide's reply, bearing in mind that it must reflect an unconditionally loving attitude toward everyone. Then continue the dialogue by responding as if what you imagined had really been said.

As already mentioned, our higher self does not always communicate as a voice. Often a thought will simply occur to us, and it is up to us to clothe it in words. It is perfectly appropriate to put words into your guide's mouth, because our higher power often prompts us through ideas, intuition, and imagination.

As you continue to practice, your interviews with your higher power will begin to seem more natural and spontaneous. Although at first you may come away feeling that you've only been told what you already knew, little by little you will relax and permit your higher power to penetrate your conscious mind. When this occurs, you will be amazed at the results!

Don't Let Your Ego Disparage the Guidance You Receive

As you play at becoming a miracle worker, you will probably find that there are times when your higher power prompts you to say or do something that makes little sense. For example, it is obvious in retrospect that "Move to the left" was good advice, but Mel's ego was not in a position to know that.

Now I am not suggesting that you simply ignore common sense or risk your health or savings on something that might or might not be divine guidance. Especially at the beginning, you should expect to have trouble telling whether a given message is truly coming from your higher self. You have a responsibility to use your best judgment in this as in all things. Your higher power will not lead you wrong, but your ego loves to masquerade as God, and it will lead you wrong every time.

Nothing is so easy as to deceive one's self; for what we wish, we readily believe.

—Demosthenes

We have only to look at the long history of religious fanaticism to realize that people can quite easily delude themselves about what God is directing them to do. There continue to be people in the world who attempt genocide in God's name, and within our own society there are individuals who appear to sincerely believe that Jesus Christ is asking them to hate and persecute people of other religions, races, and sexual orientations. The ego creates gods in its own image, and only time and practice will allow you

325

to reliably distinguish the voice that speaks for God from the many fearful and angry voices through which your ego seeks to justify its resentments and maintain separation.

Nevertheless, if we let our ego be the final judge of every inner prompting, we may limit the help we can receive. This is because our rational minds are often so confused about what the problem really is that they cannot even recognize an inspired solution, much less generate one. Take for example, my interaction with a client I'll call Susan, which occurred early in my training as a psychotherapist.

Susan

Several years earlier, Susan's daugher had nearly died from a severe electrical shock. The two-year-old stopped breathing, and a neighbor had wanted to begin artificial respiration immediately, but Susan, in her panic, was afraid that his amateur attempts at first aid would only make things worse. She insisted upon waiting for the paramedics to arrive. When they did, they were able to resuscitate the child, but by then she had suffered irreversible brain damage as a result of prolonged oxygen deprivation. Susan's daughter was now what is commonly called a "vegetable," unable to recognize anyone, communicate, or perform the simplest functions for herself.

I knew that this loving mother must have been in torment over her disastrous decision to put off artificial respiration, and I was determined to tread very lightly in this area until a good therapeutic relationship had been established. It seemed crucial that I say nothing that would suggest that I had any personal judgments about her behavior. So I was quite annoyed during one session when a sentence kept forming in my mind that pointed out what a terrible blunder Susan had made. The sentence actually made no literal sense that I could see, but it did touch upon Susan's responsibility in the matter of her daughter's disability in what seemed to me to be a very blunt and offensive manner.

Although this statement continued to resonate in my mind, I took a certain pride in my refusal to articulate it. "I might not be a very experienced therapist," I remember thinking, "but thank God I know better than to say something like that!"

Unfortunately, from that point on, the session began to go downhill. Not that anything in particular happened. It just dried up. My previous work with Susan had been characterized by a lively exchange of ideas, but suddenly neither of us had anything to say to one another. In psychotherapy, there are good silences and bad silences, but the one Susan and I eventually fell into was the worst I have ever experienced.

As the awkwardness dragged on, my ego groped in vain for some new starting place. I had a growing conviction that at the end of the session Susan would make some polite excuse not to come back, and I was dismayed to realize that I would be relieved if she did. Anything was better than the barren sense of futility that had suddenly breached our developing relationship.

And through it all that damned sentence kept echoing in my head. How was I going to think of anything to say with that infernal racket going on? Finally, desperate to break the silence and no longer caring how I did it, I blurted out the words that had been demanding my attention.

To my surprise, Susan did not appear to be offended by my comment. Instead, she took on a thoughtful expression and started off on a new verbal tack. The session picked up energy, and she really began to open up. We finished on a very upbeat note, and our subsequent therapeutic work was exciting and productive.

Several weeks later, Susan said shyly, "Carolyn, do you remember that session a while back when we had that long silence?"

I said that I certainly did, and we both laughed about how awkward it had been. Then Susan went on: "And remember when you said . . . ?" Here she repeated that stupid sentence back to me word for word. And it *still* didn't make any sense. In fact, I was frankly surprised that she could so accurately remember a meaningless string of words.

"Uh oh!" I thought. "Here it comes. She really was offended and she is just getting around to telling me how insensitive I was. Well, I guess I have it coming."

But then Susan continued, "You know, when you said that— that's when I knew that you really understood and that I could tell you everything. I had been all set to just quit therapy because I realized that I could never bring myself to tell someone else the truth about how I really felt about my daughter's accident. It just seemed hopeless. And then you said what you did, and I saw that it was all right to talk about it with you because you already knew and yet you didn't hate me. I've been thinking about it for weeks, and I just had to tell you how much it meant to me that you said that."

Afterward I puzzled over that sentence long and hard, and it still didn't make any sense to me. Even with all I eventually learned about Susan, I never did figure out exactly what those words meant to her. I am just very grateful that "something" prompted me to say them.

Here is a case where my higher power handed me the key that would unlock a client's innermost thoughts, but my ego was not in a position to understand its value and would have cast it aside unused. Examine the guidance you receive carefully, and be attentive to the possibility that it may mean more than it initially seems to.

And, finally, do not hamper yourself with the idea that you are not yet "spiritual" enough to hear the voice of God. Your higher power is eager to make conscious contact with you, and the only way you can actually fail is by not making the attempt. Every moment devoted to meditative practice succeeds beyond your wildest imaginings, so don't allow your ego to persuade you it isn't worth the effort. Miracles not worth the effort? Come on now!

The Sequel

It would be a shame to close this chapter without sharing an event that occurred as this book was nearing completion.

Arnie

For several weeks, my husband had been going through a sort of "dark night of the soul" experience. There seemed to be so much negativity in him that he questioned his ability to really help anyone. He felt like a failure and a fraud. How could he presume to guide others when his own consciousness was so imperfect?

Some of Arnie's most intense distress was focused upon the difficulty he was experiencing in hearing the voice of God in meditation. He knew that he heard it easily enough when bringing guidance through for his clients, but like most people, hearing it for himself was more challenging.

One day as we were discussing the problem, I mentioned this chapter and suggested that he glance over it to see if it might be helpful in learning to meditate. After working with it, Arnie told me that he had been able to get a dialogue going with the symbol of God in his mind but that he did not have any confidence that it was really his higher power answering him. So far, this inner voice had offered only comforting platitudes. He knew that what was being said was true in general terms, but that was just the problem. If the voice was only telling him things he already agreed with, then it was probably just his ego masquerading as God. If only his inner voice could surprise him with something he *didn't* already know, maybe then he could believe in it.

I emphasized that meditation usually starts out this way and urged him to accept the comforting philosophical generalities he was hearing as really coming from his higher power. In this way, he would become more relaxed and comfortable with the process. Only little by little would he be able to open his mind to allow information that contradicted his ego's views into awareness.

Later that afternoon, Arnie decided to share the distress he was feeling with the members of a spiritual psychotherapy group he runs for people with life-threatening illnesses. He has been doing this group weekly for seven years, but this was the first time he had ever brought up an issue of his own. Somehow it seemed important to him to let these clients know how deeply flawed their leader really was.

The group members responded to Arnie's vulnerability with great love and support. Indeed, there was a complete role reversal as these ailing clients kindly sought to guide and comfort my husband. Harry, for instance, is a former actor who has been a member of the group since its beginning. He was particularly articulate in urging Arnie to understand that his failings and mistakes were only human and meant nothing in the overall scheme of things.

Arnie said that as Harry talked to him, this man who had seemed weak and ill appeared to come alight and glow from within. Like most good stage actors, Harry is a wonderful speaker, but that day he seemed absolutely inspired. Words flowed from him in a compelling torrent of wisdom and eloquence.

Arnie was moved by Harry's kindness and deeply impressed with his brilliant grasp of the metaphysical principles they used in the group. He longed to be able to take the things he was hearing to heart. But still a destructive ego voice nagged that forgiveness would not come quite so easily for him. The mistakes of others might be easily excused, but he feared that he would be held to some higher standard.

At one point the discussion turned to hearing the voice of God within and Arnie spoke of the difficulty he was experiencing in meditation. Having just read this chapter a few hours earlier, it was fresh in his mind. He decided to use one of my examples to make his point that platitudes are one thing and real guidance quite another.

Arnie mentioned my book and then went on to say that I had once asked Jesus, "If I can perform miracles, couldn't I prevent war in the Persian Gulf?"

"And what do you think Jesus responded?" he asked the group.

Harry had no hesitation in taking up the challenge. "I think he'd say 'Why would you want to?'"

This answer stopped Arnie cold. These were exactly the words

Jesus had said to me! Harry went on to explain his reasoning, and as he did, Arnie's mind was completely blown. It was exactly the same answer I had received!

When Harry finished speaking, Arnie blurted out, "That's it!"

"You mean, what I said was like the answer Carolyn got?" Harry asked in surprise.

"It's not *like* what Carolyn got," Arnie replied. "It's *exactly* what she got. You just said the same thing she heard, word for word!"

Arnie was deeply impressed by this experience. Clearly these identical answers must have come from the same source. And that meant that perhaps the comforting message of forgiveness Harry had conveyed to him earlier, and the similar sentiments expressed in his own meditation, might also have come from this source. Maybe what he had dismissed as "platitudes" had really been God's answer to his prayer for guidance.

23

Trying Out Your
Miraculous Abilities

*Life is the art of drawing sufficient conclusions from
insufficient premises.*

—Samuel Butler

In the final analysis, you have two choices. You can treat
miracles as just another interesting issue science has not yet fully
resolved and file this book away on your bookshelf under M
(for miracles, Miller, or madness, as you prefer). Or you can
take matters into your own hands and find out for yourself if
divine grace is real by referring some of your own problems
to your higher power for solution. This latter approach requires
you to become an amateur scientist, designing private experiments that will establish the reality of miracles to your own
satisfaction.

A good way to begin your investigation is by taking an informal survey, just as I did. Ask around among your acquaintances
to find out whether anyone you know believes that he or she has
experienced a miracle, and if so, what happened. Although people often hesitate to bring miracles up themselves, many will
eagerly recount a wonderful story once they know they are not
going to be held up to ridicule. I think you will be pleasantly surprised to see how common it is for a bad situation to right itself
after someone goes into a peaceful meditative state and follows
the inspiration of the moment.

Personal Experiments

Then comes the designing of personal experiments. All this really means is that you are going to try *doing* something different, in order to see if things *work out* differently as a result. Simply begin with a situation where you are tempted to cast yourself as a victim, and try a miracle-minded attitude instead. You can use your whole lifetime of prior experience with non-miracle-minded approaches to similar problems for purposes of comparison.

Miracle mindedness means behaving like someone who is fearless, well-intentioned, innocent, and, ultimately, invulnerable. However grim the prospects, a miracle worker tries to remain calm and find some less damning construction to place on the situation. She or he listens within for guidance and follows any and all impulses toward loving and constructive action, however bizarre and inappropriate they may appear to the ego.

For example, if you regarded a hostile person as simply frightened and confused, how might you reach out to reassure him or her of your regard? If you knew that a dangerous situation taking shape before you was only a product of your own imagination, what might you think or do? If you understood that this tax audit, court case, or illness would be "no big deal" if you did your best but refused to indulge in worry, resentment, or guilt, how would you proceed?

Let me illustrate this concept of informal private experiments with one I performed while teaching.

Tiffany

My master's-level class in personality theories was constantly being disrupted by a particularly contentious student. Tiffany was a bright woman in her late twenties, but she seemed convinced that I was trying to put something over on the students and that it was her role to spearhead the opposition to this oppression.

No matter what the topic, I could always count on Tiffany to heatedly contradict whatever I had just said. If I mentioned that it was day, she would angrily insist that it was night. If I pointed out the benefits of a certain approach, she "exposed" it for what it "really" was. She was publicly denouncing my "inexcusable ignorance" and "reactionary views" several times at each class meeting.

These continual verbal confrontations took a certain emotional toll on me. For one thing, it was a struggle to keep the discussion on track in the face of Tiffany's constant efforts to subvert it. And, naturally, it is not pleasant to be treated with hostility and contempt. At the level of my ego, I felt insulted by her attitude and regarded myself as her innocent victim. I realized that I could use my legitimate authority as the teacher to insist that Tiffany behave in a more appropriate manner "or else," but something held me back from pursuing this obvious solution.

Tiffany clearly believed that her withering comments reflected what everyone else was really thinking. I could see that she expected the other students to rally to her and that she interpreted their failure to do so as evidence of the degree to which they had been intimidated and brainwashed. However, I knew that many of her classmates were fed up with her behavior.

Other students would come up after class or drop in to my office to disassociate themselves from her sentiments. In fact, one grandmotherly woman facetiously threatened that the next time Tiffany took that tone with me, she was going to personally drag her out into the hall and slap her silly! Several offered to take Tiffany aside and try to talk some sense into her, but we agreed that that would only make her feel attacked and defensive. I suggested that they leave the matter to me.

Following my inner guidance, I adopted a very permissive policy, allowing Tiffany to express her uncomplimentary views in full. When she had finished her denunciation, I would say something nonjudgmental, such as "Well, you've raised some interesting points, Tiffany, and I'm sure everyone will want to think about what you've said." Then I would go on with the business of the class. I tried to treat her with friendly courtesy, to avoid direct confrontation, and to convey that it was perfectly all right for her to disagree with me.

However, this approach didn't seem to be getting me anywhere. The verbal attacks did not lessen in either frequency or intensity. I couldn't help feeling that I must be doing something wrong, so I once again took the matter up with my higher power in meditation.

"What do you think I ought to do about Tiffany?" I asked. "She seems so angry with me. Am I doing something to cause this?"

"What you're doing is fine," Jesus responded. "This is her own problem with authority. Tiffany thinks of you as someone who has power, and she believes that the quickest way to get some for herself is to take yours. In her mind, if she can tear you down in front of the class, everyone will admire her and look to her for leadership. She unconsciously considers the students your 'followers,' and she wants to win them for herself by defeating you in 'single combat.'

"If she could get you to fight back, then she could use your repressive response as the pretext for her own hostility. When you don't defend yourself or even acknowledge that you've been attacked, it confuses her and may eventually lead her to see what she is doing."

However, this explanation didn't really satisfy me. I couldn't let go of the feeling that I must be doing something wrong.

"But, look," I said. "If I am really doing it one hundred percent right, why isn't it working? I must be doing *something* wrong. If I am really being totally nondefensive with Tiffany, why doesn't she notice that I'm not her enemy and stop attacking me? If my motives are innocent enough, shouldn't she get it that I'm not trying to hurt her?"

"Well," he pointed out reasonably, "they crucified *me.*"

This bland statement went through me like electricity. Of course! How silly of me to think that the truth would always prevail in the short run! Not even a great spiritual master like Jesus could make people understand something they didn't want to understand.

335

What made me think that my miracle-minded attitude was going to be able to instantly transform Tiffany's whole orientation toward authority? After all, she had free will, too. If she chose to construct a "reality" in which she was victimized by authority figures, she was free to do so. All I could do was to continue confounding her expectation of counterattack. It was up to her what, if any, conclusion she drew from that.

This conversation relieved the lingering sense of inadequacy I'd been feeling over these outbursts. From then on, it was much clearer in my mind. I would pray for her eventual enlightenment and do my part as well as I could. It was up to Tiffany if and when she would withdraw the insulting projections she was placing upon me.

The course ended with no sign of improvement in her attitude. I was aware of having to exercise extra vigilance to prevent Tiffany's openly expressed contempt for me from influencing my academic evaluation of her performance in the class. I confess that it was a great relief to know that I had seen the last of this troublesome student.

One day between quarters, as I was working in my office, Tiffany came in and tearfully asked if she could speak with me. She was deeply troubled about a personal problem, she said, and I was the only person she felt comfortable sharing it with. She needed some advice, and there was no one else on the faculty she could really trust—no one who understood her as I did. I was stunned to discover that she now regarded me as a respected friend and ally!

Further evidence of this inner transformation came shortly thereafter. When the following quarter began, Tiffany signed up for an elective I was teaching, which she could quite easily have avoided altogether or taken from another teacher. I am still amused to remember the expressions on the faces of the students who had been in the personality theories class the previous quarter. Many of them made no attempt to hide their astonishment when Tiffany walked in. Several nudged their neighbors to get their attention and then jerked their heads in Tiffany's direction, secretly exchanging comical glances of openmouthed incredulity with me and one another.

Those of us who had witnessed her previous performance could scarcely believe the delightful change in Tiffany. From then on, she was invariably friendly and supportive toward me. Further, I soon realized that the inner transformations hadn't stopped with her. Several students commented privately that they felt they had learned a very profound lesson about the power of defenselessness through watching me handle my conflict with Tiffany. Some said that they had already put the new technique into practice and seen it transform a difficult relationship in their own lives. I realized belatedly that this confrontation had been a valuable learning experience for everyone present. What my ego had regarded as an unwarranted imposition turned out to be a priceless opportunity to learn the value of miracle mindedness by teaching it to others.

So What?

Now some people will argue that private, uncontrolled experiments such as this one are a far cry from rigorous scientific research and that they do not "prove" anything. I will concede that they are a "cry" away from real research, but not a "far" one. This is precisely how the scientific mind works, informally testing intuitions about what is going on before investing time and money in closely controlled laboratory experiments. Rigorous scientific investigation is actually one of the last steps in a long process of scientific thinking — *a step that is necessary to persuade others of what the scientist believes she or he already knows.*

As to what informal research of this type "proves," that depends upon your standard of proof. Do you want to publish a result for the benefit of the scientific community or simply find out whether a particular strategy will work reliably for you? Discerning people continually engage in personal experimentation to see what works best. Why should you be any different?

For example, no one would fault you if you tried out a new vacuum cleaner at home and concluded that it did a superior job. Then you would simply be a "wise consumer." All I am suggesting is that you try out miracle mindedness in the same way you might test an appliance.

Simply follow the instructions for use in a conscientious manner and see whether it performs as advertised. It is not necessary to wait for a life-or-death emergency. We all have problems and interpersonal conflicts. Start with small things, and if you get positive results, you'll have more confidence in approaching bigger ones.

Holding Onto Peace

As you attempt to evaluate the results of your personal experiments, it will be well to remember that if you want to solve a problem, you must first be clear about what the problem is. The generic spiritual point of view we have been discussing always regards your *loss of peace* as the real problem. In this view, conflictual thinking causes conflict in your physical illusion, not the other way around.

When you opt to reinstate your mind in peace, you have solved your problem, and as long as you choose to remain in peace, miracles will protect you. Nevertheless, you have free will, and the decision about whether or not to relinquish your peace is always up to you. After all, whose mind is it that is not at peace? It is *your* mind, and *you* are in charge of what goes on in it. You don't have to "go to hell" every time someone tells you to!

There will always be a powerful temptation to give way to negative emotions, since indulging them feels good for a little while. For example, author and spiritual teacher Marianne Williamson aptly refers to anger as "a fifteen-minute high."[50] Truly, there is nothing like a little self-pity or righteous indignation to tone up the system. Nevertheless, if the spiritual view is correct, there is no such thing as a "good reason" to be angry or fearful.

Instead of giving way to negative emotions, miracle workers use disturbing perceptions as a cue to remember and reaffirm that they are under divine protection.

Peace Pilgrim

Consider another example from Peace Pilgrim's book.

> There was an occasion when I felt that I was indeed battling with the elements. It was my experience of walking through a dust storm which sometimes blew with such force I could scarcely stand against it, while sometimes the dust was so thick I could not see ahead and could only guide myself by the edge of the road. A policeman stopped alongside me, threw open his car door and yelled, "Get in here, woman, before you get killed." I told him I was walking a pilgrimage and did not accept rides (at that time). I also told him that God was my shield and there was nothing to fear. At that moment the winds died down, the dust settled and the sun broke from the clouds. I continued to walk. But the wonderful thing was that I felt spiritually lifted above the hardship.[47]

This is how miracles of deliverance work. If you believe that fear or anger is justified—that something outside yourself has the power to hurt you—this perception of terrifying vulnerability is hell. By buying into it, you are condemning yourself to remain in hell until you change your mind. The moment you recognize that a cause for fear or anger *cannot* be real because God did not create it, the perception of hell dissolves, and you find yourself in heaven, an alternative state of mind in which everything you see around you is conducive to peace and love.

Since we are creating the world we see through our thoughts, wise people look for the best in everything and everyone. Unless you have decided to "be grateful in all things," you will not recognize the blessings you receive, and because you do not recognize them, you will not bring them to their full flowering. Remember that miracles start out as remote possibilities in the implicate order. They exist only as potential until you make them real for yourself by believing in them.

When you learn to remain in peace at all times, you will be enlightened, and you will carry the good news that fear and anger are not real to every mind you contact. Until then, you will probably step back and forth between heaven and hell many times, taking a cold plunge into negativity one moment and then climbing back out into the sunlight as soon as you remember that suffering is optional. Like the people who shared their miracles of deliverance, you may not always be wise enough to stay out of hell, but if you keep your wits about you, you can at least make a quick exit.

Why God Sometimes Seems to Fail Us

Love always answers, being unable to deny a call for help, or not to hear the cries of pain that rise to it from every part of this strange world you made but do not want.
—A Course in Miracles

But if Divine Love is really foolproof, why is it that so many people who express complete confidence in God do not appear to be helped? The following joke about a very pious minister who is caught in a flood can serve to illustrate the problem.

The Minister

As the waters of a great flood begin to rise, a bus stops at a church to evacuate everyone. The minister, however, refuses to leave with the others, portentously proclaiming, "God will preserve me!"

When the flood has covered the first story of his church, some people come by in a boat. "Get in, Father!" they call, but the minister again declines help, affirming, "God will preserve me!"

Finally, the minister is perched upon the roof of the church, clinging to the steeple as the waters rise around him. A helicopter hovers above and lowers a ladder, but he waves it away, reaffirming, "God will preserve me!" Moments later, he is swept away and perishes in the torrent.

The indignant soul of the drowned minister goes straight to heaven. Angrily brushing by Saint Peter at the gate, he demands a personal interview with God. As he is ushered into the divine presence, the minister begins to take the Creator to task.

"I have been a good man all my life! I have done your work on earth for forty years! I had complete faith in you right up to the moment of my death! Yet You let me die! What kind of a universe are you running here?"

"So, what do you want from me?" God shrugs. "I sent you a bus, a boat, and a helicopter!"

It is easy to look at someone like this minister and think that God failed him, when the truth is that he didn't accept the help that was offered. As we have seen over and over again, listening for and following inner guidance is a vital factor in many deliverances. Onlookers have no way of knowing whether others are really doing everything their inner guidance is suggesting.

If Dennis, trapped between two gangs in that underground parking structure, had not followed his impulse to toddle up to the gang leader and call him "Dada," would he have escaped? Had Brian not burlesqued the role of a dangerous gunfighter, would the prisoners have decided to surrender to him? Would Mel have survived if he had not moved to his left?

All of these individuals might well have been killed if they had not followed inner guidance. Yet mourning their deaths afterward, who would have guessed that a viable solution to their problems had been offered and rejected? It is all very well to pray for protection, but one must also pay attention, act conscientiously, and take advantage of the help sent. As the Arab saying so eloquently puts it, "Have faith in God, but tie up your camel."

Miraculous Solutions May Not Always Be Appropriate

A miracle-minded attitude always relieves suffering, because it represents the decision not to suffer. However, miracle mindedness may or may not change the conditions that appeared to be the *reason* for suffering. Problems often serve a useful purpose in our lives, and it would be a mistake to dispense with them before we have derived full value.

For instance, if you had a disability, one way a miracle could help you would be to heal the physical condition. But another would be to show you how to regard your physical limitations as a learning experience. Perhaps the meaning of your life involves meeting the challenges of a disability, and your greatest growth and joy will come through accepting your situation and making the best of it. Miss America's story shows us God's miraculous power to heal, but so — in a different but no less profound way — does Helen Keller's.

You Ought to Be in Pictures

Perhaps because I live so close to Hollywood, I like to think in cinematic terms. Each person's life is like a movie. When we allow it to be written and directed by our ego, it takes on the aspect of a second-rate melodrama.

In the ego's production, all our aspirations end in failure, and hope is permitted only to heighten the dramatic impact when it is eventually snatched away. To use Shakespeare's inspired theatrical metaphor, life (as interpreted by the ego) is "a tale told by a fool — full of sound and fury and signifying nothing." Each of us is only "a poor player who struts and frets his hour upon the stage, and then is heard no more."

However, since we are all bent upon being actors, our higher power is generously offering to direct us in a very different sort of production. This is an improvisation where all of the players

342

work together spontaneously to create a plot that is funny, exciting, romantic, and inspirational. Here each of us gets to dream up the role we would most enjoy playing. Everyone is the star of his or her own plotline, as well as a supporting actor in the scenarios others are creating for themselves.

Our deliverance stories provide a glimpse of what is possible when the ego is dismissed and God is brought in as a consultant. With a little inspired editing, tragic scenes can be reworked into exciting adventures, spiced with humor and romance. Justice and mercy triumph, and happy endings are guaranteed. If it takes a few miracles to bring the action to this delightful conclusion, what is to stop us from writing them in? It's an improvisation, isn't it?

Thumbs Up, or Thumbs Down?

If your life were a movie, would you pay money to see it? Are you a star, or do you just "do a walk-on" in someone else's production? Is your film more worthy of winning an Oscar or of being recycled into celluloid mandolin picks?

If you aren't crazy about the way your life is shaping up, you can always try listening to your higher power's suggestions. It is just possible that Divine Omniscience will be able to think of something your ego hasn't considered. Who knows, with a little expert help, the "turkey" you've been acting in may have the makings of a cinematic triumph.

You're going to join God's production in the end anyway, you know. So what are you waiting for? A miracle?

343

Notes

1. C. S. Lewis, *Miracles: How God Intervenes in Nature and Human Affairs* (New York: Macmillan, 1947). [Editor's Note: Subsequent references to the same source will use the same note number.]

2. B. F. Skinner, *Beyond Freedom and Dignity* (New York: Alfred A. Knopf, 1971).

3. James Hansen, cited in Brendan O'Regan, "Healings, Remission and Miracle Cures," *Noetic Sciences Collection: 1980–1990 Ten Years of Consciousness Research* (Sausalito, CA: Institute of Noetic Sciences, 1991).

4. Paul Ferrini, "An Interview With Larry Dossey," *Miracles Magazine*, Fall 1994, pp. 30–33, 54–61.

5. Sophy Burnham, *A Book of Angels* (New York: Ballantine Books, 1990), pp. 199–202.

6. Bernie Siegel, *Love, Medicine and Miracles: Lessons Learned About Self-Healing From a Surgeon's Experience With Exceptional Patients* (New York: Harper & Row, 1986).

7. Marc Barasch, "A Psychology of the Miraculous," *Psychology Today*, March/April 1994, pp. 54–80.

8. Brendan O'Regan and Caryle Hirschberg, *Spontaneous Remission: An Annotated Bibliography* (Sausalito, CA: Institute of Noetic Sciences, 1993).

9. Brendan O'Regan, *Noetic Sciences Collection: 1980–1990 Ten Years of Consciousness Research* (Sausalito, CA: Institute of Noetic Sciences, 1991).

10. Gerald Jampolsky, *Teach Only Love: The Seven Principles of Attitudinal Healing* (New York: Bantam, 1983).
11. Shakti Gawain, *Creative Visualization* (Mill Valley, CA: New World Library, 1978).
12. Gallup Poll, *Religion in America: 1990* (Princeton: Princeton Religion Research Center, 1990).
13. Brian Weiss, *Through Time Into Healing* (New York: Simon and Schuster, 1992).
14. Ian Stevenson, *Twenty Cases Suggestive of Reincarnation* (New York: American Society for Psychical Research, 1966).
15. R. G. Jahn and B. J. Dunne, *Margins of Reality: The Role of Consciousness in the Physical World* (New York: Harcourt, Brace, Jovanovich, 1987).
16. S. Dowling, *Journal of the Royal Society of Medicine*, August 1984, cited in Brendan O'Regan, "Healing, Remission and Miracle Cures," *Noetic Sciences Collection: 1980–1990 Ten Years of Consciousness Research* (Sausalito, CA: Institute of Noetic Sciences, 1991).
17. "Official Report of the Lourdes Medical Commission," cited in Brendan O'Regan, "Healing, Remission and Miracle Cures," *Noetic Sciences Collection: 1980–1990 Ten Years of Consciousness Research* (Sausalito, CA: Institute of Noetic Sciences, 1991).
18. James Randi, *Flim-Flam! Psychics, ESP, Unicorns and Other Delusions* (Buffalo, NY: Prometheus Books, 1987).
19. Raymond Moody, *Life After Life* (New York: Bantam, 1976).
20. Michael Polanyi, *Personal Knowledge: Toward a Post-Critical Philosophy* (Chicago: University of Chicago Press, 1958).
21. Anonymous, *A Course in Miracles* (Tiburon: Foundation for Inner Peace, 1975).
22. Richard Feynman, *Surely You're Joking, Mr. Feynman: Adventures of a Curious Character* (New York: Bantam, 1985).
23. Abraham Maslow, *Religions, Values, and Peak-Experiences* (New York: Viking Press, 1964).
24. Jeffrey Mishlove, "Intuition: The Source of True Knowing," *Noetic Sciences Review 29* (1994), pp. 31–36.

NOTES

25. O. Jahn, *W. A. Mozart* (Leipzig: 1856–1859), vol. iii, pp. 423–25, cited in Pitirim Sorokin, *Social and Cultural Dynamics*, vol. 4 (London: Bedminster Press, 1962).
26. Friedrich Nietzsche, *Werke* (Taschenausgabe), vol. vii, pp. xxiv ff., cited in Pitirim Sorokin, *Social and Cultural Dynamics*, vol. 4 (London: Bedminster Press, 1962).
27. Sheila Rossi, personal communication, 1982.
28. Cited in Jeffrey Mishlove, *The Roots of Consciousness* (New York: Random House, 1975).
29. Pitirim Sorokin, *Social and Cultural Dynamics*, vol. 4 (London: Bedminster Press, 1962), pp. 746–64.
30. Fritjof Capra, *The Tao of Physics* (New York: Bantam Books, 1975).
31. Norman Friedman, *Bridging Science and Spirit* (St. Louis: Living Lake Books, 1994).
32. Roger Sperry, "Psychology's Mentalist Paradigm and the Religion/Science Tension," *American Psychologist* 43(8) (1988), pp. 607–13.
33. John Archibald Wheeler, "Law Without Law," in *Quantum Theory and Measurement,* edited by John Archibald Wheeler and Wojciech Hubert Zurek (Princeton: Princeton University Press, 1983), pp. 192–94.
34. Freeman Dyson, "Theology and the Origins of Life," lecture and discussion at the Center for Theology and the Natural Sciences, Berkeley, California, November 1982.
35. James Jeans, cited in Paramahansa Yogananda, *Autobiography of a Yogi* (Los Angeles: Self-Realization Fellowship, 1983).
36. David Bohm, "A Conversation with David Bohm," interviewed by Renee Weber in *ReVision* 4 (1981).
37. Paramahansa Yogananda, *Autobiography of a Yogi* (Los Angeles: Self-Realization Fellowship, 1983), pp. 113–21.
38. Serge King, *Mastering Your Hidden Self: A Guide to the Huna Way* (Wheaton: Theosophical Publishing House, 1985).
39. G. I. Gurdjieff, cited in P. D. Ouspensky, *In Search of the Miraculous* (New York: Harcourt, Brace & World, 1949).

40. Jacquelyn Small, *Transformers: The Therapists of the Future* (Marina del Rey, CA: DeVorss, 1982), p. 20.
41. Dan Millman, *Way of the Peaceful Warrior* (Tiburon: H J Kramer, 1980).
42. Terry Dobson, reprinted in Ram Dass and Paul Gorman, *How Can I Help? Stories and Reflections on Service* (New York: Alfred A. Knopf, 1985), pp. 167–71.
43. Norman Cousins, *Anatomy of an Illness as Perceived by the Patient* (New York: Norton, 1980).
44. J. McDougall, *Theaters of the Body* (New York: Norton, 1989).
45. Norman Cousins, *Head First: The Biology of Hope and the Healing Power of the Human Spirit* (New York: Penguin, 1989).
46. Elisabeth Kübler-Ross, *On Death and Dying* (New York: Macmillan, 1969).
47. Peace Pilgrim, *Peace Pilgrim: Her Life and Work in Her Own Words* (Santa Fe: Ocean Tree, 1992).
48. Alice Miller, *For Your Own Good: Hidden Cruelty in Child-Rearing and the Roots of Violence* (New York: Farrar Straus, 1983).
49. Herbert Benson, *The Mind-Body Effect* (New York: Simon & Schuster, 1979).
50. Marianne Williamson, *A Return to Love: Reflections on the Principles of* A Course in Miracles (New York: HarperCollins, 1992).

Author's Postscript

As you surely know by now, I love a good story. If you would care to share the results of your personal experiments with me, I would appreciate hearing about them and possibly including them in some future book. I can be reached through the following address:

Carolyn Miller, Ph.D.
P.O. Box 641401
Los Angeles, CA 90064

About the Author

Carolyn Miller has a doctorate in experimental psychology with specialization in the neurophysiology of motivation and emotion. She is also a licensed clinical psychologist practicing in West Los Angeles. In the course of fifteen years of graduate and undergraduate teaching, Dr. Miller has helped to train hundreds of psychotherapists, directed numerous dissertations and theses, and supervised dozens of clinical interns. She has also published many professional articles and coauthored a book on the psychology of humor.

In addition to her work as a psychologist, Carolyn Miller is also a spiritual student and teacher committed to the transformation of consciousness on the planet. Along with her husband, Arnold Weiss, Ph.D., she is a founding director of the Los Angeles–

based Foundation and Institute for the Study of *A Course in Miracles,* a nonprofit organization dedicated to spiritual psychotherapy and education. Dr. Miller is widely recognized as an expert on miracles whose lively and entertaining lectures, classes, and workshops help participants actualize their own miracle-working potential.

COMPATIBLE BOOKS

FROM H J KRAMER INC

THE EARTH LIFE SERIES
by Sanaya Roman
*A course in learning to live with joy,
sense energy, and grow spiritually.*

LIVING WITH JOY, BOOK I
*"I like this book because it describes the way I feel
about so many things."*—VIRGINIA SATIR

PERSONAL POWER THROUGH AWARENESS:
A GUIDEBOOK FOR SENSITIVE PEOPLE, BOOK II
"Every sentence contains a pearl. . . ."—LILIAS FOLAN

SPIRITUAL GROWTH:
BEING YOUR HIGHER SELF, BOOK III
*Orin teaches how to reach upward to align with the higher energies of the
universe, look inward to expand awareness, and move outward in world service.*

An Orin/DaBen Book
OPENING TO CHANNEL:
HOW TO CONNECT WITH YOUR GUIDE
by Sanaya Roman and Duane Packer, Ph.D.
*This breakthrough book is the first
step-by-step guide to the art of channeling.*

BRIDGE OF LIGHT
by LaUna Huffines
Tools of light for spiritual transformation . . . a spiritual classic.

HEALING YOURSELF WITH LIGHT
by LaUna Huffines
*A clear and precise method of esoteric healing using the
light of the soul and the angelic healers.*

UNDERSTAND YOUR DREAMS
by Alice Anne Parker
A practical book that offers the key to dream interpretation.

JOURNEY INTO ONENESS
by Michael J. Roads
*With this book, Michael Roads has established himself as an inspired
writer, storyteller, teacher, and radiant being."*—MAGICAL BLEND

COMPATIBLE BOOKS

FROM H J KRAMER INC

MESSENGERS OF LIGHT:
THE ANGELS' GUIDE TO SPIRITUAL GROWTH
by Terry Lynn Taylor
*A worldwide best-seller, this lighthearted look at the
angelic kingdom will help you create heaven in your life.*

GUARDIANS OF HOPE:
THE ANGELS' GUIDE TO PERSONAL GROWTH
by Terry Lynn Taylor
Guardians of Hope *brings the angels down to earth
with more than sixty angel practices.*

ANSWERS FROM THE ANGELS:
A BOOK OF ANGEL LETTERS
by Terry Lynn Taylor
*Terry shares the letters she has received from people
all over the world that tell of their experiences with angels.*

FULL ESTEEM AHEAD
by Diane Loomans with Julia Loomans
"Full Esteem Ahead *is the best book on parenting and self-esteem that
I've seen."*—JACK CANFIELD, Author, *Chicken Soup for the Soul*

WAY OF THE PEACEFUL WARRIOR
by Dan Millman
A tale of transformation and adventure . . . a worldwide best-seller.

SACRED JOURNEY OF THE PEACEFUL WARRIOR
by Dan Millman
"After you've read Sacred Journey, *you will know
what possibilities await you."*—WHOLE LIFE TIMES

NO ORDINARY MOMENTS
by Dan Millman
*Drawing on the premise that we can change our world by
changing ourselves, Dan shares an approach to life that turns
obstacles into opportunities and experiences into wisdom.*

THE LIFE YOU WERE BORN TO LIVE:
A GUIDE TO FINDING YOUR LIFE PURPOSE
by Dan Millman
*A modern method based on ancient wisdom that can help you
find new meaning, purpose, and direction in your life.*